"We don't use words w[illegible]eaning what we'd like them to mean rather than what they did mean. The only way to become a Bible Christian is to learn how the Bible uses words, and Keri Wyatt Kent will guide you into how to do just that. God bless this book for what it can do for Christians."

—**Scot McKnight**,
Karl A. Olsson Professor in Religious Studies,
North Park University

"The Bible says that in the beginning was the Word. Keri will help you go slower and deeper into the richness of the *logos* of God."

—**John Ortberg**,
popular author and pastor of
Menlo Park Presbyterian Church
in Menlo Park, CA

"I regularly refer to favorite commentaries and reference books as I prepare talks for retreats and conferences. Keri Wyatt Kent's *Deeper into the Word* will definitely be added to my shelf of 'go to' references. She takes New Testament words, some we know well, and opens us up to deeper meanings. This is a resource every Christ follower would benefit from."

—**Anita Lustrea**,
Host & Executive Producer of
Midday Connection

Keri Wyatt Kent

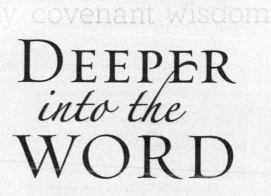

Deeper *into the* Word

New Testament

Minneapolis, Minnesota

Cover design by Lookout Design, Inc.

All emphasis in Scripture quotations is the author's.

Page 252 is a continuation of the copyright page.

Published by Bethany House Publishers
11400 Hampshire Avenue South
Bloomington, Minnesota 55438

Bethany House Publishers is a division of
Baker Publishing Group, Grand Rapids, Michigan.

Printed in the United States of America

Library of Congress Cataloging-in-Publication Data

Kent, Keri Wyatt.
Deeper into the Word : New Testament : reflections on 100 words from the New Testament / Keri Wyatt Kent.
p. cm.
Summary: "Devotional that explores the context, background, and application of 100 important New Testament words"—Provided by publisher.
Includes bibliographical references (p.) and index.
ISBN 978-0-7642-0842-3 (pbk. : alk. paper) 1. Bible. N.T.—Terminology. 2. Bible. N.T.—Meditations. I. Title.
BS2385.K396 2011
225.6—dc22

2010041172

In keeping with biblical principles of creation stewardship, Baker Publishing Group advocates the responsible use of our natural resources. As a member of the Green Press Initiative, our company uses recycled paper when possible. The text paper of this book is comprised of 30% post-consumer waste.

This book is dedicated to:

the amazing literary women
of Redbud Writers Guild

Finding all of you was like coming home,
and it seems only fitting that
a book about God's words
would be dedicated to a group
who shares my love of God,
and my love of words.
Thank you for your love, acceptance,
encouragement, and fearlessness!

CONTENTS

INTRODUCTION

The Bible is God's Word, but it's also full of words. Unfortunately, most of us do not read the Bible in its original languages. The New Testament was written in Greek, but many of the people whose stories fill its pages spoke Aramaic or Hebrew. As anyone who has read *The Little Prince* or *The Brothers Karamazov* knows, things can get lost in translation. Therefore, it is helpful to look at the original languages, as well as the historical and cultural context of those words, to give us insight into the intended meaning of the text.

When trying to understand the New Testament, we must remember that Jesus and his first followers were Jewish. Jesus was the Son of God, but he put on flesh as a Jewish rabbi in first-century Palestine. We must remember that context, and examine the text through that cultural lens.

For example, just before his trial and death, Jesus told his disciples: "And if I go and prepare a place for you, I will come back and take you to be with me that you also may be where I am. You know the way to the place where I am going" (John 14:3–4). Of course, Thomas the doubter replies: "Lord, we don't know where you are going, so how can we know the way?" (v. 5). Jesus answers with those famous words: "I am the way and the truth and the life. No one comes to the Father except through me" (v. 6).

These are verses I memorized as an obedient evangelical child because they explain that Jesus is the only way to heaven—the place he was going to prepare for us. We were told that we could use his words to refute moral relativism: If all roads led to God, then Jesus would have said, "I am a way," or "I'm one of the ways." If I told my unbelieving friends this verse, they would immediately fall to their knees in repentance and ask me what they must do to be saved, and I would tell them: Be born again (John 3:16). Or so my Sunday school teachers told me.

It didn't always work out like that, despite my good intentions. Just because something is true doesn't mean it will be immediately convincing to skeptics. I do think Jesus is the way; I'm not arguing that point. But I never learned the cultural and religious context of that verse, or what it would have meant to the people who heard it at that time. To the Jews who became his disciples, who gathered to hear his teaching or stood at a distance wondering who he was, this statement had radical implications. But he wasn't refuting moral relativism. He was fulfilling prophesy. Understanding the cultural context might actually make Christianity more interesting to skeptics, I think.

Jesus was a Jewish rabbi. The Jewish culture of which Jesus was a part absolutely revered the Torah, God's law. They learned it, memorized it, debated it, and discussed it—not because they had to, but because they loved it. Here are some of the passages they would have thought of immediately when they heard Jesus' words.

Look at Exodus 18:20: "Teach them the decrees and laws, and show them *the way* to live and the duties they are to perform" (emphasis mine). God's decrees and instructions referred to in this verse were from the Torah. It showed the Israelites the way to live. They often referred to *Torah* as "the Way."

Psalm 119:142 says, "Thy righteousness is an everlasting righteousness, and thy law is the truth" (KJV). This verse is talking about God's law, the Torah. The Truth.

In Deuteronomy 32:46–47, Moses tells the people (after reading the Torah to them), "Command your children to obey carefully all the words of this law. They are not just idle words for you—they are your life." The Torah is Life.

So when Jesus claimed to be the way, the truth, and the life, his Jewish audience would have understood that he was claiming to not just have a word from God; he was claiming to be the embodiment of God's Word. He was Torah. He was the Way. It was a radical statement, and people either embraced him as the Messiah or rejected him as a heretic.

This book is a tool to help you better understand both the words and their context so that you can engage in the spiritual discipline of the study of God's Word. As such, it is meant to be used with the Bible rather than on its own. Think of it as a shovel to help you dig deeper, or a light to help you see better.

There are several ways this book can help you connect with Scripture. First, it can be used as a reference volume, to look up words you come across in your own reading. For example, as you engage in daily Scripture reading, you may want to dig deeper. Cultivate the habit of reading slowly. As you read, notice which words in the text stand out to you or give you pause. Rather than trying to get through a chapter or section, read a shorter portion through a few times. When a specific word strikes you or puzzles you, use this book as a reference tool to look up words you've encountered in your daily reading.

Second, this book can be used as a study guide to launch your own study of specific words. If there's a word in your daily reading that is not listed in *Deeper into the Word*, you can use it in another way: as a tutorial for how to do what has been traditionally called a "word study." By reading a few chapters, you can learn this technique and try it on your own. In a word study, you take one word—say the word *love*—and by using a concordance, either printed or online, find other verses where *love* occurs. The other verses will provide insights into the word. You can use commentaries to see what scholars say about it. You can look up the words in various Bible dictionaries or even a lexicon—which gives you the Greek or Hebrew translation of the English words (there are several available online—see the appendix for suggestions).

Third, you could read this book one chapter at a time, devotionally. Don't rush—you may want to spend several days reflecting on a chapter. Look up the verses mentioned in the chapter and read their context. Or use a concordance to find other verses that use that word. Pray and journal about how God might be asking you to live out his words. You can also use this book with others—a prayer partner or a group.

However you choose to use this book, my prayer is that it will help you to more fully understand and love the Rabbi whose story unfolds in its pages.

AFRAID

What keeps you from trusting God? Perhaps you would answer that you don't have enough faith. Or put another way, you have too much fear. The word *afraid* appears thirty-five times in the New Testament; the related word *fear* appears eighty-three times. Throughout the Bible, both words are often connected with the phrase "Do not," as in "Do not be afraid," or "Fear not." It's the most-oft repeated commandment in the Bible.

Of all the commands of God, "Do not be afraid" is one of the most reassuring, yet one of the hardest to obey. And it often comes, in the biblical narrative, when God shows up and asks us to take a risk—to trust even when things look very bad, or don't seem to make sense. When the angel comes to Mary to tell her how her life will turn upside down, he begins, "Do not be afraid" (Luke 1:30). When Jairus the synagogue ruler comes pleading for Jesus to save his daughter, and she dies before Jesus can get there, Jesus looks him in the eye and says, "Don't be afraid; just believe" (Luke 8:50).

Most often the word translated "afraid" is *phobeo. Phobeo's* root word, *phobos,* is often translated "fear." *Phobeo* can mean to be scared, but it can also be used to mean reverent awe, as in, "The fear of the Lord." While the latter is more common in the Old Testament, *phobeo* is used most frequently in the New Testament in the negative sense of being fearful or afraid.

Other Greek words for afraid, used less frequently than *phobeo,* include *emphobos*, which means alarmed or trembled, as in Luke 24:5 or Acts 24:25; *deilia* or its derivative *deiliao,* which denotes timidity or cowardice (as in 2 Tim. 1:7 or John 14:27); and *ekphobos*, which essentially means being frightened out of your wits, and is used just once in the New Testament, in Matthew 9:6, to describe the disciples' response to the Transfiguration.

Fear does not come from God. "For God did not give us a spirit of timidity (*deiliao*), but a spirit of power, of love and of self-discipline" (2 Tim. 1:7).

As 1 John 4:18 says, "There is no fear in love, but perfect love casts out fear. For fear has to do with punishment, and whoever fears has not been perfected in love" (ESV). The antidote to fear is love. And how do we access that love, or be "perfected in love"? Well, this verse says fear has to do with punishment. So love, on the other hand, has to do with grace. When we let go of fear, we can trust God's grace, which makes us perfect in God's eyes.

However, the goal is not just to get rid of fear, but to replace it with love, as C. S. Lewis notes,

> Perfect love, we know, casteth out fear. But so do several other things—ignorance, alcohol, passion, presumption, and stupidity. It is very desirable that we should all advance to that perfection of love in which we shall fear no longer; but it is very undesirable, until we have reached that stage, that we should allow any inferior agent to cast out our fear.[1]

Ironically, what we'd label the "scariest" kind of love to give—self-sacrificing, generous *agape*—is the kind of love that will cast out fear. *Agape* casts out *phobeo* every time. That's why the Bible says we can approach the throne of grace with confidence rather than fear (Heb. 4:16).

There's this tension within the text: We're told to fear God, yet not be afraid. The Greek uses *phobeo* to mean both reverential fear or respect, and simply feeling alarmed or frightened. To "fear

God" means to respect, but that's something we give to our peers, our boss, or even, on a good day, those who serve us—the busboy or the dry cleaner. Fear of the Lord is so much more—it is deep reverence and awe.

Fear of God means having a right-sized view of ourselves and God. Paul said, "I can do all things through Christ who strengthens me" (Phil. 4:13 NKJV). He was not afraid because he was focused on Christ rather than life's challenges. When we fear God, we don't have to fear anything else.

ANOINT

Often when I am invited to speak at other churches, a group of people will pray with me before I get up to speak. Recently in the back room at a retreat center, the woman heading the prayer team asked if I was comfortable with people putting their hands on me as they prayed for me. I don't really have "personal space" issues, so I said sure. "And how about if we anoint you with oil?" she asked immediately.

I paused only a second—I mean, it's biblical, right?—before I agreed. She whipped out her keychain, which had a small vial of oil attached, right next to her frequent buyer card for the grocery store. I blinked, then smiled to cover my surprise. "I always like to be prepared," she said, taking me by the arm and leading me to the group of eager prayer warriors who circled around me and began to pray.

What does it mean to be anointed? Some Christians, like this dear praying sister, literally use oil and dab it on people's foreheads as they pray prayers of intercession. Others use the word to describe a movement of the Holy Spirit. The Greek verb *aleipho* is used to describe the act of anointing, typically with oil or ointment—you *aleipho* yourself with Neosporin when you get a cut, for example.

In James 5:14 we read, "Is anyone among you sick? Let him call for the elders of the church, and let them pray over him, anointing him (*aleipho*) with oil in the name of the Lord" (ESV).

The second Greek verb for *anoint* is *chrio,* which is used less often, and only to mean sacred or symbolic anointing. It can mean literally to smear with oil, or to consecrate. While *aleipho* is translated "put on" in some verses in most modern translations, those same versions always use the word *anoint* for *chrio*, as in Jesus' quote from Isaiah in Luke 4:

> The Spirit of the Lord is on me,
> because he has anointed me
> to preach good news to the poor.
> He has sent me to proclaim freedom for the prisoners
> and recovery of sight for the blind,
> to release the oppressed. (v. 18)

The name *Jesus Christ* refers to this anointing: "The title Christ signifies 'The Anointed one,' the word (*Christos*) is rendered '(His) Anointed' in Acts 4:26."[1]

The verb *chrio* is used only once to describe believers: "Now it is God who makes both us and you stand firm in Christ. He anointed us, set his seal of ownership on us, and put his Spirit in our hearts as a deposit, guaranteeing what is to come" (2 Cor. 1:21–22).

The corresponding noun, *chrisma*, however, is used to describe what believers have. The word literally means an unguent made from oil and aromatic herbs. However, in the New Testament it is used only metaphorically.

I've heard people describe preaching, worship, or ministry that was particularly powerful as "anointed." Interestingly, the word *anointed* is never used as an adjective in the Bible. But the New

Testament does describe having an anointing (*chrisma*) from God. Who has this anointing? Is it only super preachers? Or pastors? Those with the gift of prophesy? Do they have it only once in a while, when they hit one out of the park with a great sermon? The Bible doesn't seem to indicate that. First John 2:20, 27 says, "But you have an anointing (*chrisma*) from the Holy One, and all of you know the truth. . . . As for you, the anointing you received from him remains in you, and you do not need anyone to teach you. But as his anointing teaches you about all things and as that anointing is real, not counterfeit—just as it has taught you, remain in him."

Who is the "you" to whom John refers? Throughout the letter, John addresses his readers as "dear children." We must assume he was writing to ordinary believers just like us. But because we have this anointing, ordinary believers can do extraordinary things for God.

APOSTLE

The word *apostle* comes directly from the Greek *apostolos*, which literally means one sent forth (it comes from the Greek verb *apostello*, meaning to send forth or send out). Often the word translated "sent" in the Bible is *apostello*, which Jesus uses to describe himself (sent from the Father, see Heb. 3:1 or John 17:3), and the twelve disciples selected by Jesus (see Luke 6:13; 9:10) for special training to teach and preach. After Jesus' death and resurrection, we see the meaning of the word evolving, broadening like ripples in a pond.

Acts 1 describes the eleven apostles (Judas having left the group) gathering with other men and women who were followers (disciples) of Jesus, and choosing one to replace Judas. Peter leads this endeavor, and he says he has certain standards for those who would be selected as apostles: "Therefore it is necessary to choose one of the men who have been with us the whole time the Lord Jesus went in and out among us, beginning from John's baptism to the time when Jesus was taken up from us. For one of these must become a witness with us of his resurrection" (Acts 1:21–22).

This gives us some important information. When Jesus walked the earth, he had a group of followers larger than just the twelve apostles who were with him all the time—otherwise there would not have been additional men to choose from. This group of disciples included several women, who are mentioned both in Acts 1 and Luke 8. The apostles continued to teach and preach Jesus' message.

The word *apostle* is used frequently in the New Testament to describe Paul. Although he did not meet the standard of having been with Jesus during his earthly ministry, he encountered the risen Christ on the road to Damascus. And apparently some people didn't think that was good enough. Paul's rant in 1 Corinthians 9 seems to indicate that some didn't want to confer the title (or the benefits, including financial support) of apostleship on Paul.

Gradually the word *apostle* broadened in meaning to include other messengers or preachers of the Word. The Bible says apostles were mostly teachers, but it also mentions other tasks, such as working miracles, discerning spirits, ordaining elders, administering rites, and making laws. It is mentioned first in the lists of spiritual gifts in Ephesians 4:11–13 and 1 Corinthians 12:28. Eventually it was used to describe Barnabas as well as Paul. In 2 Corinthians 8:23, Paul mentions two brothers who are apostles. (Though the word is often translated "messengers" or "representatives," the Greek is again *apostolos*.) In Philippians 2:25, Paul mentions "Epaphroditus, my brother, fellow worker and fellow soldier, who is also your messenger (*apostolos*), whom you sent to take care of my needs."

In Romans 16:7, Paul asks the church at Rome to "Greet

Andronicus and Junia, my fellow Jews who have been in prison with me. They are outstanding among the apostles, and they were in Christ before I was" (TNIV).

This raises an interesting question, as Junia is a woman's name. Was there a woman apostle? This debate has simmered among academics for centuries. While the King James Version, New Revised Standard Version, and English Standard Verson also say "Junia," many translators added a letter to change Junia to Junias, making it a masculine name. But a growing number of scholars believe that the correct name is Junia. Could it be that apostleship was not limited to men in the first-century church?[1] And are there still those who are called to be apostles today?

BELIEVE

What does it mean to believe? Someone who offers you support may exclaim, "I believe in you!" We believe in politicians (an arguably foolish move). We're told we should just believe in ourselves in order to be successful. We tell the underdog team they just have to believe. It seems the word loses some of its punch in this context, expecting our team will win if we just "believe" they will. In that instance, you could argue that to believe means to hope against all odds and sound reasoning—which is not at all what the Bible means by that word.

To believe, in the biblical sense, is so much more than just to agree with, hope for, or even support. To be a believer in Christ is not merely to consider yourself to be his biggest fan. Rather, it means you stake your life on his claims: his proclamation of divinity, his assertion that he can forgive sin, his radical statement about being "the way, the truth, and the life." To believe is not just to give intellectual assent, but to stake your life on the premise that such truth will save you.

This belief affects not only our future, but our present, as it ushers us into intimacy with the object of our belief. Believers are not just those who agree, but those who are adopted. (See Rom. 8, especially verses 12–17.)

The four gospels that begin the New Testament exhort us to believe, but none so vehemently as John's gospel. The Greek verb *pisteuo*, to believe, appears in Matthew and Mark ten times each, in Luke nine times, but in John ninety-nine times.

John's gospel is markedly different from the synoptic gospels of Matthew, Mark, and Luke, and not just in word choices. Those words support his purpose. Rather than biography, John's story of Jesus' life is much more focused on theology and uses stories to back up his points. John was focused on trying to convince people that Jesus was more than just a rabbi, or a good teacher, or a prophet sent from God. Rather, John focuses on Jesus' claim to be God in the flesh. So it makes sense that someone who is trying to prove the deity of Christ would use the word *believe* a lot more often than those just trying to tell his life story and record his teachings.

John often links *pisteuo* and *zoe*, life, as in "whoever believes in him shall not perish but have eternal life" (3:16) and "everyone who looks to the Son and believes in him shall have eternal life" (6:40).

One commentary notes that John's purpose in writing was "specifically evangelistic. It was aimed to produce faith in Jesus Christ as the son of God. The record of the various signs was intended to produce this result, and with this in mind the many references to believe and to non-believing become significant."[1]

Pisteuo means not only to believe but to place your confidence in something, to rely upon it. It is often translated "commit to," or "commit to one's trust."

Belief does not simply change our mind about God, it changes who we are. We are filled with life—not just for eternity, but for now. Belief means we live differently, because we live fully.

BLESS/BLESSED/BLESSING

Ancient Jews (including Jesus) prayed countless prayers throughout their day, all of which began, "Blessed are you, Lord God, who . . ." Although these prayers named the blessings God had given, they focused on the giver of all good things.

More often than instructing us to pray for God to bless us, the Bible exhorts us to bless God. Or it presents a countercultural view of blessing. Jesus said nothing about health and wealth; rather, he said you are blessed if you are poor in spirit, mourning, merciful, pure in heart, hungry for righteousness, persecuted, and falsely accused. (See Matt. 5.)

In the Greek, the word *eulogeo* means literally to speak well of, and is used to address God and also to ask God's blessing on a thing or person. The adjective form, *eulogetos*, is applied only to God in the New Testament. The verb *makarizo*, which means to pronounce happy or blessed, is used only twice. Its adjective form, *makarios*, is used most frequently. It is the "blessed" we see in the Beatitudes of Matthew 5 and Luke 6, and also in Revelation. It means supremely blessed, fortunate, happy, and well-off.

I imagine people scratching their heads in confusion as they listened to Jesus' words:

> Blessed (*makarios*) are the poor in spirit. . . . Blessed (*makarios*) are those who mourn. . . . Blessed (*makarios*) are those who are persecuted because of righteousness, for theirs is the kingdom of heaven. Blessed (*makarios*) are you when people insult you, persecute you and falsely say all kinds of evil against you

> because of me. Rejoice and be glad, because great is your reward in heaven, for in the same way they persecuted the prophets who were before you. (Matt. 5:3–4, 11–12)

Really? So if you're spiritually impoverished, sad, meek, or persecuted, you should be considered fortunate, happy, well-off? God's economy is an odd one—we often feel anything but blessed when we mourn or face opposition. But the blessing comes not just in the struggles of life, but in the promises Jesus makes. For example, when Jesus says "blessed are those who mourn, for they will be comforted," it's the second half of the sentence that is the blessing part. The blessing, when you mourn, is the comfort God gives. The blessing, when you're persecuted, is the promise of the kingdom. Jesus urges us to take a long-term view of our life, which is, after all, eternal.

Jesus is not recommending seeking out suffering in order to find blessings. Such challenges will come our way without looking for them. But someone who is poor in spirit is someone who is not proud in spirit. That's really about how we choose to react to the challenges of life—with humility and patience, rather than anger. And if you are able to respond to difficulty in that way, well, that's evidence of God's blessing your life.

Someone who mourns has chosen mourning rather than anger or revenge. Someone who is meek has chosen humility. Likewise, the other examples in Jesus' list exhort us to hunger and thirst for righteousness, to be merciful, pure in heart, peacemakers. Blessing is often connected to our choices. Maybe happiness is a choice—whether we will be blessed or not depends on our perspective, on our willingness to choose humility over pride, peace over strife. The secret to joy lies in choosing to live God's way rather than our own way—and to lean into the comfort he offers in the midst of our struggles.

BLIND

In Jesus' public preaching debut, he took for his text a messianic prophesy from Isaiah that predicted, among other things, "recovery of sight for the blind" (see Luke 4:18), then boldly declared, "Today this Scripture is fulfilled in your hearing" (Luke 4:21).

One mark of Jesus' ministry, and in fact, of his divinity, was the healing of blindness. With mud, spit, or words, he granted sight. The Greek word *tuphlos* (meaning blind) appears in the gospels forty-nine times. It derives from the verb *tupho*, which means roughly to make "a smoke"—the idea is something is smoldering, but the smoke obscures it. The related word *tuphoo* means to be proud or conceited. (See 1 Tim. 3:6.) It is very accurate since pride often blinds us, and because the proud person is often all smoke and no real fire.

John 9 contains rich detail of the story of Jesus' healing of a man born blind. When the disciples ask whose sin caused him to be born blind (reflecting their cultural belief that physical infirmities were meted out for sin), Jesus answers that neither he nor his parents were to blame, "but this happened so that the work of God might be displayed in his life" (John 9:3). In other words, so that others might *see* God. After the man is healed, the Pharisees demand to know who healed him on the Sabbath, and thus broke the rules—unwittingly admitting that their legalism had blinded them. When the now-seeing man tries to help them see (verses 30–32), they throw him out of the synagogue.

When Jesus hears this man has been cast out of the community, he seeks him out and invites him into belief—offers him the grace that will heal his spiritual blindness. And Jesus makes this stunning statement: "For judgment I have come into this world, so that the blind will see and those who see will become blind" (v. 39). Jesus turns the religious order of the day upside down by pointing out the blindness of the Pharisees.

In this passage and others, Jesus accused the religious leaders of his day of hypocrisy and legalism, calling them "blind guides" (see Matthew 15:14). Rather than be healed of their blindness, they conspired to bring about his death.

In my book *Simple Compassion*, I wrote:

> The Christian faith is a journey in which God increasingly improves our vision. One in which we learn to see. Sometimes, the first step is asking God not for vision, but for the *desire* to ask for vision—which only comes to those who acknowledge their blindness.
>
> When God called Saul, a man who had dedicated his life to persecuting Christians, to be his messenger, he first physically blinded him, knocking him off his horse. The thing is, Saul was already blind—spiritually. Like most of us when we are spiritually blind, he thought he knew and saw everything. He was a man, he thought, with a vision: to stamp out this heresy called Christianity. I know that in many areas of my life, I live with that kind of blindness—oblivious to my own lack of vision.[1]

Growing spiritually means seeing more clearly and acting on that vision.

Saul, whose name was changed to Paul, later wrote, "When I was a child, I talked like a child, I thought like a child, I reasoned like a child. When I became a man, I put childish ways behind me. Now we see but a poor reflection as in a mirror; then we shall see face to face. Now I know in part; then I shall know fully, even as I am fully known" (1 Cor. 13:11–12). Temporary blindness put things in perspective for Paul.

As the famous hymn declares, "I once was . . . blind, but now I see." An encounter with God, and with grace, opens our eyes. When we realize our blindness, we can ask for healing, for sight. And we realize that our healing is a way for others to see God, to see his work displayed in our lives.

BODY

One of the first heresies to threaten the early church was Gnosticism, a philosophy that argued that salvation came through special higher knowledge (the Greek word *gnosis* means to know) attained by a select few. They also believed that physical matter, including the human body, was inherently bad, and spirit was inherently good. This dualism led them to deny the incarnation. They argued that because he was good, Christ could not truly have a human body, but only appeared to have one. As a result, they denied the resurrection and even the need for Christ's atoning death on the cross.

One Gnostic teacher in the early second century, Basilides, "held that Christ did not suffer, but that Simon of Cyrene was crucified in his place, while the invisible Christ stood by laughing."[1]

So it is little wonder that Paul's letters, especially those to the church at Corinth (a pagan center), emphasized the bodily resurrection of Christ, and our connection with one another as a body and with Christ as his body. As it was in the first century, our Communion table is set with the body and blood of Christ, and we take these into our bodies as a spiritual practice and a reminder and affirmation of Christ's actual death and resurrection.

The Greek word for body, *soma,* appears more than 150 times in the New Testament. It is used to describe the physical body and the physical nature (as opposed to the spiritual nature). It's also used as a metaphor to describe the church as a whole, or even a local church, which is made up of various members or parts, but remains a whole connected unit.

Dallas Willard writes,

> The physical human frame as created was designed for interaction with the spiritual realm and . . . this interaction can be resumed at the initiative of God. . . . People have a body for one reason—that we might have at our disposal the resources

> that would allow us to be persons in fellowship and cooperation with a personal God.[2]

In other words, we live out our spiritual lives through our physical bodies. We, in our bodies, are the means by which God acts in the world—in and through his body, he is able to bring the kingdom, to bring healing and salvation.

When Paul describes spiritual gifts in passages like 1 Corinthians 12 (where he uses the word *soma* seventeen times), he uses the analogy of a body to describe how all the gifts work cooperatively in the church. It's a well-thought-out metaphor, true on more than one level. Yes, it's a way of thinking about the differences in functions of various people within the church, but it's also a reminder that faith is meant to be lived out. In and through our physical bodies, we are able to do things like care for the sick and the poor, share the good news, and so forth. Whether our spiritual gift is mercy or preaching, we do it with our hands or our voices—in other words, with our physical bodies.

The word *body* in the New Testament points to our unity with Christ and with each other. Ephesians 1:22–23 states, "And God placed all things under his feet and appointed him to be head over everything for the church, which is his body, the fullness of him who fills everything in every way."

Paul is giving us heavy theology but in an almost playful way—God appointed him to be the head, yet placed all things under Christ's feet. Aren't the feet part of the body? If Christ is the head and the church is the body, how can he have feet to put things under? And how can the church be the fullness of him who already fills everything? The only way for these riddles to be resolved is this: the unity of Christ and his body, the church. Jesus prayed for this in John 17: "I have given them the glory that you gave me, that they may be one as we are one: I in them and you in me. May they be brought to complete unity to let the world know that you sent me and have loved them even as you have loved me" (vv. 22–23).

BREAD

The Greek word *artos* appears in the New Testament ninety-nine times, and even when it literally means a loaf, it still carries a rich symbolism—of life, sustenance, nourishment, and God himself.

For centuries before Jesus' birth, the Jews had used bread in worship. Their weekly Sabbath table was set with two loaves of bread to remind them of the manna God provided to the children of Israel in the wilderness—and God's command to gather double portions on the sixth day in preparation for the Sabbath.

The Passover, or Feast of Unleavened Bread, was an annual festival that included ritual meals. Among other things, the Jews would eat unleavened bread to remember their hasty but miraculous departure from slavery in Egypt. The sacrifices outlined in Leviticus and other Old Testament books include not only lambs or bulls but grain and bread. Every week in synagogue the "loaves of presentation" or shewbread was consecrated to the Lord—again, a reminder of provision and how God satisfies our spiritual hunger.

Jesus was born in Bethlehem, a town whose name literally means house of bread.

Jesus refuted Satan's temptation to turn stones to bread by saying, "Man does not live on bread alone, but on every word that comes from the mouth of God" (Matt. 4:4). A statement filled with rich symbolism, since Jesus later referred to himself as the bread that comes down from God (in John 6, where the word *artos* appears seventeen times). The chapter opens with the feeding of the five thousand, where Jesus takes five loaves and two fish and feeds a multitude. Amazingly, there are twelve baskets of leftovers (perhaps symbolizing Israel and its twelve tribes).

The next scene in the chapter is Jesus walking on water. When he gets to the other side of the lake, people wonder how he got there. He gets into a discussion with them about, of all things, bread. He challenges them to look beyond the hunger of their stomachs to the hunger of their souls, which only he can satisfy.

> Jesus said to them, "I tell you the truth, it is not Moses who has given you the bread from heaven, but it is my Father who gives you the true bread from heaven. For the bread of God is he who comes down from heaven and gives life to the world."
>
> "Sir," they said, "from now on give us this bread."
>
> Then Jesus declared, "I am the bread of life. He who comes to me will never go hungry, and he who believes in me will never be thirsty. But as I told you, you have seen me and still you do not believe." (John 6:32–36)

Jesus was talking about spiritual hunger and thirst, though most of his listeners didn't catch on. Even as they spoke of the manna their forefathers received in the wilderness, they missed the symbolic meaning of that bread—and didn't see that it was a physical foreshadowing of Jesus' life and, ultimately, his sacrifice.

All of these discussions build to the climactic scene of the last supper, a Passover meal, where Jesus bridges the ancient traditions with his new covenant by declaring that the Passover loaves are now his body, broken for us.

The image of bread is an apt one. Simply believing that bread exists will not feed our hunger. Even believing it is the best bread in the world, or that it is truly satisfying, is not enough to alleviate our hunger. We must take it in, make it a part of us. In the same way, we must take him into our hearts and trust him fully if we are to truly be satisfied. How can we partake of this bread? We must come to him and believe in him. The offer to never be hungry is an offer not just of spiritual nourishment but of eternal life.

BREAK/BROKEN

About a dozen different Greek words are used to describe breaking or broken. *Klao,* in its various forms, refers to the breaking of bread, both literally and symbolically. *Klao* is used in 1 Corinthians 11:24, the verse we read so often when we celebrate Communion: "This is my body, which is broken for you" (KJV).

Different individual verbs are used to describe a broken heart, breaking forth, broken bones, breaking the law. Because all of them are translated into the same English word, we must look at the context to determine what the writer intended. This is true not just with certain words but with all of Scripture.

One of the more interesting words that can be translated "break" is the verb *luo,* which appears forty-three times in the New Testament. Its primary meaning is to loosen, unbind, or release. John the Baptist uses the word *luo* when he says, "After me will come one more powerful than I, the thongs of whose sandals I am not worthy to stoop down and untie" (Mark 1:7; see also Luke 3:16 and John 1:27). In that culture, loosing the ties of a sandal was an act performed by Gentile servants prior to the lowly task of washing feet—a foreshadowing, perhaps, of the last night of Jesus' life when he did this for his disciples.

Luo also means breaking destructively, as in the breaking of commandments. This can mean to refuse to follow the commands, but it is also used to describe "loosing the force of them, rendering them not binding."[1] However, in other contexts it has a more positive connotation.

In the ancient Jewish tradition in which Jesus lived and taught, rabbis like him would interpret the Torah, teaching people what it meant, and offering their opinion on how to live out its precepts. Each rabbi had his take on the commandments, and what he would forbid or permit. Scholar David Bivin writes,

> The sages were called upon constantly by their community to interpret scriptural commands. The Bible forbids working on the Sabbath, for instance, but it does not define what constitutes work. As a result, the sages were required to rule on which activities were permitted on the Sabbath. They "bound," or prohibited, certain activities, and "loosed," or allowed, others.[2]

When the Pharisees criticized Jesus, they said he would break, or *luo*, the rules of their tradition by doing things like healing on the Sabbath. But Jesus was loosing in the sense of allowing, because he wanted people to focus on the heart of God rather than legalistic traditions. It was something other rabbis had done before him and would continue to do.

Now, the interesting part about loosing (and binding) is that Jesus gave his disciples permission to do it. In Matthew 16:19 he tells Peter and the other disciples, "I will give you the keys of the kingdom of heaven; whatever you bind on earth will be bound in heaven, and whatever you loose (*luo*) on earth will be loosed in heaven."

Rob Bell writes,

> Now the rabbis had technical terms for this endless process of forbidding and permitting and making interpretations. They called it "binding and loosing." To "bind" something was to forbid it. To "loose" something was to allow it. So a rabbi would bind certain practices and loose other practices. And when he gave his disciples the authority to bind and loose, it was called "giving the keys of the kingdom." . . . What he is doing here is significant. He is giving his followers the authority to make *new* interpretations of the Bible.[3]

This is part of what it means to live in Christian community—to help each other figure out how to live out the commands of Scripture. When Jesus gave his disciples (and consequently, us) the keys to the kingdom, he gave us the power to bind and loose. While Scripture does not change, it is living and active. While God is immutable, he is continually making all things new.

BURDEN

People facing struggles and trials often refer to them as burdens—a weighty word. Jesus said that to follow him, we may have to take up our cross daily. A cross is a heavy burden indeed, whether you're talking literally or metaphorically. But Jesus, seemingly contradicting himself, said his burden was light. So what are we to make of this word *burden*?

The Greek word typically translated "burden" is *phortion,* which means something carried, but is used metaphorically in the New Testament.[1] For example, in Matthew 23:4 and Luke 11:46, the word describes the oppressive rules of the Pharisees: "So you must obey them and do everything they tell you. But do not do what they do, for they do not practice what they preach. They tie up heavy loads (*phortion*) and put them on men's shoulders, but they themselves are not willing to lift a finger to move them" (Matt. 23:3–4 TNIV).

In contrast, in Matthew 11:28–30, Jesus invites all who are "weary and burdened" (*phortizo*, from the same root as *phortion*) to follow him, to take his yoke upon them, "for my yoke is easy and my burden (*phortion*) is light."

What was Jesus' "yoke"? (See ***Yoke.***) It was the way of life he both taught and lived. Unlike the Pharisees, he did practice what he preached and didn't put any burden on his followers that he was unwilling to bear himself.

The burden of the Christian life is to live as Jesus would if he were in our place. That is the yoke he calls us to take upon ourselves—a requirement that would be impossible had he not offered to do it with us, to bear our burdens with us. And how do we engage his assistance? We must, as he says in verse 28, come to him. We must live our lives in fellowship with him, daily deciding to live as he lived in small ways, so that we are strengthened for the heavier burdens when they come. We must emulate his practices of solitude, service, prayer, and more, in order that we may live like him in more demanding situations. We must come to him over and over, seeking his presence and assistance as we try to live as he would.

Dallas Willard wisely notes,

> Asking ourselves "What would Jesus do?" when suddenly in the face of an important situation simply is not an adequate discipline or preparation to enable one to live as he lived. . . . The secret of the easy yoke, then, is to learn from Christ how to live our total lives, how to invest all our time and our energies of mind and body as he did.[2]

And indeed, this becomes the role of the church, to be Christ to one another, as we "bear one another's burdens." (The Greek in this instance is *baros*.) We do this not just to be kind or out of obligation, but because doing so will "fulfill the law of Christ" (Gal. 6:2). And what law is that? Christ's law refers to his teachings, or to the way he lived those out—in other words, his yoke.

A few verses later in Galatians, Paul says that "each one should carry his own load (*phortion*)." Why when we are bearing others' burdens does he use *baros*, and a few sentences later use *phortion*?

Baros refers to a heavy weight pressing down on a person (whether physical or spiritual). *Phortion* is something carried. We need others to help us with our *baros,* but we can each, with God's help, handle our own *phortion*.

CALL/CALLED/CALLING

When someone decides to become a vocational minister, they often speak of being called into ministry, or receiving a "calling." But what about the rest of us? Does God call only some?

Anyone who professes to be a Christian has come to that faith (whether they realize it or not) in response to an invitation, a calling. Even if a person believes their spiritual journey was the result of private study or philosophical seeking, the ultimate impetus for their quest is always the gentle whisper of God, often so subtle we do not even realize that the longing in our deepest hearts actually is from God.

So to put faith in Christ is to answer a call. God calls all people to himself, to put their faith in him, to trust him as Savior and Redeemer. This is the call on every human heart, to accept God's offer of adoption and forgiveness, though not all will respond. For example, in Romans 1, Paul writes to "all in Rome who are loved by God and called to be saints" (Rom. 1:7).

For those who do respond, whether in a dramatic moment or via a slow process, God offers both acceptance and a more specific calling, often related to our spiritual gifts. In the same letter to the church at Rome, Paul refers to himself as one "called to be an apostle," a much more specific assignment within the body of saints. He uses a similar structure in his first letter to the church at Corinth: "Paul, *called* to be an apostle of Christ Jesus by the will of God, and our brother Sosthenes, to the church of God in Corinth, to those sanctified in Christ Jesus and *called* to be holy" (1 Cor. 1:1–2). In each of these instances, the verb is *kletos*, meaning called, invited, or appointed. It also means to be a saint. The related *klesis,* which appears eleven times in the New Testament, means calling and always refers to a heavenly calling.

There are nearly thirty different words translated as "call," "called," or "calling" in the New Testament. They range in meaning from call into question (as in *egkaleo* or *krino*), to summon, or to call after (*metakaleo*), and more. Often a Greek word will be translated as "call" or "called" in some verses, while it might mean sound, speak, or say in other contexts.

Most frequently, we see the word *kaleo*, or some form or derivative of it. *Kaleo* is used 146 times in the New Testament, and it literally means to call aloud, or summon. "It is used particularly of the divine call to partake of the blessings of redemption,"[1] and it can be used to mean vocation or destination, bid in the sense of invite, or cry out for a purpose. Derivatives include *epikaleo* (to be called by name); *metakaleo* (to call from one place to another); *proskaleo* (to call to oneself, or God's call to the Gentiles in Acts 2:39); and *sunkaleo* (to call together).

The Bible twice mentions the idea of being "worthy of God's calling." Do we strive to become worthy, or does God make us worthy? In 2 Thessalonians 1:11, Paul writes: "To this end we always pray for you, that our God may make you worthy of his calling (*klesis*) and may fulfill every resolve for good and every work of faith by his power" (ESV). Note in this instance Paul emphasizes God's power to change us.

But in Ephesians, Paul writes, "As a prisoner for the Lord, then, I urge you to live a life worthy of the calling (*klesis*) you have received. Be completely humble and gentle; be patient, bearing with one another in love. Make every effort to keep the unity of the Spirit through the bond of peace" (Eph. 4:1–3). Here he focuses on what we can do to cooperate with God and live up to his calling. Rather than a contradiction, this is a glimpse into the different facets of our life with God. God calls, we respond. God transforms us when we are willing to cooperate obediently with the work he's doing in us—when we listen with our lives to his holy calling.

CARE

In English, the word *care* has two nearly opposite meanings. If someone cares, they are interested and concerned. If someone *has* a care, they perhaps have an anxiety or worry. Having someone care for us can alleviate our cares.

Likewise, in New Testament Greek there are different meanings, but in some cases several different words signify those meanings. *Merimna* (and the verb form *merimnao*) means anxiety, or to have a care; *spoude* means carefulness or watchful interest, as in taking care of someone or something. Four other verbs are also used to designate different types of care: The verb *melei* denotes care of interest and concern, not anxiety. *Epimeleomai* means to take care of, to provide for. It is used both in Luke 10 to describe the Good Samaritan's care for the wounded man, and in 1 Timothy 3:5 to describe the role of a bishop or overseer of the church—perhaps, some scholars suggest, alluding to a parallel between these two roles.

The verbs *phrontizo* and *phroneo*, which also mean to think or consider, are translated "be careful" in some translations. But even the word *merimnao* can have different meanings in different contexts.

First Peter 5:7 exhorts believers to give our anxiety over to the care of Jesus: "casting all your care (*merimna*) upon Him, for He cares (*melei*) for you" (NKJV). I remember singing (and loving) a song based on this verse when I was a child in Sunday school. It's an interesting play on words—we can release our cares (our anxiety, worries) to Jesus because of his care (his deep concern and provision) for us. This word *care*, when it refers to God, reminds us of his amazing love for us.

Jesus noted in Matthew 13:22 that the "cares (*merimna*) of this world" can choke out our spiritual growth. He uses the same word in the Sermon on the Mount when he says, "Do not worry (*merimnao*) about your life, what you will eat or drink; or about your body, what you will wear" (Matt. 6:25).

In fact, Jesus' teaching in Matthew 6:19–34, which begins, "Do not store up for yourselves treasures on earth," is all about not letting *merimna* have control of our hearts, and subsequently, our lives. When we are focused on obtaining and hoarding wealth, we worry about moths, rust, and thieves, and of course we are distracted from following Jesus. We are blocked, in a way, from receiving his love and his care for us. Our worry and anxiety flows out of our fear—again, something Jesus told us not to do. (See ***Afraid***.)

However, Paul uses the same verb to mean something a bit different when he describes his own burden of care for all the churches in 2 Corinthians 11:28–29. At the end of a long description of the hardships Paul has faced, he adds, "Besides everything else, I face daily the pressure of my concern (*merimnao*) for all the churches. Who is weak, and I do not feel weak? Who is led into sin, and I do not inwardly burn?" In other words, in addition to facing dangers like shipwrecks and beatings, Paul cares so much for the young churches he's planted that his care for them is a daily pressure in his life. He literally feels their pain and identifies with their struggle as if it were his own.

New Testament scholar William Barclay notes, "*Merimna* is a word that has a double flavor, for obviously *the cares of life* which choke the seed are not the same thing as *the care of all the churches* which was laid upon the heart of Paul."[1] Barclay points out that in secular Greek texts as well as the New Testament, there are times when "care" is understood to be a good thing, and times it is "a distracting, a distressing and an evil thing."[2]

Likewise, in 1 Corinthians 12:25–26, Paul exhorts the church "there should be no division in the body, but that its parts should have equal concern (*merimnao*) for each other. If one part suffers, every part suffers with it; if one part is honored, every part rejoices with it."

When we care for others within the body of Christ, we share their pain. When we are willing to bear another's burdens (see ***Burden***), our own burdens and cares are lightened.

CHOSEN

In our culture, we are overly attuned to what's in and what's out, what's hot and what's not. Reality television allows us to choose which contestant will stay and which will go home. We know the chosen ones stay on the island, the others get voted off.

So when we read the New Testament from our twenty-first-century vantage point, we tend to see the word *chosen* as an exclusive term. If some are chosen, our mind jumps to those who are not chosen, who are left out. While the New Testament culture was just as stratified as ours, the word *chosen* didn't carry a connotation of rejection.

God's grace is extended to all, and if we accept this gift, we are indeed chosen ones. The verb most often translated "chose" is *eklego*, which means to pick out or select, but with the motivation of love or kindness. Its adjective form, meaning chosen, is *eklektos*. (In some versions, *eklektos* is translated "elect," as in God's elect.)

The apostle Paul wrote to the church at Colosse,

> Here there is no Greek or Jew, circumcised or uncircumcised, barbarian, Scythian, slave or free, but Christ is all, and

> is in all. Therefore, as God's chosen (*eklektos*) people, holy and dearly loved, clothe yourselves with compassion, kindness, humility, gentleness and patience. Bear with each other and forgive whatever grievances you may have against one another. Forgive as the Lord forgave you. (Col. 3:11–13)

A tension exists: In verse 11, Paul seems to be pointing to the inclusiveness of God and the flattening of social hierarchy. And yet in verse 12 he points out what seems to be exclusion—we are God's chosen ones, the implication (at least in our minds) being that if some are chosen, others are not. But that's a misreading of the text. Paul urges the Colossian Christians (and us) to live out their faith, to act in loving and kind ways, and in fact extend the offer of God's love to others rather than resting smugly on their chosenness. In other words, he chose to love us, and we must choose to love others. God has chosen us in spite of our shortcomings. Our social standing or material wealth mean nothing to him—he chooses us purely out of love. He chooses to be kind to us.

Jesus told his disciples, "You did not choose (*eklego*) me, but I chose (*eklego*) you and appointed you to go and bear fruit—fruit that will last. Then the Father will give you whatever you ask in my name" (John 15:16).

We are not robots who follow God when he chooses us as if we had no will. We must choose whether or not to accept God's offer. And yet God's love is sometimes so compelling we feel it drawing us like a magnet.

A related word, which appears only in the writings of Paul, is *huiothesia*, typically translated "adoption." God has made us heirs; he has adopted us.

These two words come together in the opening greetings of Paul's letter to the church at Ephesus: "For he chose (*eklego*) us in him before the creation of the world to be holy and blameless in his sight. In love he predestined us to be adopted (*huiothesia*) as his sons through Jesus Christ, in accordance with his pleasure and will—to the praise of his glorious grace, which he has freely given us in the One he loves" (Eph. 1:4–6).

The notes on the TNIV say this about verse 5: "The Greek word for *adoption to sonship* is a legal term referring to the full legal standing of an adopted male heir in Roman culture."[1] In both ancient Jewish and Greco-Roman culture, adoption was an honor. A wealthy person might choose to adopt a young man to help him financially and socially. And if you were adopted in this way, you had the same rights and privileges a natural-born son had.

It's important to note that God chose and adopted us not because of something we've done to earn this privilege, but as a free gift. Certainly that is something to celebrate.

CHURCH

In New Testament times, people did not speak of "going to church"—because the word *church* (*ekklesia*) referred not to a building or even a worship service, but to a group of people. They gathered in homes, or even, as Acts 2:46 points out, in the courts of the Jewish temple. The emphasis was on who they were and that they were together. The services did not look much like our modern church services. The earliest church, described in Acts 2, met daily and shared all their resources. They were a community, a body. They were known at first only as followers of the Way.

Ekklesia was used in ancient Greece to refer to the conferred assembly of Greek citizens who would gather in true democracy to decide on matters of state, so it would have been familiar to Christians and pagans alike. In fact, when the apostle Paul writes his letters to the churches, he often opens with something like, "to the church *of God* in Corinth," perhaps to differentiate the group of believers from other groups of citizens in the same city.

Barclay notes: "The church, the *ekklesia*, is a body of people, not so much assembling because they have chosen to come together but assembling because God has called them to himself; not so much assembling to share their own thoughts and opinions, but assembling to listen to the voice of God."[1]

Ekklesia contains the root *kaleo,* to call. (See ***Call***.) The church is a group of people called by God to be his body in the world. The entire New Testament never uses *ekklesia* to refer to a building.

A church is far more than the building where it meets. It's also something way beyond entertainment. I sometimes find myself saying, "Wow, church was really good today," as if it were a performance. Church, in the New Testament sense of the word, is not a meeting we attend, but a group of which we are a part, and a group we serve within.

Paul compares the church at large, as well as individual churches, to a body—implying that we don't just sit there, but we move and act and serve. We serve others in the church, and together with others in the church, we serve those in need outside of the church. We are meant to be the hands and feet of Christ in the world.

Local churches were often led by the men and women who owned the homes that served as gathering places. And yet the church service was highly participatory—there was no such thing as a senior pastor or worship leader. Everyone brought their gifts to the gatherings, and they listened to God together. Look at this passage from Paul's letter to the believers at Corinth, with instructions for their worship gatherings:

> So here's what I want you to do. When you gather for worship, each one of you be prepared with something that will be useful for all: Sing a hymn, teach a lesson, tell a story, lead a prayer, provide an insight. If prayers are offered in tongues, two or three's the limit, and then only if someone is present who can interpret what you're saying. Otherwise, keep it between

> God and yourself. And no more than two or three speakers at a meeting, with the rest of you listening and taking it to heart. Take your turn, no one person taking over. Then each speaker gets a chance to say something special from God, and you all learn from each other. If you choose to speak, you're also responsible for how and when you speak. When we worship the right way, God doesn't stir us up into confusion; he brings us into harmony. This goes for all the churches—no exceptions. (1 Cor. 14:26–33 THE MESSAGE)

What would the church in our culture look like if we assembled to hear the voice of God and expected that voice to flow through all the people of the congregation, not just one person? What if church was not a building or even an organization, but a group of people who were called by God together and were responding to that call together?

CLEAN/CLEANSE

We cannot even begin to understand the New Testament word *katharizo* (to make clean, cleanse, purify, or heal) without some understanding of the Old Testament laws and promises. Over and over the word *clean* or *cleanse* is used as a metaphor for God's forgiveness. Psalm 51, written by King David in remorse and repentance after he committed adultery with Bathsheba, asks for and affirms God's mercy: "Cleanse me with hyssop, and I will be clean; wash me, and I will be whiter than snow" (v. 7).

Jewish traditions reflect this—ritual baths were required for purifying before the Levites could enter the holy of holies, after a woman had given birth, and so forth. Like all Old Testament laws, the rules for bathing were prophetic in nature, a foreshadowing of the day when Christ's blood would wash sinners clean.

In both Mark 1 and Matthew 8, we read a story of a leper

who asks for healing, if Jesus is willing. Jesus is indeed willing, and says to him simply, "Be clean (*katharizo*)!" The text says the man is cured immediately.

We are cleansed by God, and also by our own decisions. First John 1:6–9 describes this tension: We must walk in the light; if we confess our sins, then God forgives and purifies (*katharizo*) us from all unrighteousness. Second Corinthians 7:1 exhorts us to "purify (*katharizo*) ourselves." This does not mean we can expunge our own sins, but that our submission is, by definition, a cleansing act. Both human beings and God are involved in the process of sanctification.

John 15 contains Jesus' words to his disciples about this continual process. He notes that even when our lives are spiritually fruitful, God continues to make us clean (*kathairo*—meaning to cleanse or prune). He then tells his disciples that they are "already clean (*katharos*) because of the word I have spoken to you." This adjective, *katharos*, means pure, free from impurities, without blemish.

Jesus also said, "Blessed are the pure (*katharoi,* plural of *katharos*) in heart, for they will see God" (Matt. 5:8). What an amazing promise. For who has a pure heart except someone who has submitted to the loving pruning of our heavenly Father?

C. S. Lewis's book *The Voyage of the Dawn Treader* tells the story of a miserable boy named Eustace, who is so selfish and greedy he turns into a dragon. He finds this situation rather unpleasant, especially because a gold bracelet around his arm (which fit when he was human but is too tight on his dragon self) is causing him discomfort. He becomes even more frightened when a lion approaches him.

The lion (Aslan, the Christ figure in the stories, but Eustace doesn't know this) bids him to follow, and leads him to a large marble pool. Eustace wants to bathe in it, thinking it will ease the pain. The lion tells him he must first undress. Eustace realizes he might be able to scratch the dragon skin (which itches) off. And while he actually is able to shed several layers of skin, like a snake, he remains a dragon. Then Aslan tells Eustace that he must allow the lion to undress him. Despite his fear, Eustace is desperate enough to agree to submit to the lion's claws. Aslan cuts off and completely removes the dragon skin, which is undeniably painful, yet incredibly freeing. Eustace, telling his incredible story later, concludes:

> And there was I as smooth and soft as a peeled switch and smaller than I had been. Then he caught hold of me—I didn't like that much for I was very tender underneath now that I'd no skin on—and threw me into the water. It smarted like anything but only for a moment. After that it became perfectly delicious and as soon as I started swimming and splashing I found that all the pain had gone from my arm. And then I saw why. I'd turned into a boy again.[1]

What a beautiful picture of what Jesus' cleansing does to us—strips away our grandiosity to leave us smaller and more vulnerable, but ultimately makes us what we are meant to be. To submit to him is the only way we will become truly pure in heart.

COMPASSION

The English word *compassion* comes from two Latin words, *cum* (with) and *pati* (to suffer—the same root as passion). To have compassion is not just a vague concern for someone; it means to join in their struggle, to come alongside of them and "suffer with" them. It is closely related to love, of course—both *agape* and *phileo*. (See ***Love***.)

In the New Testament, there are several words that are

translated "compassion." One, *sypatheo* (the root of our English word *sympathy*), means to share the same suffering or emotion, to be compassionate. Like our English word, it is a compound of the words *syn* and *pathos*. Again, the idea is to share suffering, to undergo similar trials.

New Testament scholar Ceslas Spicq writes: "If compassion means participating in another's pain, it is tinged with pity and includes a tendency to help the unfortunate."[1]

Throughout the gospels we read that Jesus was "moved with compassion" on the people. The Greek word in these cases is one of the richest in the Greek New Testament: *splagchnizomai*. It is the verb form of the noun *splagchna,* which means not only the heart but the lungs, liver, and bowels or intestines as well. In our culture, we tend to think that the physical seat of our emotions is the heart, or even the brain. The Greeks believed emotions ranging from tenderness to anger were centered in the *splagchnas*, or the guts. *Splagchnizomai* means to be deeply moved with compassion, to feel it in your guts in a yearning, visceral way.

This is the sort of compassion Jesus had for crowds that were like sheep without a shepherd (see for example Matt. 9:36; 14:14; or 15:32), and for the individuals who sought his healing touch. His very nature and attitude toward us is marked by this deep compassion—a longing in his guts to touch us and care for us. He is not only deeply moved by our predicament of being lost in our sins; he has become a human being and suffered the same things we've suffered. His sympathy is not hypothetical.

William Barclay writes, "The greatness of Jesus was his willingness to enter into the human situation and to be moved by its poignancy to that compassion which compelled him to help and heal."[2]

Barclay goes on to note that in Greek culture, the very idea of a compassionate God was incredible. The Stoics argued that the gods were so far above mere mortals that they were unaffected by them. If a god were affected by a person, that would make the person greater than the god, which could not be, to their thinking. "The Greeks believed in a God who could not feel. To them a divine being who was moved with compassion was incredible."[3]

While our culture values compassion (even if we don't always practice it), Barclay notes that because pagan Greeks thought gods were emotionally detached, their spiritual goal was also detachment. They did not value compassion because they didn't believe their gods were compassionate. "The idea of a god who could be moved with compassion, and of a life whose motive force was pitying love, must have come to such a world literally like a new revelation."[4]

Jesus brought a whole new perspective. Because of this, we likewise ought to have a similar gut-wrenching compassion for others. First Peter 3:8 and Ephesians 4:32 implore us to treat others with compassion, to be *esplagchnos* (from *splagchnos*). Knowing that Christ has "suffered with" us enables us to show compassion to others, to live like Jesus did: "Finally, all of you, have unity of spirit, sympathy (*sympathes*), love (*philadelphos*) for one another, a tender heart (*esplagchnos*), and a humble (*philophron*) mind" (1 Peter 3:8 NRSV).

Colossians 3:12 says, "Clothe yourselves with compassion" (NIV) or "Put on a heart of compassion" (NASB). The KJV translates more literally: "Put on . . . bowels of mercies," which sounds odd in English, but the Greek noun again is *splagchnon*, that idea of being moved in your inner being with deep empathy.

What we have received from God—tender, heartfelt compassion—we should freely and lovingly give to others. What moves God should also stir our hearts (and our guts) with empathy and tenderness.

CONTENT/CONTENTMENT

The apostle Paul, though he suffered much, wrote profound and compelling words about the important theme of contentment. For example, Paul wrote to his young protégé Timothy, warning him about those who would use preaching the gospel for their own personal gain, people "who have been robbed of the truth and who think that godliness is a means to financial gain" (1 Tim. 6:5). He then contrasts this false teaching with the truth:

> Now there is great gain in godliness with contentment (*autarkeia*), for we brought nothing into the world, and we cannot take anything out of the world. But if we have food and clothing, with these we will be content (*arkeo*). But those who desire to be rich fall into temptation, into a snare, into many senseless and harmful desires that plunge people into ruin and destruction. (1 Tim. 6:6–9 ESV)

The noun *autarkeia* appears only twice in the text, here and in 2 Corinthians 9:8, where it is translated "sufficiency." The verb form *arkeo* is found only eight times. Still, it is a major New Testament theme, the subject of both parables and true heroic stories.

Paul contrasts contentment with chasing after riches, or loving money, echoing the teachings of Jesus in Matthew 6, when he said that no one can serve two masters, but must choose between God and money.

A spiritual discipline that will help us cultivate contentment is the practice of detachment. Adele Calhoun writes: "As followers of Jesus we are called to live as Jesus did. . . . We are to relinquish worldly values and detach from anything that stands in the way of desiring and knowing God."[1]

Choosing to serve God, and allowing him to guide and help us, brings contentment. Letting go of our grip on earthly goods and ambitions allows us to live in the freedom of contentment.

How do we attain contentment, which seems so elusive? In Philippians 4, Paul writes, "Rejoice in the Lord always. I will say it again: Rejoice!" (v. 4). In a way, this exhortation, and the one in the next paragraph urging his readers to think about good and pure things, are setting up his comments about contentment. Choosing to rejoice despite your circumstances, choosing to focus on what is good and pure and lovely—these are important steps in gaining contentment—as Paul goes on to explain. "I have learned to be content whatever the circumstances. I know what it is to be in need, and I know what it is to have plenty. I have learned the secret of being content in any and every situation, whether well fed or hungry, whether living in plenty or in want. I can do everything through him who gives me strength" (vv. 11–13).

How can we be content in any and every situation? By not focusing on our situation at all, but rather, focusing on the sufficiency (*autarkeia*) of Christ. And by remembering that we will not live forever in this world, where Jesus told us we would have trouble. An eternal perspective cultivates contentment.

Lisa Graham McMinn writes, "Being content does not mean we are satisfied. In fact, to be content is to know we will always be groaning this side of eternity. Yet when we believe that fullness will come, that there is more than this life, we live with contentment."[2]

John the Baptist, when asked by repentant listeners how they should live, urged them to be both generous and content (see Luke 3:10–14), as these two characteristics are linked. When you are content, you believe you have enough, and you are able to be generous. When you are discontent, you live in fear. When you are discontent, believing in scarcity rather than abundance, you cannot be generous—a sin in God's eyes.

Contentment doesn't mean blind acceptance of our suffering. Paul writes about wrestling with God over the struggles in his life:

> There was given me a thorn in my flesh, a messenger of Satan, to torment me. Three times I pleaded with the Lord to take it away from me. But he said to me, "My grace is sufficient (*arkeo*) for you, for my power is made perfect in weakness." Therefore I will boast all the more gladly about my weaknesses, so that Christ's power may rest on me. (2 Cor. 12:7–9)

COVENANT

Jesus' declaration of a "new covenant" was astonishing to his Jewish disciples, as the Jews were a covenanted people.

In the Middle East, then and today, covenants are serious business—much more than a simple agreement or contract. Often, people making a covenant would sacrifice an animal, then cut it in half and lay the halves on the ground. The two people making the covenant would walk together between the halves, splashing the blood on themselves, essentially giving one another the right to do what they'd done to the animal if either broke the covenant. God's covenant with Abram (see Gen. 15) was unique because only God walked between the halves of the animals. But the covenant with Moses described in Exodus 24 seems to indicate that the people were sprinkled with blood, as they would be had they stomped through the blood of animals on the ground. And they declare to God, "We will do everything the Lord has said; we will obey" (Ex. 24:7).

The Greek word translated "covenant" in the New Testament is *diatheke*, meaning a disposition, contract, covenant, or testament (as in someone's last will and testament disposing of their property after they die). The reason we call the two sections of the Bible the Old Testament and New Testament is that the first describes the old covenant of the law, while the second describes the details of the new covenant, which is essentially salvation by grace alone, through Christ's death and resurrection and subsequent life in us.

The old covenant was based on sacrifice of animals, which were a prophetic symbol of Christ's death. Although the Jews were God's chosen people, God remained at a distance. Only the priests could go into the "Holy of Holies," the inner sanctum of the tabernacle, and then only once a year to make atonement for the sins of the people. Moses received the covenant on Mount Sinai, again, far from the people.

Christ's death established the new covenant. At that moment, the curtain that separated the Holy of Holies from the people was torn from top to bottom (as if God himself had reached down to rend it). (See Matt. 27:51; Mark 15:38.) Because of this, the writer of Hebrews reminds us that we may now approach the throne of grace with confidence (Heb. 4:16).

One commentary notes, "The Sinaitic *diatheke* to Moses, however, was a conditional dispensation or series of promises . . . which God made for the Jews only if they obeyed. In the NT, God provided His Son in the execution of His plan and dispensation but not as a result of the obedience to any rule that He preset. However, the giving of eternal life to individuals depends on their acceptance of that sacrifice of the Son of God."[1]

Hebrews 8–10 describes the old and new covenants. Another commentary states, "This new covenant is declared to involve a different relationship between God and his people from that under the old covenant, precisely because the old covenant did not keep the people from failure and God had to turn away from them."[2]

Most English translations of Hebrews 9 use the words *covenant* and *will* (or sometimes, *testament*). But in the Greek, the word translated both "covenant" and "will" is *diatheke*.

> For this reason Christ is the mediator of a new covenant (*diatheke*), that those who are called may receive the promised

> eternal inheritance—now that he has died as a ransom to set them free from the sins committed under the first covenant (*diatheke*). In the case of a will (*diatheke*), it is necessary to prove the death of the one who made it, because a will (*diatheke*) is in force only when somebody has died; it never takes effect while the one who made it is living. This is why even the first covenant (*diatheke*) was not put into effect without blood. (Heb. 9:15–18)

This passage reminds us of a holy mystery: Jesus is both the mediator of a covenant and the sacrifice required for it. He invites us to enter into a covenant with him.

CROSS

What does it mean to "take up your cross"?

In Matthew 16:24–26 we read,

> Then Jesus told his disciples, "If any want to become my followers, let them deny themselves and take up their cross and follow me. For those who want to save their life will lose it, and those who lose their life for my sake will find it. For what will it profit them if they gain the whole world but forfeit their life? Or what will they give in return for their life?" (NRSV) (See also Matt. 10:38; Mark 8:34 and 10:21; Luke 9:23 and 14:37; John 12:25.)

In parts of the world where the church is persecuted, the idea of taking up one's cross is understood in a completely different way than it is in the United States, where, despite our diversity, the majority of the population claims to be Christian. Certainly there is a growing resistance to certain Christian values, but we don't go to church on Sunday wondering if we will be arrested on the way out just for attending. Consequently, it is much easier for a twenty-first-century Christian in say, Indonesia, to understand Jesus' words than it is for the average American Christian to do so.

The cross was used regularly in Jesus' lifetime to publically torture, humiliate, and kill criminals. When Jesus first told his followers to take up their cross, even though they saw public executions on crosses on a regular basis, I'm sure they hoped he was speaking metaphorically. They probably had no idea he would actually be killed on one, much less that eventually some of them would suffer the same fate for being his followers.

"It seems unconscionable that God submitted to the cross, a symbol that opposed his message of love and forgiveness," writes Judith Couchman. "In the Roman world, it represented paganism, cruelty, hatred, bondage and death. With humility, Christ faced down humanity's worst to give us God's best."[1]

Scholar Stuart K. Weber comments,

> The moment we become Christ's followers, our own lives and will become forfeit; we die with Christ to sin (that is, to the right to make selfish choices; Rom. 6:3–4) and choose a path that could lead any day to our execution in Christ's name. Although we may speak glibly today of "our cross" as the need to put up with Aunt Molly or a leaky roof, "taking up the cross" in Jesus' day meant being forced to bear the instrument of one's execution past a jeering mob to the site of one's imminent death as a condemned criminal.[2]

The word *cross* appears twenty-eight times in the New Testament. The Greek is *stauros*—a stake often with a cross piece on which criminals were nailed for execution. The Greek name comes from the verb *histemi*, which means to stand, either literally or figuratively. One concordance notes that *histemi* can also mean "abide, appoint, bring, continue, covenant, establish, hold up, lay, present, or stanch."[3] This rich etymology flows into the metaphorical meanings of the cross—it represents God's covenant, it establishes our place in God's family.

In Colossians 1:20, Paul writes that Jesus' violent death had the purpose of reconciliation, "by making peace through his blood, shed on the cross."

One commentary notes,

> Where other NT authors (and Paul elsewhere) employ the word *blood* (*haima*) as a symbol for Christ's sacrificial death, Paul often uses the word *cross*. Although both terms refer to Christ's death, each emphasizes a particular aspect regarding it. Christ's blood represents His death as sacrifice and connects it with the OT sacrifices. The cross of Christ represents His death as suffering and connects it with the curse of sin.[4]

So when Jesus asks us to take up our cross, he's asking us to be ready to suffer for him and to forsake our worldly ambitions (see Phil. 2). In a way, the stark symbol of the cross is a call to simplicity. As one commentary notes, "Jesus was not saying that we need to create pain or deprivation for ourselves, but that we need to be prepared to let go of anything that competes with his kingdom."[5]

DAUGHTER

All three synoptic gospels report on the raising of a synagogue ruler's daughter from the dead. While each account offers different details, all include the interruption of a sick woman who is healed when she surreptitiously touches Jesus' cloak.

This beautiful story gives us light into the various meanings of the Greek word *thugater*, which refers to a person's female offspring, but also to a woman's spiritual relationship to God.

Just as Jairus, the synagogue ruler, is deeply concerned for his daughter, so Jesus is deeply concerned for his. He does not let the woman who had been "subject to bleeding" get away with pickpocketing a healing. Because of her reproductive ailment, this woman would have been considered "unclean." To get caught touching a rabbi would have serious consequences. With the large crowd pressing around him, no one noticed the woman's touch except Jesus.

He calls her out, not to bring her shame or punishment, but to restore her fully. The one who has been shunned and taken advantage of is now welcomed. He calls her "daughter." Can you imagine her fear melting into joy as she hears that tender word?

And then, as they are speaking, word comes that Jairus' daughter has died. Jesus remains calm and tells the leader, "Do not be afraid, just believe." I imagine that as he said those words, Jesus looked at Jairus and then again at the woman before them, implying, "Just believe—as this woman did." Jesus takes a person from the lowest rung in the social hierarchy and makes her a role model of faith for a venerated religious leader. God loves all of his daughters, just as Jairus loves his daughter.

In first-century Jewish culture (as in many cultures today), daughters were not as highly valued as sons. For example, only male heirs inherited their father's property. Daughters typically got nothing.

And yet, there is a subtle thread of inclusiveness running through Scripture, which reminds us that God values each of his children equally. When Jesus heals a woman who cannot stand straight, he calls her a "daughter of Abraham" (see Luke 13:15–17) to show her value as a person.

In the Old Testament, the nation of Israel was often referred to in a feminine form, as "Daughter Zion" or "Daughter Jerusalem." (See Jer. 4:31; Lam. 2:12–14; and Zeph. 3:13–15.) Certainly Jesus was alluding to those ancient Scriptures on his way to the cross when he called his female followers Daughters of Jerusalem (see Luke 23:27–29).

On the day of Pentecost, Peter explains the believers' ability to speak in other languages by quoting the prophet Joel:

> In the last days, God says,
> I will pour out my Spirit on all people.
> Your sons and daughters will prophesy,
> your young men will see visions,
> your old men will dream dreams.
>
> Even on my servants, both men and women,
> I will pour out my Spirit in those days,
> and they will prophesy. (Acts 2:17–18; see also Joel 2:28–29)

The Holy Spirit was an inheritance given not only to sons, but to daughters as well. The New Testament makes this very clear. The word *thugater* also appears in 2 Corinthians 6:18, which reads "I will be a Father to you, and you will be my sons and daughters, says the Lord Almighty." In this passage, Paul is quoting 2 Samuel 7:14. However, that Old Testament passage does not mention daughters. It reads: "I will be his father, and he will be my son." The Holy Spirit has come to fulfill the prophesy, and is poured out on ALL people, sons and daughters, women and men. Still, this was a radical departure from a culture that considered sons an asset and daughters a liability.

No wonder Paul wrote to the young church at Galatia, "There is neither Jew nor Greek, slave nor free, male nor female, for you are all one in Christ Jesus" (Gal. 3:28). The prevailing social hierarchy was flattened at the cross and in the church.

Unfortunately, history shows that the church has not lived out these verses, and has often injured and devalued its daughters. The New Testament calls us away from patriarchy, into a culture in which "both men and women" are filled with God's spirit and seen as equals.

DEACON

The word *deacon* is an anglicized version of the Greek word *diakonos*, even though that word is most typically translated "servant" in the New Testament. (The noun *diakonos* appears thirty-one times; the verb *diakoneo* thirty-seven times; these terms are translated "servant," "minister," "serve," "ministry," etc.). In passages like Romans 15:8, it is translated "servant" or "minister," and refers to Jesus. Jesus used the word to describe himself and his followers. (See ***Serve***.)

Originally *diakonos* meant someone who serves food at a table. Indeed, there is a description of what seems to be early deacons in Acts 6 (a group of men known later as "the Seven") who took over "the daily distribution of the food" in the church so that the apostles (whose primary service was prayer, teaching, and leadership) would not have to do so. In order to understand this statement, we must remember that the early church functioned financially in a much different way than the modern church.

Acts 2 states that the believers "held all things in common." They pooled their resources so that no one would be in need. So these seven leaders were chosen to be in charge of distributing food (and some scholars believe money) to the church members, especially the widows, who were complaining that things were inequitable. The situation allows us to see the way that the early church functioned: people served according to their giftedness, and they shared their resources completely with the poor.

This disagreement was between the Hellenic (Greek) Jewish widows and the Hebraic Jewish widows. Even at its infancy, the church was multicultural. Notice the names of these early deacons: all Hellenic names. The apostles wisely chose members of the minority for this important role. The story provides a model for conflict resolution, an affirmation of diversity within the church, and a reminder that each part of the church body plays a different but important role.

This word highlights an interesting dilemma for the church: the challenge of reading the Bible and figuring out how to apply it today. While most churches do not "hold all things in common," that is, pool all the resources of all the members, they do need financial management and oversight of benevolence to the poor or to members in need.

The *IVP Bible Commentary*, as quoted on Biblegateway.com, states:

> That the diaconate is a function and not an office is clear from Luke's wording. He never uses the noun "deacon" (compare Phil. 1:1; 1 Tim. 3:8–13), though a noun and verb to describe the function are present (*diakonia*, Acts 6:1; *diakoneo*, 6:2; contrast 1:25). This passage probably did contribute, however, to the origin of the office.[1]

Other scholars argue that this same passage (Acts 6) establishes the office of deacon.[2] They point out that the early Christians, who were Jewish, based the governing structure of their congregations on that of the synagogues, where official leadership positions were standard.

In 1 Timothy 3, we see some qualifications for what appears to be a church office or leadership position. This suggests that this role continued to be an important one in the early church. In some translations, this is the only passage where we find *diakonos* consistently translated "deacon" (plus Phil. 1:1, where Paul addresses his letter to the church at Philippi with the bishops and deacons).

Romans 16:1 mentions Phoebe, and calls her a *diakonos* of the church. The word is variously translated "servant," "deacon," "deaconess." So is she simply one who serves, or did she hold the office of deacon? If she was a deacon, did other women hold this position in local churches? Either way, she was deemed responsible and important enough to be the courier of Paul's letter to the church at Rome, a high honor. Since her service is mentioned as a credential, she likely had some position of respect in the church.

The New Testament also mentions the positions of elder and bishop, with similar qualifications of honorable living. Some churches today have deacons, others have elders; some have both and some have neither.

Whether deacon is an office or just a function, whether it can be held only by men or also by women (such as Phoebe), is of course a question that churches continue to debate, or at least, choose to interpret differently. Such conversations are important, but regardless of our opinions on church government, we are all called to follow Jesus' example of servanthood—which is the original meaning of deacon.

DEATH/DIE

Though it seems like a morbid subject, and one of our culture's few remaining taboo subjects, death is inevitable. Everyone, like it or not, eventually dies. Consequently, every religion in the world, including Christianity, has crafted an eschatology that addresses the big questions: What happens when you die? How does the story end? And how does that connect with how you live?

So it's not surprising that words meaning dead, death, or die appear hundreds of times in the New Testament. The most common verb for "die" is *apothnesko*, which means literally to die off or out. It appears 112 times in the New Testament. A handful of Greek words may be translated "death": *anairesis, apothnesko, apago, apookteino, teleute*, and most commonly, *thanatos*. Like *apothnesko*, *thanatos* is understood as a separation of the body and soul, of the spiritual and material aspects of our lives. It can also refer to separation of man from God. The verb form, *thanatoo*, means to kill, put to death, or in some cases, mortify. *Thnesko* means to die or to be dead.

The word *nekros*, used as both a noun and an adjective, means dead. Its verb form, *nekroo*, to put to death, appears only a few times. (See especially Col. 3:5.)

These words appear frequently in the New Testament, not just because of discussions of the afterlife, or even the atoning death of Christ, but because they are used at times metaphorically to describe someone who is spiritually separated from God. Ephesians 2 explores the basic (if paradoxical) human condition of living in a way that's dead. Paul writes: "As for you, you were dead (*nekros*) in your transgressions and sins. . . . But because of his great love for us, God, who is rich in mercy, made us alive with Christ even when we were dead (*nekros*) in transgressions—it is by grace you have been saved" (Eph. 2:1, 4–5).

Jesus said, "I tell you the truth, whoever hears my word and believes him who sent me has eternal life and will not be condemned; he has crossed over from death to life" (John 5:24).

This is the problem that Christianity addresses, again paradoxically, by inviting us to die to self and live in Christ. The question, of course, is how do we do that? What does it look like in our daily lives to die to sin? What does it mean to be alive in Christ?

The apostle Paul wrote, "For me, to live is Christ and to die (*apothnesko*) is gain" (Phil. 1:21). His life, despite its difficulties, had no bad options. Through the beatings, shipwrecks, struggles, and health problems Paul faced, Christ was with him. Heaven would be better, but his ministry was fruitful because he was following Christ in fearless obedience.

Likewise, Paul writes in 1 Corinthians 15:55 (quoting the Old Testament prophet Hosea), "Where, O death, is your victory? Where, O death, is your sting?" He is confident and unafraid of death because of God's grace through Jesus.

This entire chapter explores Christ's resurrection—the linchpin of Christian theology. As Paul writes, "For if the dead are not raised, then Christ has not been raised either. And if Christ has not been raised, your faith is futile; you are still in your sins" (1 Cor. 15:16–17). He concludes with Christ's ultimate victory, not only over sin, but death itself: "The last enemy to be destroyed is death" (v. 26).

Just before his own death, Jesus said, "I tell you the truth, unless a kernel of wheat falls to the ground and dies, it remains only a single seed. But if it dies, it produces many seeds. The man who loves his life will lose it, while the man who hates his life in this world will keep it for eternal life" (John 12:24–25). He was referring to his own death, which would bring a great harvest of souls, and he was also calling his followers to an attitude of self-sacrifice and eternal perspective.

While we may not have to face martyrdom, every Christ follower must grapple with the question—what does it mean to die to self, not just once, but daily? For that is the call of Christ on our lives.

DISCIPLE

In order to understand the word *disciple* in the New Testament, we must first understand that Jesus was a Jewish rabbi, or teacher. And like other rabbis of his time, he had disciples. The word *disciple* is *mathetes* in the Greek, and it appears 269 times. While the New Testament was of course written in Greek, Jesus and his contemporaries spoke Hebrew and Aramaic, and would have called them *talmidim*, a Hebrew word that was defined in part by the culture that revolved around the learning of, discussion of, and reverence for the Torah.

The Greek word *mathetes* comes from the word *manthano*, to learn, "from a root math—, indicating thought accompanied by endeavor."[1]

"Thought accompanied by endeavor." This was the type of learning that *talmidim* did. The rabbi would live out application of the Scripture in front of them, and their knowledge was immediately put into action. So often, our own discipleship seems to lean heavily on thought and less on endeavor. But the two were inextricably linked in Jesus' culture.

Jewish children were taught the Torah from age five or six. The most talented students would continue to study the Torah, often memorizing the entire Scriptures, in what was known as *beth midrash*. From there, pastor Ray VanderLaan explains,

> A few (very few) of the most outstanding *Beth Midrash* students sought permission to study with a famous rabbi often leaving home to travel with him for a lengthy period of time. These students were called *talmidim* (*talmid*, s.) in Hebrew, which is translated *disciple*. There is much more to a *talmid* than what we call student. A student wants to know what the teacher knows for the grade, to complete the class or the degree or even out of respect for the teacher. A *talmid* wants to [be] like the teacher, that is to become what the teacher is. That meant that students were passionately devoted to their rabbi and noted everything he did or said. This meant the *rabbi/talmid* relationship was a very intense and personal system of education. As the rabbi lived and taught his understanding of the Scripture his students (*talmidim*) listened and watched and imitated so

as to become like him. Eventually they would become teachers passing on a lifestyle to their *talmidim*.[2]

Authors Ann Spangler and Lois Tverberg provide great insight into the "Jewishness of Jesus" in their book *Sitting at the Feet of Rabbi Jesus*. They write:

> Along with instructing the crowds, a rabbi's greatest goal was to raise up disciples who would carry on his teaching. . . . As important as knowledge of Scripture was, there was one thing more important—a rabbi's moral character. . . . The mission of a rabbi was to become a living example of what it means to apply God's Word to one's life.[3]

The New Testament mentions not just Jesus' disciples but the disciples of John, Moses, and the Pharisees. The term is used not just to refer to the twelve apostles but to the large group of men and women who followed Jesus. Jesus himself uses the word only a handful of times.

In John 8:31, we read, "To the Jews who had believed him, Jesus said, 'If you hold to my teaching, you are really my disciples.'" In John 13:34–35, Jesus says, "A new command I give you: Love one another. As I have loved you, so you must love one another. By this everyone will know that you are my disciples, if you love one another."

Likewise, in his famous teaching in John 15 about the vine and the branches, the central point is that the mark of a disciple is a life that bears the fruit of love. Just as our rabbi went to great extremes to show us the extent of his love, so should we love others. As his disciples, we want not just to know what he knows, but to live as he lived. In other words, thought accompanied by endeavor. It is what we are called to as disciples of Rabbi Jesus.

DOUBT

Even Mother Teresa had doubts.

Considered an icon of faith and of faithful action, this diminutive Nobel Peace Prize-winning nun admitted to living the last several years of her life in a dark night of the soul, even as she continued to serve the poor in Calcutta. In private letters to a superior, she shared her anguished longing to feel God's presence, and admitted it was difficult to pray. She doubted perhaps not his existence, but his presence in her life.

We all have times, if we are honest, when we wonder if our beliefs are merely wishful thinking. God seems coolly distant, disinterested even when senseless tragedies befall us (or other seemingly innocent people).

I am often amazed at the Bible and how it fits together like an intricate multidimensional puzzle. Other times, though, I wonder if it is true at all, and even if it is, why does it contain so much violence? There are times when Jesus' presence is a sweet and very near gift, yet other times when prayer seems dusty and dysfunctional.

John Ortberg notes that faith and doubt coexist in every human heart. "The birth of every infant whispers of a God who loves stories; the death of every infant calls his existence into question . . . the reality is, we all have believing and doubting inside us."[1]

The Greek word *poros* means transit, or a way. So the opposite, *aporeo*, literally means to be without a way. The word connotes confusion and perplexity and lack of resources, and doubt.

Doubt takes us off track, pulls us away from the Way. But not completely. In 2 Corinthians 4:8, Paul writes words that resonate deep in the soul: We are "perplexed (*aporeo*), but not in despair (*exaporeomai*)."

This second Greek adjective adds the prefix *ex-* and the suffix

-mai to the root word *aporeo*. It's the more intensive form of the word (like adding an -est suffix to an English word).

Paul's subtle word play reminds us that although we doubt, but we're not the doubting-est, so to speak. This superlative, *exaporeomai*, is found only twice in the New Testament. In 2 Corinthians 1:8, Paul writes of persecution so intense that he "despaired even of life." Yet three chapters later he says he is not *exaporeomai*, but only *aporeo*.

Our doubts somehow seem less daunting when we realize faith heroes like Mother Teresa and the apostle Paul wrestled with doubt. Jesus, when he encountered doubters, did not walk away, but encouraged them to see that doubt is the flip side of faith. The father of the demon possessed son asked Jesus to heal his son, "*if* you can do anything." He voiced what so many of us keep hidden in our hearts: "I do believe; help me overcome my unbelief!" (Mark 9:24).

Ortberg comments: "*I believe and I doubt. I hope and I fear. I pray and I waver. I ask and I worry. I believe; help my unbelief.* I get that prayer. That's the Doubter's Prayer. Take away my *if*. I believe; help my unbelief."[2]

There are other Greek words for doubt. Add the prefix *dia-* which means asunder, to the root and you get *diaporeo*, another word for doubt meaning completely perplexed and confused.

When Peter tries a stroll on a stormy lake, and starts to sink, Jesus says, "Oh, you of little faith. Why did you doubt?" The Greek word is *distazo*, which means literally to stand in two ways or to be uncertain. Peter didn't doubt Jesus, he doubted himself. It describes a shrinking or weakened faith rather than a rejection of truth.

A lack of faith, on the other hand, is described by the Greek verb *diakrino*, which we find in James 1:6, and encourages us not to doubt (or in some translations, "waver"), and in Jude 22, which says simply, "Be merciful to those who doubt."

Perhaps the doubt that is hardest for us to be merciful toward is the doubt we find in our own hearts. That was Mother Teresa's dilemma, it seems. And yet she persisted in following a God she could not feel or see. Doubt can coexist not only with faith but also with obedience.

EYE/EYES

In the collection of Jesus' teachings known as the Sermon on the Mount, we read these words: "The eye is the lamp of the body. If your eyes are good, your whole body will be full of light. But if your eyes are bad, your whole body will be full of darkness. If then the light within you is darkness, how great is that darkness!" (Matt. 6:22–23). Some other versions say if your eyes are "clear" or "healthy." The King James Version says, "If thine eye be single…" The phrase is an attempt to translate an idiom related to single-mindedness and focus, but it's so much more. Richard Foster explains: "The ancient term 'single eye' has a rich connotation, which our English has difficulty capturing. It refers both to a single aim in life and to a generous unselfish spirit. The two ideas have such a close connection in the Hebrew mind that they cannot be expressed in a single phrase. Singleness of purpose toward God and generosity of spirit are twins."[1]

To understand these verses, it's important to understand that when the New Testament was written, popular science taught that the mechanics of the human vision involved rays that beamed outward from the eye, allowing people to see.

One scholar notes,

> Beginning with Euclid, treatises on optical geometry do not represent vision as involving the reflection of light from the things we see onto our retinas but rather attribute an active role

> to the eye. Vision is a movement of the eye toward things; the eye emits rays that are propagated along a straight line, a sort of invisible fire.[2]

The Greek word for *eye* is *ophthalmos* (the obvious root for English words like ophthalmologist).

A few verses later, in Matthew 7 (and in Luke 6, where the teaching is repeated), Jesus uses the word *eye* again, this time metaphorically, to remind them not to judge one another.

> Why do you see the speck in your neighbour's eye, but do not notice the log in your own eye? Or how can you say to your neighbour, "Let me take the speck out of your eye," while the log is in your own eye? You hypocrite, first take the log out of your own eye, and then you will see clearly to take the speck out of your neighbour's eye. (Matt. 7:3–5 NRSV)

The word *ophthalmos* is also used to refer to God's omniscience, as in Hebrews 4:13: "Nothing in all creation is hidden from God's sight. Everything is uncovered and laid bare before the eyes of him to whom we must give account."

All three synoptic gospels record Jesus' startling statement that it is harder for a camel to go through the eye of a needle than for a rich man to enter the kingdom. Mark and Luke use the Greek word *trumalia*, the eye of a needle. In Matthew 19:24, the word is *trupema*, again meaning the eye of a needle, but which one commentary notes is smaller than *trumalia*.

Again, the use is idiomatic. A popular, if widely debated, explanation of Jesus' words states that there was a gate in Jerusalem nicknamed "The Eye of the Needle" that camels could only pass through if they were stripped of their burdens and went through on their knees. There's no archeological evidence of this gate's existence, although it is a charming story and a reminder of the need for humility. But that's likely not what Jesus was talking about.

Perhaps the best explanation is the simplest. In Jesus' day, suffering and poverty were seen as signs of a person's sin and God's subsequent wrath. Wealth was evidence of God's blessings. So Jesus uses hyperbole to shatter that thinking and to make an observation about human nature: When we have material wealth, we are often distracted and busy because of it, and we cannot focus on the priorities of the kingdom of God. He's not making a judgment, but rather an observation: It's really hard for a wealthy person to focus on kingdom priorities.

The common theme in all of these verses is this: Jesus calls us to see clearly and live generously.

FAITH/FAITHFUL

When New Testament authors write of faith in God, they use the Greek word *pistis*, which means a firm persuasion. The related word, *pistos*, means faithful, and as it is in English, can be used as either a noun (as in "the faithful," meaning believers) or as an adjective (as in "good and faithful servant").

Scholar Ceslas Spicq points out that *pistis* has a unique meaning in the Bible (and other Christian texts) when compared to secular writings of the time, but we can understand its nuances by understanding how the word was used in that culture nonetheless.

> *Pistis*, which derives from *peithomai* ("be persuaded, have confidence, obey"), connotes persuasion, conviction, and commitment, and always implies confidence, which is expressed in human relationships as fidelity, trust, assurance, oath, proof, guarantee. Only this richness of meaning can account for the faith (*pistei, kata pistin, dia pisteos*) that inspired the conduct of the great Israelite ancestors of Hebrews 11.[1]

Spicq argues that in the phrase, "Now faith (*pistis*) is the assurance (*hypostasis*) of things hoped for" (Heb. 11:1 ESV), *hypostasis* should be translated "guarantee." He adds: "Thus faith is the true title attesting to one's ownership of the heavenly property that one hopes for, and thus the guarantee that one will obtain them in the future."

To put faith into action is not easy, but if we understand that our faith is based on God's guarantee, it makes it easier to follow in the footsteps of the Old Testament faithful cataloged in Hebrews 11. This passage points out that faith is not just a mental exercise but requires action: Abel brought an offering, Noah built a boat, Abraham "obeyed and went" to a strange land.

In the Greek, the link between *pistis* and words like *pisteuo* (to believe) is obvious. The Bible instructs us to have faith, but it also provides countless reminders of the faithfulness of God. In fact, it is because of God's initiative of faithfulness that we can be faithful. We are, in essence, putting our faith in God's faithfulness.

We sometimes confuse faith and religion, but they are two different things. When Jesus encounters a Roman centurion (who was certainly not a part of the Jewish religion), he marveled at his faith, saying, "I tell you the truth, I have not found anyone in Israel with such great faith" (Matt. 8:10). Jesus held up this pagan (a hated Roman military leader no less) as an example of faith.[2]

Sometimes when Jesus would heal people, he would tell them "your faith has saved you" or "your faith has made you whole" (see Mark 5:34; 10:52; Luke 8:48). He also tells us to have faith in God (see Mark 11:22). The faith that Jesus commends is not purely intellectual but is tied to action—even the small action of grabbing the hem of his garment.

The phrase "of little faith" is a single Greek word: *oligopistos*. It is used only by Jesus to gently rebuke his followers for their fear or worry. Still, 2 Timothy 2:13 assures us that even "if we are faithless, he remains faithful." God's faith is greater than our own, yet he calls us to trust when it seems impossible.

God's faithfulness exceeds, yet inspires, ours to him. But the relationship is not one-sided. Our faith needs an object and begins with action. First John 1:9 states, "If we confess our sins, he is faithful and just and will forgive us our sins and purify us from all unrighteousness." The object is God; the action is confession.

Which sins would we have to confess? Many would fall under the broad heading of faithlessness, or fear. We have not trusted, we have not lived as if we truly believed that God is in charge of the universe or in charge of us. God's faithfulness stands in stark contrast to our faithlessness. His purity floods our souls and washes away our lack of faith, our impurity, our wrong choices. In simply admitting our unrighteousness, we take a step toward righteousness, divinely assisted by the faithfulness of God.

FATHER

When the Bible speaks of God as a Father, what sort of person comes to mind? Someone warm and kind? Distant? Loving? Controlling? Attentive? Too busy for you?

Our view of God is framed in many ways, particularly by our view of our earthly parents. An important step of spiritual growth is to give some careful consideration to how much our earthly fathers, and especially their imperfections, have colored and skewed our view of God, and then to let go of those misconceptions to try to understand God better. Though God is beyond our full comprehension, Jesus came to show us what God is like, and to show us what intimacy with the Father could be.

The Greek word is *pater* (the Latin word is also *pater*, and many English words like *paternal* and *paternity*, and even *father*, derive from both these words). In ancient cultures, people usually didn't have last names, but they would often refer to themselves with names like "Jeshua son of Joseph" or "James son of Zebedee."

In the Sermon on the Mount (Matt. 5–7), Jesus uses the word *Father* seventeen times, referring to him as "our Father," and "your heavenly Father," and "your Father in heaven." In all four gospels Jesus taught his disciples to pray, "Our Father," and he typically referred to God as "my Father" or, when teaching, "your Father." The idea of God as a father was not a new one to his first listeners. Still, before Jesus, Jews would refer to God as the "God of our fathers" or "the father of Israel" or even the father of all people. (See Mal. 2:10.) For many Jews, the name of God was too sacred to even pronounce out loud. Even the name Yahweh (Jehovah) is actually a collection of Hebrew consonants that simply mean "I am."

But Jesus, when speaking of God, modeled a startling familiarity, speaking often of "my Father," which of course made the Jews want to stone him immediately for blasphemy.

He uses stronger language in Matthew 10:32–33: "Whoever acknowledges me before men, I will also acknowledge before my Father in heaven. But whoever disowns me before men, I will disown him before my Father in heaven."

And then this kicker in Matthew 11:27 (see also Luke 10:22): "All things have been committed to me by my Father. No one knows the Son except the Father, and no one knows the Father except the Son and those to whom the Son chooses to reveal him."

Jesus knew that earthly fathers were imperfect, and yet they provided a glimpse of what God was like. He asks, "If you, then, though you are evil, know how to give good gifts to your children, how much more will your Father in heaven give good gifts to those who ask him!" (Matt. 7:11; Luke 11:13).

Jesus was also the first to refer to God as "Abba, Father" (Mark 14:36). Abba, a familiar name like Daddy or Papa, is easy for a child to say; it might even be a child's first word. Jesus combines this sweet, intimate name with the more formal *Father*—perhaps conveying a combination of intimacy and respect.

He claimed that no one could come to the Father except through him (John 14:6), but also that no one could come to him unless the Father had enabled them (John 6:65). He told people that if they knew him, they would know the Father (John 8:20). He also taught that although their heavenly Father knew what they needed, he still wanted them to ask.

The context of this last claim (John 10:22–39) makes an interesting study of the word *Father* and the authority Jesus claimed to have. His Messianic claims shocked and outraged the religious leaders of his day, because Jesus did not seem to fit their preconceptions of what a messiah ought to be.

The question becomes for us, What do we expect a Father to be, especially a heavenly Father? Does he offer us guidance, or exist merely to be a provider of material blessings? If we return to the Sermon on the Mount, we see that God is a Father who "knows what you need" and "sees what is done in secret" and "will reward you." Jesus provided a glimpse, through his teaching and his life, of the spiritual intimacy we can have with the Father.

FELLOWSHIP

In the small church where I grew up, my first-grade Sunday school class met in a low-ceilinged room called the Fellowship Hall. Not far from the kitchen, this room might be called a "multipurpose room" in more modern churches. It was not quite as casual as the gym (where the church basketball league had games, and the adult Sunday school class met), but it was certainly much less formal than the sanctuary.

Fellowship, I discerned as a first grader, meant grown-ups standing around chatting. There was always coffee involved, brewed in large metal urns, and if we were lucky, donuts. The announcements for meetings and so on would sometimes note that they would be followed by a time of fellowship. Ours was a friendly church, so we fellowshipped a lot—not just when and where it was designated, but in the church lobby after services, at people's homes, at local restaurants. When I got to be in high school and my friends and I would sometimes skip out during the Sunday school hour, we tried to overcome our parents' objections by saying we were going out for "fellowship" (i.e., pancakes).

In the New Testament, fellowship is so much more than standing about drinking bitter coffee and nibbling donuts, a Sunday morning church-style version of a cocktail party.

The Greek word *koinonia* comes from the word *koinonos*, meaning a partnership or having in common. *Koinonia* has various shades of meaning, but it is used in the New Testament to express community, generosity, and deep connection.

One scholar points out, "In later Greek, *koinonia* is used as the opposite and contrast to *pleonexia*, which is the grasping spirit which is out for itself. *Koinonia* is the spirit of generous sharing as contrasted with the spirit of selfish getting."[1]

The word *koinonia* is also translated "communion," "communication," "contribution," and "distribution." These give us the shades of its meaning, and remind us of the connection between fellowship and generosity. The church exists not just to be a gathering place for Christians but a means of making a difference in the world. We gather not just to be edified but to offer concrete, practical care to those in need—both within and outside of our immediate fellowship. (See Rom. 15:26; 2 Cor. 8:4; 9:13; Heb. 13:16, which all contain the word *koinonia*.)

Koinonia and the related words *koinoneo* and *koinonos* appear a total of thirty-eight times in the New Testament, but the idea of fellowship and community is a theme throughout. The Christian life is not meant to be lived in isolation. Almost always, when the writers refer to "you," the reference is plural. It's too bad Bible translators can't use the dialect of the American South—they'd get plenty of use of the helpful term *y'all*.

Without using the word, Jesus prayed that his followers would experience *koinonia* when he prayed in John 17:20–23:

> I pray also for those who will believe in me through their message, that all of them may be one, Father, just as you are in me and I am in you. May they also be in us so that the world may believe that you have sent me. . . . May they be brought to complete unity to let the world know that you sent me and have loved them even as you have loved me.

Koinonia consists of this "being in" one another and God.

Acts 2:42 says, "They devoted themselves to the apostles' teaching and to fellowship (*koinonia*), to the breaking of bread and to prayer." The next few verses describe the church in the wake of Pentecost—an amazing glimpse into what *koinonia* meant at that time: sharing of all resources, eating meals together, gathering daily, signs and wonders performed, conversions on a daily basis. People were drawn to this inclusive and exciting community, which offered an irresistible combination of learning and loving. Does our twenty-first-century fellowship have this effect on unbelievers?

How can we experience *koinonia* today? Despite our high-tech communication, we are often isolated or lonely. Fellowship is a necessary component of a Christian's spiritual growth and formation. Perhaps we will find the intimate community we seek when we invite others into it.

FILL/FULFILL/FULLNESS

Judging by the number of times in the New Testament we find various forms of words that mean to fill, fulfill, or fullness, we cannot help but conclude that the Christian life is meant to be one of abundance. God is not miserly or stingy, but generous. Our faith is not empty, but full. Prophesy does not stand waiting, but is fulfilled. The hungry are filled with good things. Jesus offers us life to the full, and came that we may be full of joy.

In the Greek, the word *pleroo* means, depending on context, either to make full, to fill to the full, or to fulfill. It appears ninety times in the text. In addition, it is the root of several other words, each conveying a subtly different facet of meaning. Together, these words appear more than seventy-five times: *anapleroo, antanapleroo, sumpleroo, pleo, pleres, plerophoreo. Pleroo*'s noun form, *pleroma*, means that which fills up, or fullness, completion. The related *empiplemi, empletho, empiplao* mean to fill full, to satisfy; the latter being used to describe God's provision for human beings.

The Greek word *teleo* means to end in a variety of ways, and is translated "fulfill" in a number of verses, as are its related words *sunteleo* (to complete), and *teleioo*, and the noun *teleiosis* (fulfillment).

Sumpleroo means to fill completely. It is used not only to describe a swamped boat in Luke 8:23, but also to describe fulfillment of time—connoting perhaps the fulfillment of prophesy, or perhaps God's perfect timing for events, as in Luke 9:51: "As the time approached for him to be taken up to heaven, Jesus resolutely set out for Jerusalem." The KJV says, "when the time was come." The same word and tense is used in Acts 2:1, "when the day of Pentecost was fully come" (KJV).

Anapleroo, to "fill up completely" is used to describe fulfilled prophesy, but also to describe a person who fills a position, or of how our care for one another fulfills the law of Christ (see Gal. 6:2).

Luke 1:1 also refers to the fulfillment of prophesy about Jesus, and he chooses the word *plerophoreo*, which means to carry out fully, to convince or completely assure, or even to be persuaded. Paul uses the same word in 2 Timothy 4:17, when he writes of his own message being fully known or fully proclaimed.

In Luke 4:1, we read that Jesus was "full (*pleres*) of the Holy Spirit." *Pleres* means full either materially or spiritually.

The Greek words *pimplemi* and *pletho*, which are lengthened forms of the verb *pleo* (to fill or complete) are used of both things (say, a boat full of fish) and people (full of emotion, or of the Holy Spirit).

One of the more interesting things Jesus said was, "Do not think that I have come to abolish the Law or the Prophets; I have not come to abolish them but to fulfill (*pleroo*) them" (Matt. 5:17). What does that mean, exactly? Jesus taught not just to share ideas, but with the expectation that his listeners would apply his teaching to their daily life.

Rob Bell writes,

> Rabbis would spend hours discussing with their students what it meant to live out a certain text. If a student made a suggestion about what a certain text meant and the rabbi thought the student had totally missed the point, the rabbi would say, "You have abolished the Torah," which meant that in the rabbi's opinion, the student wasn't anywhere near what God wanted. But if the student got it right, if the rabbi thought the student had grasped God's intention in the text, the rabbi would say, "You have fulfilled Torah."[1]

It's a bold claim for someone to make: that his interpretation of the Old Testament (the Law and the Prophets) was the right one. But such a claim was an essential foundation to the invitation he issued: "Follow me."

If we respond with our lives to that invitation, if we follow him and try to live as he lived, Jesus promises that our joy will be full (*pleroo*—see John 15:11 and 16:24). He said that he came that we might have life, and life to the full (John 10:10). Here we see yet another word: *perissos*. It means super-abundant, superior in quality, over and above. It is an extravagant, abundant word, full of promise and hope. It's a word I want my life to embody.

FIRE

The Greek word *pur* appears seventy-four times in the New Testament, and while it sometimes refers to literal fire, it is also used to describe God's holiness, his judgment, or even the fire of hell. Sometimes the metaphor is multifaceted, as in Luke 12:49–51, where Jesus says, "I have come to bring fire on the earth, and how I wish it were already kindled! But I have a baptism to undergo, and how distressed I am until it is completed! Do you think I came to bring peace on earth? No, I tell you, but division." Was the fire Jesus was bringing the fire of conflict, or the purifying fire of his message? Or was he saying that when his message spread, conflict would be an inevitable result?

We get our English word *pure* from this root, for that is one function of fire—to refine or purify. This is not always a painless process, because it always involves change.

Pur is a violent word in some ways. I sometimes want to skim over this word in my Bible, especially when I find it in the words inked in red, that is, words from Jesus' mouth. Jesus talked about the fire of hell, and as unpalatable as that is, we need to examine the context of these references.

He uses the image of a fire as part of an extended metaphor, talking of tree branches and weeds (representing people and things that are evil or cause evil) that will be destroyed. For example, in Matthew 13:40–43, Jesus explained a parable:

> As the weeds are pulled up and burned in the fire, so it will be at the end of the age. The Son of Man will send out his angels, and they will weed out of his kingdom everything that causes sin and all who do evil. They will throw them into the fiery furnace, where there will be weeping and gnashing of teeth. Then the righteous will shine like the sun in the kingdom of their Father.

Here Jesus contrasts two fires: a fiery furnace, a metaphor for eternal punishment and regret; and the shining sun, a metaphor for the righteous.

Both Matthew 18 and Mark 9 record Jesus' teaching on temptation, where the word *pur* is combined with the word *hell*—as in "hell fire"—a favorite of preachers exacting repentance for centuries. Here the word *fire* comes in the context of extreme hyperbole: "If your eye causes you to sin, gouge it out and throw it away. It is better for you to enter life with one eye than to have two eyes and be thrown into the fire of hell" (Matt. 18:9).

Mark's gospel reiterates these same words in chapter 9. The word translated "hell" in this passage is the Greek *geenna.* One commentary notes: "This is a loose transliteration of the Hebrew *ge-hinnom*, 'the valley of Hinnom,' a gorge just outside Jerusalem which had in ancient times been the scene of human sacrifices (Jer. 7:31), but later, during the reforms of Josiah (2 Kings 23:10), became the refuse-heap of the city. It was a natural metaphor for the place of future punishment."[1]

John the Baptist said this of Jesus:

> The ax is already at the root of the trees, and every tree that does not produce good fruit will be cut down and thrown into

> the fire. I baptize you with water for repentance. But after me will come one who is more powerful than I, whose sandals I am not fit to carry. He will baptize you with the Holy Spirit and with fire. His winnowing fork is in his hand, and he will clear his threshing floor, gathering the wheat into his barn and burning up the chaff with unquenchable fire. (Matt. 3:10–12)

In my life, I have both wheat and chaff. I follow Jesus, yet make mistakes. I act loving, then selfish, then loving again. While John's words may describe any number of different things (including ultimate judgment), they serve as an apt metaphor for the process of sanctification, which is sometimes scary and difficult but ultimately purifies our hearts and actions.

FORGIVE/FORGIVEN/FORGIVENESS

Since ancient times, revenge has been a human instinct. Forgiveness remains a rare commodity in our litigious culture. We cannot stand to be wronged, and yet we find a perverse pleasure in holding a grudge. We don't see the damage that bitterness does to our own soul.

In my previous book, *Simple Compassion*, I wrote: "To forgive is to access the power of God. To forgive is to enter into deep community with Jesus, the ultimate forgiver. To forgive doesn't let the person who wronged you off the hook. It lets *you* off the hook."[1]

Lew Smedes, a former professor at Fuller Theological Seminary, said: "When you refuse to forgive, you are giving the person who walloped you once the privilege of hurting you all over again—in your memory. . . . The first person to get the benefits of forgiving is the person who does the forgiving. Forgiving is, first of all, a way of helping yourself to get free of the unfair pain somebody caused you."[2]

The familiar refrain "Christians aren't perfect, just forgiven" has unfortunately evolved into a way to brush our own sin off our shoulders like a bit of dandruff—unsightly but not exactly our fault. Perhaps Jesus would want us to remember instead: "Christians aren't perfect, that's why they're forgivers."

Right after teaching his disciples to pray, "Forgive us our debts, as we forgive our debtors," Jesus adds: "For if you forgive [others] when they sin against you, your heavenly Father will also forgive you. But if you do not forgive [others] their sins, your Father will not forgive your sins" (Matt. 6:14–15). Similar passages in Mark 11 and Luke 11 seem at first glance to make God's forgiveness conditional upon our forgiveness of others. But as Frederick Buechner points out, "In the first place, forgiveness that's conditional isn't really forgiveness at all, just Fair Warning; and in the second place, our unforgivingness is among those things about us which we need to have God forgive us most."[3]

The Greek word is *aphiemi*. It appears in the New Testament 146 times, but is translated "forgive" only forty-seven of those times. More frequently, it is translated "leave," but it also can mean to suffer, to forsake, to let alone, and more. Its primary meaning is to send forth, send away. And that's what forgiveness is—to send the offense and our anger about it packing.

In Luke 4:18, Jesus declares that he has come to "release the oppressed, to proclaim the year of the Lord's favor." The word for "set free" in the Greek is *aphesis*, the noun form of *aphiemi*. The term "the year of the Lord's favor" reminded his listeners of the ancient command to observe the Year of Jubilee, in which debts were forgiven, slaves set free, and land restored to its original owners. It was supposed to be observed every fifty years—after seven periods of seven years each (Lev. 25).

In Matthew 18, Peter asks Jesus how many times he must forgive someone who wrongs him, and Jesus answers "seventy times seven." Jesus is not saying that on the four hundred and ninety-first offense you no longer have to forgive. He's alluding to Jubilee, and the spirit of that law, which is radical, God-focused forgiveness.

To drive home his point, he tells a story of a wicked servant who, though his huge debts had been forgiven, refused to forgive the small debt another man owed him. Jesus' point is that we have all been forgiven much, and if we fully understood that, we would be joyful forgivers, anxious to extend the grace we've received.

Ephesians 4:32 says: "Be kind and compassionate to one another, forgiving each other, just as in Christ God forgave you." The word *forgiving* in this verse is *charizomai*, which derives from *charis*, grace. It means literally to bestow a favor unconditionally. On our own, such generous forgiveness would be impossible. It is only when we truly grasp the extent of God's forgiveness to us that we are able to forgive in this grace-giving, tenderhearted way.

FREE/FREEDOM

To understand freedom in the biblical context, it would behoove us to look at the words found in the same sentences: words like *truth*, *give*, *gift*, *grace*, *justified*, and *Spirit*. Freedom is always related to grace, but also, paradoxically, to obedience. James 1:22–25 instructs us to not only hear God's Word, but to do what it says, to "look intently into the perfect law that gives freedom."

We look at the law of love not just to know it intellectually, but to live it. By definition, a person has freedom *from* something—freedom from sin, freedom from the desires of the flesh, freedom from fear. We also have freedom to do something—to go where we want, to choose whom we will love or follow, to act in a certain way. While we are free from the Mosaic Law, James echoes Paul's teachings in Galatians that freedom from the Old Testament law is not the same as freedom to indulge in sin. We are called to a higher law—the law of love. Our obedience to that law brings us freedom.

A key part of our identity in Christ is that we are a people who have been set free. And yet it is our obedience to Christ, and his Spirit in us, that brings that freedom.

In 2 Corinthians 3:17, freedom is connected with the presence of the Spirit and with spiritual transformation. "And where the Spirit of the Lord is, there is freedom." The context of this verse compares the veil that remained between God and his people in the Old Testament, and the freedom that we experience when the veil is taken away and we are transformed by Christ.

The Greek word *eleutheros* means freedom to go wherever one likes, or a free person. The related *eleutheria* means liberty, and *eleutheroo* means to set free or make free. To drive home his point in Galatians 5:1, Paul uses two forms of this word: "It is for freedom (*eleutheria*) that Christ has set us free (*eleutheroo*). Stand firm, then, and do not let yourselves be burdened again by a yoke of slavery." We should not abuse our freedom by indulging the sinful nature (which ultimately will enslave us), but rather, live by the Spirit, which brings freedom.

John 8:32 records Jesus' promise: "The truth will set you free (*eleutheroo*)." This verb means to make free. Truth doesn't just release us from sin; it changes who we are, our identity. We are made into new people, who are at our core free indeed.

This verse is found in a conversation between Jesus and a group of Jews. The text says this group had believed Jesus' teaching. And so Jesus challenges them to go a little deeper. He tells them the truth will set them free—but it is not an easy truth to swallow. Freedom sometimes involves letting go of our preconceptions, our pride, our old ways of thinking.

Clearly, freedom is not passive, but active. It manifests itself in actions that are directed by the Spirit, reflect the will of God, and follow the example of Christ. He tells them, "If you hold to my teaching, you are really my disciples. Then you will know the truth, and the truth will set you free" (John 8:31–32). He goes on to accuse them of obeying not God but Satan. They are, not surprisingly, incensed.

Freedom is a major theme in the book of Romans, where Paul uses metaphorical language to help us examine our hearts: Are we slaves to sin, or slaves to righteousness? Romans 5:15–18 explores the themes of sin, justification, and the free gift of life. While some versions merely speak of justification as a gift, several versions, including the KJV, emphasize that this is a *free* gift— one we cannot pay for even if we try. The Greek word is *charisma*, which means, of course, a free gift, bestowed by pure grace, not because of any merit on the part of the receiver. *The Message* translation captures it beautifully: "If death got the upper hand through one man's wrongdoing, can you imagine the breathtaking recovery life makes, sovereign life, in those who grasp with both hands this wildly extravagant life-gift, this grand setting-everything-right, that the one man Jesus Christ provides?"

FRIEND

In the ancient world, young men would approach established rabbis and ask to become their disciples (*talmidim* in Hebrew). If, after being quizzed by the rabbi on both their knowledge and their motives, they were granted this privilege, they would give up everything to follow the rabbi. Their lives would be dedicated to learning from him, discussing theology with him, asking him questions, and even imitating him in his every daily habit. (See ***Disciple***.) Jesus' highly unorthodox method of inviting people to follow him instead of waiting for them to come to him would have raised eyebrows.

Both in ancient times and today, Jewish students study not only with a rabbi but in a *havruta*, a gathering where they pair up to discuss and debate the Scriptures. Spangler and Tverberg write: "Each student is studying with a *haver* (pronounced hah-VAIR; literally a "friend") to master the text. . . . The word *haver* can simply mean a companion or close friend. But here it actually means someone who is willing to partner with you in grappling with Scripture and the rabbinic texts."[1]

Again breaking with convention, Jesus said to his disciples, "I have called you friends." His *talmidim* were also his *haverim*. They would have talked about the meaning of the Scriptures as they walked along, not just with Jesus but among themselves. He invited them to learn from each other. And Jewish learning often answered a question with a question. Occasionally the gospels record conversations between the disciples, where they ask each other what Jesus meant when he said certain things. The disciples were not clueless. What if they were engaging in *havruta*, where they would question each other as a learning method?

In John 15:12–17, we read,

> My command is this: Love each other as I have loved you. Greater love has no one than this, that he lay down his life for his friends. You are my friends if you do what I command. I no longer call you servants, because a servant does not know his master's business. Instead, I have called you friends, for everything that I learned from my Father I have made known to you. You did not choose me, but I chose you and appointed you to go and bear fruit—fruit that will last. Then the Father will give you whatever you ask in my name. This is my command: Love each other.

Jesus' words, bookended by the command to love one another, are an amazing offer of intimacy. He calls us friends (*philoi* in Greek, meaning those who are dearly loved) if we do what he commands

(v. 14). And what does he command? Love others. We live out our friendship with Jesus through friendship with others.

Our closest friends are those with whom we share confidences, the people who know and guard our secrets. He's chosen us not just to follow him but to be entrusted with all of what the Father has revealed to him. He's held nothing back.

Scholar Ceslas Spicq notes, "We should also recall a specific meaning of *philos*, namely, 'confidant, one to whom a secret is entrusted,' not only because the master-disciple relationship is assimilated to a friendship relationship, but because people entrust their most intimate and precious secrets only to those whom they love and in whom they have confidence."[2]

In contrast, the word *hetairos* means a comrade, but not an intimate. It appears only three times in the New Testament, always in Matthew. Jesus always refers to his disciples as *philoi* (plural of *philos*) except once: when he says to Judas, "Friend, do what you came for," as he comes to betray him. The word Jesus chooses to greet Judas is *hetairos*, the word he might use for a stranger—which indeed Judas has become.

Friendship with Jesus involves loving as he loved. It requires us to love each other, but beyond that, to help each other to work out what it means to follow him, and to do so together.

FRUIT

Jesus' teachings are full of botanical metaphors, which should come as no surprise, as he lived in an agrarian society. In our culture, many people have little to no idea where their food comes from or how it grows. They have never watched a plant develop from a seed, never had to coax tiny seedlings to maturity in order to eat.

But Jesus' contemporaries understood his stories of seeds, trees, plants, and sheep in a visceral way. The story of their lives had been illustrated with many of the same images. So it's not surprising that Jesus tried to explain the kingdom with words they would be able to relate to, and it's certainly not surprising that the words *fruit* or *fruitful* appear in his recorded teachings fifty times.

Fruit is the offspring of a plant—it's what a plant produces, not just to feed animals and people, but so that the plant can reproduce. By definition, the seed of the plant is always found within the fruit, making it a perfect metaphor. Fruit lasts because the seed within it can be planted to produce yet more fruit.

The term *fruit* in both ancient Greek and English metaphorically describes a person's actions—what a person reproduces, or leaves as a legacy. In Greek, the word is *karpos*, which is used in the Bible to describe both the fruit of plants and also "the visible expression of power working inwardly and invisibly, the character of the 'fruit' being evidence of the character of the power producing it."[1]

The three synoptic gospels all include Jesus' parable of the sower (Matt. 13; Mark 4; Luke 8). Jesus tells this story to a large crowd that has gathered to hear him teach. He talks of seed that falls on a hard-packed path, on rocky soil, on thorny soil, and on good soil. Later, in each account, the disciples ask privately for an interpretation, which he gives.

The Greek word *karpophoreo* (which means to bear or bring forth fruit) appears at the end of each of these passages, where Jesus is explaining what happens to seed that falls on good soil. It produces a crop thirty, sixty, or even a hundred times what was sown.

What brings forth this kind of fruit in our lives? According to Jesus' explanation, it is hearing and understanding (or retaining) the Word of God. Fruit seems to be produced as a result of what God plants in us and how we respond. It is not all of our doing, nor entirely God's job.

How do we know if we are living fruitful lives? Galatians 5:22–23 describes the fruit of the Spirit, which is "love, joy, peace, patience, kindness, goodness, faithfulness, gentleness and self-control." Notice the verse does not say the "fruits" of the Spirit, but fruit. The fruit, or result, of the Spirit working in our lives is that we become not just some but all of these things: more loving, more patient, more faithful, and so forth. This verse is not a to-do list for us to work through, but a description of the transformation that occurs when God's Spirit begins to work in us. When we remain open to that work, cooperating with it, hearing and retaining God's word, fruit will result. We will be transformed and become agents of transformation in the world.

John's gospel doesn't include the parable of the sower, but the fifteenth chapter records Jesus' teaching on the vine and the branches, another garden metaphor. In this passage, Jesus is talking about fruit bearing again. In this text, as others, there is an underlying tension about the miracle of growth—we cannot force ourselves to grow, but we can cooperate with God to create the right conditions for growth in our lives. John 15:2 says that branches that don't produce fruit will be cut off, which sounds frightening, but two verses later he points out that no branch can produce fruit by itself. Our focus should not be primarily on trying to produce fruit, but on clinging to the vine. When we do that, Jesus promised, spiritual fruit is the inevitable and joyful result.

GIFT/GIFTS

Nearly half the New Testament is not history or narrative, but correspondence: letters, mostly from the apostle Paul to churches. It is unfortunate that we don't have any letters from the churches to

Paul. We hear, as it were, only one half the conversation. Investigating the cultural context can only help.

First Corinthians appears to be a response to a letter from the church at Corinth. Paul writes in chapter 7, "Now for the matters you wrote about . . ." (v. 1). The church had obviously written asking questions, which he addresses in the subsequent chapters. We see the phrase "Now about . . ." repeatedly as he turns to yet another topic they'd evidently queried him about.

In chapter 12, he writes: "Now about the gifts of the Spirit, brothers, I do not want you to be ignorant. You know that when you were pagans . . ." (v. 1). The believers at Corinth were converted pagans, not Jewish Christians. (Even if Paul hadn't stated it so clearly, their questions about things like eating meat sacrificed to idols tips us off to the fact that they did not exactly keep kosher.) They had been part of a pantheistic religion whose belief and practice was quite different from Judaism, which was the religious background of the first disciples, Paul himself, and the very earliest Christians. Corinth was a center for pagan worship, especially of the Greek god Apollo. These converts had to learn a whole new way of worship.

Throughout his letter, Paul is advocating orderly worship, self-control (whether in worship or shared meals or in sexual morals), and self-discipline—all in stark contrast to pagan practice.

Paul reminds his readers of the unity they are called to, and that the different gifts are given by "one Spirit." He then lists various gifts (in Greek, *charisma*) of the Spirit, such as prophesy, healing, wisdom, and knowledge. He explains how these gifts are meant to work together for the common good of the church. (See ***Body***.) The gifts did not come from within the person, but from the Holy Spirit. They were not earned or bought, but a free gift from a loving God—another idea that would be new to these former pagans.

All gifts had equal value—a gift of speaking in tongues or teaching was not more valuable than a less "glamorous" gift like helps or encouragement. Paul emphasizes that no gift is more important than the others. The gifts were not for the benefit of the person with the gift, but rather, for the benefit of others, and all are necessary for the functioning of the body of Christ.

A *charisma* is a free gift of grace, and also a calling. Its root, *charis*, means grace. *Charisma* can also mean unmerited favor or grace, or can refer to the gifts of the Spirit listed both here in 1 Corinthians 12 and also in Romans 12—divinely given endowments such as the gift of teaching, prophesy, mercy, or helps.

While entire denominations have formed and split over the interpretation of this passage, we can agree that the Bible teaches that every believer is given these gifts, by the Holy Spirit, for the edification and encouragement of the body of believers. Do you know what your spiritual gift is? Has the Spirit given you, for example, the ability to show mercy to those in pain? To explain theological truth in a way that brings light? Are you using that gift within the body of Christ?[1]

Paul uses the same word, *charisma*, in Romans 5:15, to describe the gift of God's grace, and in Romans 1:1 when he speaks of his longing to give the believers at Rome a "spiritual gift" of mutual encouragement.

There are several other Greek words that are translated "gift" or "gifts." *Doron*, for example, appears nineteen times in the text and refers to a gift given to honor someone or to support the temple or the poor. It's also used once, in Ephesians 2:8, to refer to the gift of salvation by grace from God. *Dorea* appears eleven times in the New Testament and always refers to a spiritual or supernatural gift.

Paul writes to his young protégé Timothy: "Do not neglect your gift (*charisma*), which was given you through a prophetic message when the body of elders laid their hands on you" (1 Tim. 4:14). In his next letter to Timothy, Paul reiterates, "For this reason I remind you to fan into flame the gift (*charisma*) of God, which is in you through the laying on of my hands" (2 Tim. 1:6). Each of us, likewise, has a responsibility to discover and develop our spiritual gift.

GOOD/GOODNESS

Three of the four gospel accounts include the story of a rich young ruler who addresses Jesus as "Good teacher"—only to have Jesus retort, "Why do you call me good? No one is good—except God alone." (See Matt. 19:16–17; Mark 10:17–18; Luke 18:18–19.) He and Jesus have a very interesting discussion about rule-keeping in contrast with full-out discipleship, about pride in contrast with compassion.

The Greek adjective in this and many other passages is *agathos*, which can be used as either an adjective meaning good or a noun meaning good thing. The related noun *agathosune* is the moral quality of goodness. Jesus often told parables about the fruitfulness of good trees, good ground, good fish. The Greek word in these stories is *kalos.* While it is a synonym for *agathos, kalos* refers to something beautiful, either physically or morally, or honorable.

Jesus said only God is good, and yet, the Bible calls us to goodness, both in character and actions. Paul also wrote, in an important nugget of theological truth, that God's goodness (or in some translations, kindness) leads us to repentance. The word in Greek is *chrestotes*, a noun related to the adjective *chrestos,* both of which might be translated "goodness" or "kindness" or "gentleness." These words describe the inner character of a person, rather than simply goodness as an attribute or their propensity to occasionally do good deeds. Spicq notes: "*Chrestos* in that period is a title of honor conferred upon a mother, a grandmother, parents . . . Tertullian noted that pagans called Christians not *christiani* but *chrestiani,* 'made up of mildness or kindness.' "[1]

We see this word in Matthew 11:30, where Jesus says, "my yoke is easy (*chrestos*)." (See ***Yoke***.) He didn't mean his yoke (his way of life) was frivolous or required no effort. Rather, being yoked together with Jesus gives us access to true goodness. The life he asks us to live will result in character development toward goodness. It will be a joyful undertaking because we will be linked with Jesus.

The fruit of the Spirit (see previous entry), the result of the Spirit's work in our lives, is, among other things, goodness. Galatians 5:22–23 says, "But the fruit of the Spirit is love, joy, peace, patience, kindness (*chrestotes*), goodness (*agathosune*), faithfulness, gentleness (*praiotes*) and self-control. Against such things there is no law." In some translations, *chrestotes* is translated "gentleness" instead of "kindness." And *praiotes* is translated "meekness," but means a gentleness of spirit or humility. This list, then, has words that are so close in meaning it is obvious that Paul is describing not nine different qualities but different facets of one beautiful gem—a life shaped and formed by the Spirit. Our goodness, kindness, and gentleness flow out of a transformed soul.

The paradoxical first step toward goodness is to come face-to-face with our depravity. We cannot be good on our own, at least not for very long or with any kind of purity. Our efforts to be good, if we are truthful, are often motivated by our desire to gain the approval of other people or perhaps, in our futile thinking, to impress God.

Goodness is the result of cooperation with and submission to God. As Ephesians 2:10 says, "For we are God's workmanship, created in Christ Jesus to do good (*agathos*) works, which God prepared in advance for us to do." The context of this verse makes it clear that our good works will not save us, but they are our grateful and humble response to the gracious love of God.

As C. S. Lewis wrote,

> The Christian is in a different position from other people who are trying to be good. They hope, by being good, to please God if there is one; or—if they think there is not—at least they hope to deserve approval from good men. But the Christian thinks any good he does comes from the Christ-life inside him. He does not think God will love us because we are good, but that God will make us good because he loves us.[2]

GOSPEL

In some churches, the liturgy includes this proclamation of faith: "Christ has died, Christ is risen, Christ will come again!" Whether or not you recite those words in your Sunday service, they are the heart of the gospel, or good news. It is the Message.

The Greek word *euaggelion* occurs seventy-seven times in the New Testament. William Barclay notes: "The word *euaggelion* means 'gospel' or 'good news,' and when we come to study it we are of necessity at the very heart and centre of the Christian faith."[1]

Euaggelion, one dictionary notes, "originally denoted a reward for good tidings; later, the idea of a reward dropped, and the word stood for 'the good news' itself."[2]

The related Greek verb *euaggelizo*, which means to announce good news, is typically translated "to preach the gospel." (See ***Preach***.) It occurs fifty-five times in the New Testament. This word is often used to describe the ministry of Jesus. This word is used when Jesus stands up in the temple and quotes Isaiah (as recorded in Luke 4) by saying "the Spirit of the Lord is on me, because he has anointed me to preach good news (*euaggelizo*) to the poor" (Luke 4:18).

And what is this news? The heart of the good news, or gospel, is that "God so loved the world, he gave his one and only son, that whoever believes in him shall not perish but have eternal life" (John

3:16). This is the good news, which is from God but is also about God—God is loving, and beyond that, he *is* Love—it is his essential nature. The astonishing message, or gospel, is that God is not just concerned, but embodies love to such an extent that he is willing to sacrifice for humankind in order to show love toward us. This is what makes the news so good, and unique among religions.

The apostle Paul wrote that *euaggelion* is this: "That the Messiah died for our sins, exactly as Scripture tells it; that he was buried; that he was raised from death on the third day, again exactly as Scripture says; that he presented himself alive to Peter, then to his closest followers" (1 Cor. 15:3–5 THE MESSAGE).

Euaggelion appears a handful of times in the gospels of Matthew and Mark, in one passage of Acts, and in 1 Peter 4:17, but it appears most frequently in the letters of Paul. Paul writes not only of the gospel as the facts of Jesus' death and resurrection, but he also uses the same word to refer to the theological doctrine that interprets those facts. For example, in the opening paragraphs of his letter to the church at Galatia, Paul admonishes the church for "turning to a different gospel—which is really no gospel at all!" (Gal.1:6–7).

Here Paul is arguing not just about the facts of Christ's death and resurrection, but about the doctrine he extrapolates from those facts. He's defending his teaching, his theology, and warning the church to not be taken in by false teaching. Specifically, he was refuting doctrine espoused by a group of Jewish Christians called the Judaizers, who were making headway in the churches in Galatia. They taught that even those who followed Jesus also had to obey all of the Jewish law—from keeping kosher to being circumcised.

Paul says to follow this doctrine would be the wrong choice. Which makes an important point: the gospel presents us with a choice. Although God goes to great lengths to show his love, love is not love if it forces reciprocity. We have the freedom to accept and appropriate the gospel into our lives, or not. And if we choose to believe it, we begin to live by it and share it with others. We do this not out of obligation, but because we simply cannot keep such good news to ourselves. Paul wrote that he had been "entrusted with the gospel" (1 Thess. 2:4) and that he was "compelled to preach" the good news. When we fully comprehend the good tidings of God's love, we will feel the same way.

GRACE

Although the gospels are the ultimate story of God's grace, the word *grace* itself, *charis* in the Greek, appears within the gospels only four times: once in Luke and three times in the first chapter of John. But of course, Jesus told (and showed) his followers how to live graciously: "Love your enemies and pray for those who persecute you" (Matt. 5:44), "If someone strikes you on the right cheek, turn to him the other also" (Matt. 5:39), or most radically, "Father, forgive them, for they do not know what they are doing" (Luke 23:34) uttered from what should have been a graceless place, the cross.

And of course, grace, both the word and the idea, dances through the rest of the New Testament. Its fair countenance shines from nearly every page. *Charis*, which is translated "grace," "favor," "thanks," and so on, appears 156 times in the Greek New Testament. Its context is often "the grace of God" or "the grace of our Lord Jesus," because his grace is unlike any other.

Charis is the obvious root of *charisma*, gift, and is in itself a gift. It's been said that justice is getting what you deserve, mercy is not getting what you deserve, but grace is getting what you don't deserve. In a nutshell, this is the theology of grace: "For the wages of sin is death, but the free gift (*charisma*) of God is eternal life in Christ Jesus our Lord" (Rom. 6:23 NASB). Grace comes to us not through our efforts but through divine initiative. It cannot be earned, only received.

Grace is related to freedom. (See ***Freedom***.) It offers freedom from the consequences of sin, but not the freedom to sin. (See all of Romans, especially chapters 5 and 6.) It is freely given by God (see Eph. 2:4–9), and must be received as such.

One commentary offers this insight:

> Grace indicates favor on the part of the giver, thanks on the part of the receiver. Although *charis* is related to sins and is the attribute of God that they evoke, God's *eleos*, the free gift for the forgiveness of sins, is related to the misery that sin brings. God's tender sense of our misery displays itself in his efforts to lessen and entirely remove it—efforts that are hindered and defeated only by man's continued perverseness.[1]

In his book *What's So Amazing About Grace?* author Philip Yancey writes:

> The many uses of the word in English convince me that *grace* is indeed amazing—truly our last best word. It contains the essence of the gospel as a drop of water can contain the image of the sun. The world thirsts for grace in ways it does not even recognize. . . . Trace the roots of grace, or *charis* in Greek, and you will find a verb that means "I rejoice, I am glad."[2]

Although my life has been changed by grace, I don't always find myself rejoicing. But choosing to be glad and rejoice enables me to extend grace to those who need it most. If we let it, grace enables us to live in such a way as we could not otherwise—we become, through its influence on our souls, better people than we would be without it. The problem is, we can easily come to believe that the transformation effected by grace is one that we have orchestrated ourselves, that we have somehow engineered through sheer will. Our tendency to forget what grace has done only shows us that we never outgrow our need for grace.

In her excellent book *Sin Boldly: A Field Guide for Grace*,

Cathleen Falsani writes: "When I understood, in God's grace, that there was nothing—not a thing—I could do to make God love me any less or any more, when I understood that there was nothing wrong or right about who I am in God's eyes, that I'm just loved, I started to live. Boldly. Or at least as boldly as I can muster much of the time."[3]

When we fully grasp that nothing we do can make God love us any more or any less, we can live boldly. We can let our lives tell the story of God's grace.

HARVEST

One of Jesus' more disturbing parables is found in Matthew 13. Sandwiched between two other "seed" parables (the parable of the sower and the parable of the mustard seed), we find the parable of the weeds, or as the King James Version calls it, the wheat and the tares.

In it, a farmer sows good seed, only to have it tainted by an enemy who sows weeds in the same field. Rather than pull up the weeds and uproot the crop, the farmer instructs his workers to leave them all growing together until harvest day, and then pull up the weeds to be burned, and gather the wheat into the barn.

When Jesus' disciples ask about this curious parable, he explains that the wheat symbolizes "the sons of the kingdom" and the weeds are "the sons of the evil one." He then notes, "The harvest is the end of the age, and the harvesters are angels."

Jesus is warning his listeners about a day of reckoning, and about how people will be separated according to whom they have served, God or Satan. Those who do evil will be thrown into a furnace where there is "weeping and gnashing of teeth."

In this parable, *harvest* is a metaphor for judgment. But in other passages, *harvest* connotes spiritual readiness. One commentary notes, "Significantly, it is the person and work of Christ that functions as the catalyst for gathering both citizens of the kingdom of God and those who will be condemned to eternal separation from God. 'Harvesting' in the New Testament is a profoundly eschatological concept—one which is already anticipated in the Old Testament."[1]

Growing up evangelical, I remember hearing Jesus' words, "The fields...are white already to harvest" (John 4:35 KJV), or as other versions put it, "ripe for harvest." Jesus tells his disciples that the harvest is plentiful and ready and abundant. I was taught that this meant there are sinners out there just ready to be plucked, like apples from trees or wheat in a field, if we would just go out and tell them to repent and be saved. One part of the harvest metaphor we may have missed was the importance of timing—there is a season for both sowing and reaping, and sometimes there is a season of simply waiting and watering.

The Greek word for harvest is *therismos*, which is related to the word *therizo*, to reap, and is used figuratively in the New Testament. The parable of the sower promises a spiritual harvest of plenty for those who "hear and understand" God's Word—the phrase implies not just intellectual assent to God's truth but obedient action to live it out.

Our culture is far removed from the whole idea of a harvest—of the waiting for the correct time of year, of the careful watching and hoping for well-timed rains. If the rains came too early, they could destroy tender seedlings; if they came too late, they might knock the ripened grain from the stalks. For Jesus' contemporaries, harvest was a metaphor they lived in fully.

Harvest was a time of feasting—which is only logical because that was when food was most plentiful. Consequently, the Hebrew calendar was built around feasts that coincided with the harvest of various crops. "The three principal feasts of the Jews corresponded to the three harvest seasons (Ex. 23:16; 34:21–22); (1) the feast of the Passover in April at the time of the barley harvest (compare Ruth 1:22); (2) the feast of Pentecost (7 weeks later) at the wheat harvest (Ex. 34:22), and (3) the feast of Tabernacles at the end of the year (October) during the fruit harvest."[2]

I keep a garden, but I don't depend on it for sustenance. My lack of farming experience limits my understanding of the biblical word *therismos*. While I eagerly anticipate the first tomato from my garden, I can't really fully grasp the idea of the urgency of looking forward to harvest time as the means by which I will survive the coming year—or not.

I have to ask myself—do I similarly lack urgency about the spiritual harvest in which God has called me to be a worker?

HOLY SPIRIT

From the time the last book of the Old Testament was written until the annunciation, there is a yawning silence of four hundred years. Four centuries of waiting and looking for the promised Messiah, during which God says—nothing. And then, with sudden vengeance, the Holy Spirit shows up. Immediately, things get interesting in very concrete ways: a young virgin and a post-menopausal woman both end up pregnant, for starters.

No one is described as having just a smidgen of the Spirit—instead, like Elizabeth, they're described as "filled with the Holy Spirit" (Luke 1:41). As the gospel narrative unfolds, we see Jesus, "full of the Holy Spirit," led by that Spirit into the wilderness for a time of testing (see Luke 4). In Luke 10:21, Jesus is described as being "full of joy through the Holy Spirit" when he prays.

In Luke 11:13, Jesus says that the Spirit is ours for the asking: "If you then, though you are evil, know how to give good gifts to your children, how much more will your Father in heaven give the Holy Spirit to those who ask him!"

The Spirit cannot, therefore, be earned, but can of course be invited into our lives. When a child invites Jesus to live in her heart, that's really what she's asking for—an indwelling of the Holy Spirit.

The word *spirit* in Greek is *pneuma*, which comes from the word *pneo*, to breathe. So *pneuma* means both breath (or wind) and spirit. By itself, it can mean the spirit of a person. Add the Greek word *hagios*, holy, and you describe the third person of the Trinity. Jesus uses this double meaning in a wonderful play on words in his conversation with Nicodemus in John 3.

Jesus answered,

> I tell you the truth, no one can enter the kingdom of God unless he is born of water and the Spirit (*pneuma*). Flesh gives birth to flesh, but the Spirit (*pneuma*) gives birth to spirit (*pneuma*). You should not be surprised at my saying, "You must be born again." The wind (*pneuma*) blows wherever it pleases. You hear its sound, but you cannot tell where it comes from or where it is going. So it is with everyone born of the Spirit (*pneuma*) (vv. 5–8).

No wonder that Nicodemus responds, "How can this be?" His actual response may have been, "Huh?"

Like wind or breath, the Spirit has power, yet is invisible; is everywhere and yet impossible to pin down. We see the results of his action but can't see or fully understand him.

The Holy Spirit is also referred to with the Greek word *parakletos*. Just before he died, Jesus told his followers, "It is for your good that I am going away. Unless I go away, the Counselor will not come to you; but if I go, I will send him to you" (John 16:7).

Other versions translate *parakletos* as "Advocate," "Comforter," or "Helper." Why so many different words? One commentary notes,

> A precise translation of *parakletos* is difficult to determine. The underlying sense of the term is that of "one who stands alongside another in order to offer encouragement, comfort." . . . The designations "Advocate" and "Counselor," while accurate, are not comprehensive. No one English term expresses the full semantic range of *parakletos*.[1]

Jesus then told his disciples, "When he comes, he will convict the world of guilt in regard to sin and righteousness and judgment" (John 16:8).

The Holy Spirit convicts us, not from far off, but from within us. God speaks to us through the Spirit, and the Spirit prays on our behalf. (See Rom. 8:26.)

On the day of Pentecost described in Acts 2, the Holy Spirit comes, as promised, on the believers gathered in Jerusalem. They hear and feel a violent wind (*pneuma*), then see tongues of fire resting over each of them. The text says they were filled with the Spirit and began to speak in tongues.

We may not see the Holy Spirit in tongues of fire or feel him in a strong wind, but his presence in our souls and in our lives is unmistakable, and, if we let it be, incredibly empowering.

HOPE

Hope, in the biblical sense, is not a vague longing, but a confident assurance that things will turn out the way that they should in the end—even though they may not seem to in this life. To truly have hope in God requires putting all of our eggs into one basket. That is frightening, or would be, were the basket not firmly in the grasp of Jesus, who conquered, among other things, death—a very hopeful thing indeed.

In English, *hope* can be a noun or a verb. We can hope or trust (in Greek, the verb is *elpizo*), or we can have hope, a confident expectation (the Greek noun is *elpis*). The word *hope* is typically combined with prepositions—hope *in* God, or hope *of* glory, for example. Our hope is directed and specific, not vague and uncertain. It is connected with the virtues of patience or suffering, but ultimately, these do not give us hope. Rather, God gives us hope in spite of suffering, and enables us to be patient, so that we are able to grow in faith—which is the hope of things unseen.

Both *elpizo* and *elpis* appear frequently in the writings of Paul, though interestingly, not at all in the teachings of Jesus (though he did tell his followers not to worry, which is perhaps another way of telling them to have hope). And of course, when Paul writes of hope, he talks about putting our hope in nothing less than the most profoundly hopeful event in history, the resurrection of Jesus Christ.

When the Bible mentions hope, you'll often find the word *faith* in the same sentence. Our faith in God is the basis and foundation for our hope. "Now faith is being sure of what we hope for and certain of what we do not see" (Heb. 11:1); "And now these three remain: faith, hope and love" (1 Cor. 13:13); "But by faith we eagerly await through the Spirit the righteousness for which we hope" (Gal. 5:5).

Stoic philosophers of Paul's time taught endurance or acceptance without complaint, but this is not at all what Paul is teaching. One commentary offers this insight:

> The majority of secular thinkers in the ancient world did not regard hope as a virtue, but merely as a temporary illusion; and Paul was giving an accurate description of pagans when he said they have no hope (Eph. 2:12; *cf.* 1 Thess. 4:13), the fundamental reason for this being that they were "without God." . . . Faith, hope and love are thus inseparable. Hope cannot exist apart from faith, and love cannot be exercised without hope.

> These three are the things that abide (1 Cor. 13:13) and together they comprise the Christian way of life.[1]

Hope is, then, impossible apart from God, since God is the object of our hope. Hope is also one of the outcomes of our spiritual formation. Paul writes in his letter to the Romans:

> Therefore, since we have been justified through faith, we have peace with God through our Lord Jesus Christ, through whom we have gained access by faith into this grace in which we now stand. And we rejoice in the hope of the glory of God. Not only so, but we also rejoice in our sufferings, because we know that suffering produces perseverance; perseverance, character; and character, hope. And hope does not disappoint us, because God has poured out his love into our hearts by the Holy Spirit, whom he has given us. (Rom. 5:1–5)

Look at the progression outlined in this passage: We put our faith in God, which justifies us. That justification brings us peace with God and access to his grace. That grace enables us to endure suffering. And even our sufferings ultimately lead us to hope.

William Barclay writes, "The Christian hope is not simply a trembling, hesitant hope that perhaps the promises of God may be true. It is the confident expectation that they cannot be anything else than true."[2]

HUMBLE

Jesus' disciples came to him, on more than one occasion, asking which of them was the greatest. They seem, at times, obsessed with position and power. Jesus' answers confound them. In Matthew 18 we read, "He called a little child, whom he placed among them. And he said: 'Truly I tell you, unless you change and become like little children, you will never enter the kingdom of heaven. Therefore, whoever takes a humble place—becoming like this child—is the greatest in the kingdom of heaven' " (Matt. 18:2–4 TNIV).

Did you catch that? Unless you become humble, you will never enter the kingdom. You must, Jesus says, change. Transformation is required, and the means to that transformation is humility. Admitting our sinfulness and asking Christ to forgive us requires deep humility. Unfortunately, we've sometimes reduced this important step to a formulaic prayer, and then judged others (not exactly a humble move) based on whether they have said a prayer, rather than on whether or not they have actually humbled themselves. This is a serious mistake.

The phrase "takes a humble place," or as other versions say, "shall humble himself," is a rendering of the Greek verb *tapeinoo*. It means to make low, to bring low, to abase.

As an aside, how did Jesus happen to have a little child nearby for this object lesson? Perhaps some of the crowd following Jesus—or even some of the women who were among his more devoted followers—were mothers who had their children with them. In another instance, Jesus welcomed little children—who, in his culture, were looked at as a nuisance. He modeled humility himself, being willing to converse with children and their mothers.

In other verses, the word translated "humble" is *tapeinos*, meaning depressed or humiliated, that which is low, lowly, or of no degree or low degree.

These two Greek words appear a total of only twenty-two times in the New Testament, and yet humility is a key Christian virtue and mark of Jesus' life. One of the most profound passages on humility is found in Philippians 2:1–11. There, Paul exhorts his readers to humbly "consider others better than yourselves" and to be concerned about the interests of others. We read of Jesus' descent from the wonders of heaven to the abasement of the incarnation. The text says that he "made himself nothing" and that "he humbled himself." This detailed description of Jesus' steps of humility is prefaced by these words: "Your attitude should be the same as that of Christ Jesus."

In their book *Descending into Greatness*, Bill Hybels and Rob Wilkins examine this passage in detail, outlining Jesus' loving steps of "downward mobility" from heaven to the cross. They write,

> If you want to be truly great, then the direction you must go is down. You must descend into greatness. At the heart of this paradox is still another paradox: Greatness is not a measure of self-will, but rather self-abandonment. The more you lose, the more you gain. . . . Throughout history, few Christians have really come to grips with the concept of downward mobility. . . . Difficult as the concept is to act on, Philippians makes it clear that moving down is the only way to become great in God's eyes. Downward mobility is not simply the best of many optional paths a Christian can take to bring God pleasure. It is the only path.[1]

Humility is the only path to greatness. Jesus repeatedly told his followers, "Everyone who exalts himself will be humbled, and he who humbles himself will be exalted" (Luke 18:14; Matt. 23:12; and elsewhere).

Humility enables us to extend grace to others. As it says in Ephesians, "Always be humble and gentle. Be patient with each other, making allowance for each other's faults because of your love" (Eph. 4:2 NLT).

Frederick Buechner writes, "True humility doesn't consist of thinking ill of yourself but of not thinking of yourself much differently from the way you'd be apt to think of anybody else. It is the capacity for being no more and no less pleased when you play your own hand well than when your opponents do."[2]

HUNGRY

Have you ever been hungry? For the last few years, our church family has together embarked on a Five-Day Challenge to raise money for the poor. Once a year, we eat as the majority of the world's population eats, for five days. A typical meal might consist of about a one-cup serving of rice and beans wrapped in a tortilla. As a church, we take the money we save on groceries and give it to an organization called Feed My Starving Children, which provides meals for hungry children around the world.

To fast in this way has a profound impact on your awareness and on your soul. The growling in your stomach becomes an ache in your heart, as you slowly (often on about the third day) realize—this is the plight of millions. And they don't get to be "done" with the fast after five days. The meager portions of a narrow variety of foods—perhaps the occasional addition of a small portion of meat—that's just normal, all the time.

As my family debriefed the experience of eating this way, my daughter, who was about thirteen at the time, said, "I will never say 'I'm starving' again." She had learned the difference between simply desiring something to eat and true hunger.

When we embrace the experience of physical hunger for a short time, we gain insight into our spiritual hunger. For me, the week of rice and beans is both exhausting and exhilarating. Eating these simple foods reminds me of the beauty of feasting on the simple words of Jesus. I become aware of how often the spiritual junk food of busyness and mindless activity has dulled my appetite for God. I felt both satiated with God's presence, and yet longing for more. It was a longing that brought me joy—so often I feel a bit of guilt for not wanting God more, for not being spiritually hungry enough.

Fasting is a spiritual discipline that is tied to prayer and self-examination. Author Lynne M. Baab writes, "What is my true hunger? In what ways am I satisfying myself too easily with toys and mindless pleasures? What does my desire for God really look like? These are some of the questions we may find ourselves considering when we fast, and the answer to these questions will nourish our life of prayer."[1]

When I fast, questions like these rise to the surface. Prayerfully working through them feeds my soul.

The words *hungry* and *hunger* appear less than two dozen times in the text, but are nonetheless a major theme in the teachings of Jesus. He spoke of himself as the only answer to our spiritual hunger. For example, in John 6:35 we read, "Then Jesus declared, 'I am the bread of life. Whoever comes to me will never go hungry, and whoever believes in me will never be thirsty' " (TNIV).

The Greek word is *peinao*, meaning to hunger or be hungry. The word is used literally or metaphorically, or sometimes both. In Mary's Magnificat, for example, she praises God because "he has filled the hungry with good things but has sent the rich away empty" (Luke 1:53). Mary's song is a prophetic word about the ministry of Jesus, spoken before he was even born. Jesus did indeed offer us spiritual food, but he also told us to feed the poor—and not just feed them with truth, but with physical food as well (see Matt. 25).

Jesus said, "Blessed are those who hunger and thirst for righteousness, for they will be filled" (Matt. 5:6). *The Message* translation renders this verse: "You're blessed when you've worked up a good appetite for God. He's food and drink in the best meal you'll ever eat."

What does that mean, to hunger for righteousness, to have an appetite for God? And what does that metaphorical filling, that spiritual "best meal," look like? In a culture where we can numb ourselves with cheap junk food, mindless entertainment, or electronic distractions, we often avoid ever experiencing true hunger—physical or spiritual. It is in our hunger that God meets us, and shows us what true satisfaction tastes like.

INHERITANCE

In order to understand the idea of inheritance in the New Testament, we must look back to the Old Testament covenant between God and Abraham. God promised Abraham and Sarah, a childless couple, an heir, through whom they would become parents of a great nation. As if that weren't enough, God promised that those descendants would inherit the Promised Land of Canaan.

Against this backdrop of covenantal promise, the New Testament speaks of a spiritual inheritance. The Promised Land becomes the New Jerusalem; the allotment of land becomes an allotment of spiritual glory and blessing.

One dictionary notes,

> The range of words referring to "inheritance" in both Old and New Testaments is quite broad. . . . "Inheritance" in the Old Testament manifests itself primarily in material terms. In the New Testament, "inheritance" takes on the aspect of blessing that moves from the earthly to the spiritual plane. No longer does "inheritance" focus on the land of Canaan, but rather on the heritage of the eternal promise of salvation.[1]

Still, when Jesus came with this new message, those who were accustomed to the former system (of the Law) had a bit of trouble adjusting. Consider the story of a rich young man who came to Jesus asking, "What must I do to inherit eternal life?"

Jesus discerns that this young man is looking to accumulate more, to inherit in a material sense. He wants to add to his already bulging portfolio an annuity, an eternal life insurance policy. Jesus quickly discerns that the man is spiritually bankrupt, as he proudly claims to have kept all of God's commandments without error since he was a child. Hearing this, Jesus tells him to give away all of his wealth (Mark 10:17–31; Luke 18:18–30).

Jesus preached a kingdom upside down, one in which you gain by losing, you receive by letting go. The inheritance offered by Jesus is the pearl of great price, for which we trade all that we hold dear.

The Greek word *kleros* means a portion, but its primary meaning is a lot that is given or cast. It can also be translated "inheritance" or "heritage." The other New Testament Greek words for inheritance are rooted in this word: *kleronomia, kleronomeo, kleroo.* The similar *kleronomos* means inheritor or heir. The root *kleros* is itself a derivative of the word *klao*, which means to break (as in breaking bread). The idea of getting your share or portion is imbedded in all these words.

Kleronomeo, which appears eighteen times in the New Testament, literally means to receive by lot. It encompasses the ideas of being given a birthright or a gift, a reward. Although the Bible is clear that such an inheritance is a gift that cannot be earned, it is also a reward for "faith and patience" (see Heb. 6:12) and for meekness (see Matt. 5:5).

The opening chapter of Ephesians talks about our spiritual inheritance. While some translations render Ephesians 1:11, "We were chosen," the word in the Greek is *kleroo*, which is the only time that word appears in the text. A more literal rendering would say that we were made heirs, or given an inheritance, specifically of salvation. A few verses later, Paul writes: "Having believed, you were marked in him with a seal, the promised Holy Spirit, who is a deposit guaranteeing our inheritance (*kleronomia*) until the redemption of those who are God's possession—to the praise of his glory" (Eph. 1:13–14).

Inheritance in the New Testament embraces a paradox: We

receive our spiritual inheritance through faith in Jesus when we relinquish our lives to him. We become "God's possession," yet also "co-heirs" or "fellow heirs" with Jesus. Romans 8:17 says, "Now if we are children, then we are heirs—heirs of God and co-heirs with Christ, if indeed we share in his sufferings in order that we may also share in his glory." The Greek word is *sugkleronomos*, the prefix meaning "with" added to *kleronomos*.

Jesus said the meek will inherit the earth. Dietrich Bonhoeffer comments, "But Jesus says: 'They shall inherit the earth.' To these, the powerless and the disenfranchised, the very earth belongs. Those who now possess it by violence and injustice shall lose it, and those who here have utterly renounced it, who were meek to the point of the cross, shall rule the new earth."[2]

JOY

Joy is elusive in many ways. It is not happiness, which is dependent on circumstances. Joy is something we experience in spite of our circumstances, and goes far beyond simply feeling happy or well. Because we cannot obtain it by possessing things or even experiences, joy refuses to be pinned down. It's a gift we receive when we stop trying to get it.

C. S. Lewis wrote extensively on Joy. His life was marked by what he labeled *Sehnsucht*—a longing for joy. It was the longing itself that brought joy, not the attaining. And it was that longing that led him to eventually renounce atheism and become one of the greatest Christian apologists of the twentieth century.

In his wonderful book *Surprised by Joy*, he writes,

> In a sense the central story of my life is about nothing else. . . . . It is that of an unsatisfied desire which is itself more desirable than any other satisfaction. I call it Joy, which is here

> a technical term and must be sharply distinguished both from Happiness and from Pleasure. Joy (in my sense) has indeed one characteristic, and one only, in common with them; the fact that anyone who has experienced it will want it again.[1]

Jesus told his disciples that they would find joy by staying intimately connected to him (see John 15). When Jesus told his disciples he would be leaving them but then returning (referring to his death and resurrection), he told them those events would cause them to grieve but then to rejoice. Sometimes the path to joy leads us first through disappointment or pain. Sometimes we find joy in the midst of that pain, in spite of it, because we experience the presence of God.

The Greek word most frequently translated "joy" is *chara*, meaning cheerfulness or delight. The related verb *chairo* means to be glad or to rejoice. These are obviously related to *charis*, which primarily means grace but also can be translated "joy."

"*Chairo* is used in a whole range of situations in which the emotion of joy is evoked. Predominant in the usage of this term is the focus on rejoicing over the redemptive deeds of God that come to fruition in the gospel in the person of the Messiah, Jesus Christ."[2]

If we examine Paul's writings about joy, we find that he often experienced joy in the midst of difficulties. It is not an emotion we can manufacture by our own effort, but a gift of God. He opens his letter to the church at Philippi by encouraging them to be unified, which will make his joy complete.

Galatians 5 describes the fruit of the Spirit. We often mistakenly read "fruits" of the Spirit, as if they were separate and individual fruits, like apples and oranges. But the text says the "fruit of the Spirit is . . ." It's more akin to saying an apple is crunchy, sweet, juicy, delicious, etc. Joy is an inextricable part of the list—you cannot be loving without being joyful, if you are peaceful you will be patient, and so on. All of the characteristics, including joy, are interdependent, and none of them, again, can we produce on our own. They are the fruit, the product, the result of the Spirit's influence in our lives.

Joy is not produced by the absence of conflict or struggle—rather, it is what results from those trials when we understand them from God's perspective, and when we experience his presence in the midst of them. As James 1:2–4 says, "My brothers and sisters, whenever you face trials of any kind, consider it nothing but joy, because you know that the testing of your faith produces endurance; and let endurance have its full effect, so that you may be mature and complete, lacking in nothing" (NRSV).

Many of us want to be "mature and complete" but don't want to endure the trials that will hone our character. When we are able to see those difficulties as God's tools for strengthening and maturing our faith, we can have joy.

JUSTIFY/JUSTIFICATION

Justification is being made right with God, and it's a very important theological concept. The word itself, as a noun (*dikaiosis* in Greek), appears only three times in the New Testament, in the fourth and fifth chapters of Romans. The verb form, *dikaioo*, which essentially means to be made right or righteous, appears thirty-nine times, twenty-nine of those in the writings of Paul.

It is a prevalent theme in Romans, the longest of all the Pauline epistles, which summarizes Paul's theology. Obviously, justification is foundational to Paul, and to Christian doctrine.

The *New Bible Dictionary* notes, "Justification means to Paul God's act of remitting the sins of guilty men, and accounting them righteous, freely, by his grace, through faith in Christ, on the ground, not of their own works, but of the representative law-keeping and redemptive blood-shedding of the Lord Jesus Christ on their behalf."[1]

We cannot keep God's law perfectly, which means we are in need of justification. But just as we cannot keep the law perfectly, neither can we keep it even partially in hopes that we do it well enough to earn God's favor. The only way we can be justified is by putting our faith in Christ. As Paul writes: "For there is no distinction, since all have sinned and fall short of the glory of God; they are now justified (*dikaioo*) by his grace as a gift, through the redemption that is in Christ Jesus . . . For we hold that a person is justified (*dikaioo*) by faith apart from works prescribed by the law" (Rom. 3:23–24, 28 NRSV).

I have so many friends, some of whom go to church and agree philosophically that Jesus is the Son of God, who use phrases like, "Well, I am a pretty good person" or, "You'll go to heaven if you're good." Their theology is muddled at best.

The doctrine of justification points out that none of us is good. God does want us to be good (see ***Good***), but that goodness does not justify us. Goodness flows out of justification, which comes only through faith. Good works flow out of a justified soul. The book of James, especially the second chapter, explores this tension between faith and works. Although James appears to contradict Paul in James 2:24, James is writing not about how to be justified, but how to tell authentic faith (i.e., a justified person) from inauthentic faith (someone who has not really experienced justification by grace).

One commentary on this verse notes, "An opinion, or assent to the gospel, without works, is not faith. There is no way to show we really believe in Christ, but by being diligent in good works, from gospel motives, and for gospel purposes."[2] Our good works are not a means of earning God's favor, which we already have, but a means of furthering the gospel by living consistently with Jesus' teachings.

The Old Testament law did not justify God's people, only showed them their need for forgiveness. In Galatians 3:11, Paul quotes the prophet Habakkuk as if to point out that even before Jesus came, justification still occurred not by works but by faith: "Clearly no one is justified before God by the law, because 'the righteous will live by faith.' " Some versions say, "The just shall live by faith," because this word, *dikaios*, means both righteous and just. These two concepts are deeply intertwined. You cannot separate God's righteousness from his justice. In the same way, our lives ought to be about living rightly and living justly.

Jesus said, "And I tell you this, you must give an account on judgment day for every idle word you speak. The words you say will either acquit you or condemn you" (Matt. 12:36–37 NLT). Jesus is telling the Pharisees that what is in their heart flows out in their words. So they will be justified, or judged, based on their words, because they accurately reflect their hearts. A heart given over to God will be justified not because of the work of the person, but because of the work of Jesus.

LAMB

The words *lamb* and *sheep* both appear in the New Testament numerous times. Both words are used metaphorically, but their meanings are quite different. (See ***Sheep/Shepherd***.)

The term *lamb* (*arnion*) often refers symbolically to Christ. Of the thirty-one times the singular word *lamb* appears, twenty seven are in the book of Revelation, referring to the glorified Christ as the Lamb with a capital *L*. The Lamb is worthy, worshiped, seated on a throne.

In Revelation 5, Jesus is referred to as a lion, a root, and also a lamb (vv. 5–6). This is obviously symbolic language, not to mention freely mixed metaphors. This type of writing was common in the first century. In this chapter, the throne is surrounded by creatures who cry out:

> Worthy is the Lamb, who was slain,
> to receive power and wealth and wisdom and strength
> and honor and glory and praise! (Rev. 5:12)

The Lamb referenced in Revelation is not only the sacrificed Christ but the resurrected Christ—one whose submission and death has resulted in power and strength.

Scholar R. J. Krejcir of Into Thy Word Ministries wrote:

> In "apocalyptic" literature or *genre*, the language is clear, such as the word, "lamb," which is used often. We know what a lamb is and we may know that Christ is described as a lamb, but do we also know that Jesus is the *Lamb . . . been slain,* which means that Christ is the sacrifice? A lamb is the common animal that was "slain" and sacrificed for the atonement of sin and used for commerce. . . . The image of the lamb was common in apocalyptic literature, also meaning victory and power through, and sometimes over death. (Ex. 12:12–13; Isaiah 53:7; John 1:29; 21:15; Rev. 17:14)[1]

The Bible is not the only ancient text to contain apocalyptic literature, or even to use the symbol of a lamb. This does not negate the power of this word or compromise the truth of the Bible, but only helps us understand it in light of its cultural context.

In Revelation, the Greek word for *Lamb* is always *arnion*. In the other four New Testament uses, the word is *amnos*, meaning a lamb, as opposed to the Lamb. *Amnos* is still used figuratively of Christ, but focuses on his sacrifice. *Arnion* focuses on his glory.

The plural *lambs* is used only twice: in Luke 10:3, where Jesus sends out his disciples "as lambs (*aren*) among wolves" (the only time that Greek word is used), and in John 21:15, where it is used alternately with sheep when Jesus restores Peter and tells him to "feed my lambs," referring to his followers both present and future.

John the Baptist declares, "Behold, the Lamb (*amnos*) of God who takes away the sin of the world" (John 1:29 NASB), and in that moment everything is upended in a way that had never been before and hasn't since.

One commentary notes,

> The idea of a spotless lamb as a substitutionary sacrifice for the sin of the worshiper is a paradigm for forgiveness in the Old Testament ceremonial sphere. The theological significance of such a sacrifice is captured perfectly in the figure of Jesus Christ, whose designation by John the Baptist as the "Lamb of God" is perhaps the most sublime metaphor of the supreme efficacy of Christ's death in the New Testament.[2]

Everything in the Old Testament points toward the coming Messiah. Not just the prophesies, but also the Law and even the sacrifices, the stories, the songs. Each year, the Hebrew people would celebrate Passover and kill an innocent lamb, putting its blood on the doorpost. And they would tell the story of God's deliverance of their people from slavery in Egypt. That lamb's blood on the doorpost would protect God's people from the angel of death.

Christ's death, which happened during the Passover, was the fulfillment of the prophesy woven into that festival and its stories and rituals, and it foiled the angel of death not just for a year but for eternity.

LIGHT

According to the creation story in Genesis, light was the very first thing God created. He set the earth in motion, establishing a rhythm of day and night, darkness and light. Light was the beginning of life. In the New Testament, John opens his gospel narrative with allusions to the creation story:

> In the beginning the Word already existed. The Word was with God, and the Word was God. . . . The Word gave life to everything that was created, and his life brought light to everyone. The light shines in the darkness, and the darkness can never extinguish it. . . . The one who is the true light, who gives light to everyone, was coming into the world. (John 1:1, 4–5, 9 NLT)

The Greek word in this passage is *phos*, meaning light, a word that derives from *phao*, which means to shine, or luminousness. It's the most frequently used Greek word for *light*, although there are several others. Vine notes that *phos* means "light as seen by the eye, and, metaphorically, as reaching the mind. . . . Hence believers are called 'sons of light,' Luke 16:8, not merely because they have received a revelation from God, but because in the new Birth they have received the spiritual capacity for it."[1]

Other Greek words include *kaio* (to burn or light, as a candle); *lampo* (to shine, give light, or radiate); *pheggos* (brilliancy, a more concrete light, like a beam); *epiphaino* (to become visible); and *luchnos* (a portable lamp or candle, used both literally and metaphorically).

Jesus said, "I am the light (*phos*) of the world" (John 8:12; 9:5).

Jesus told his followers that they too were the light of the world. In just a few sentences from the Sermon on the Mount, we see several different Greek words for *light*:

> You are the light (*phos*) of the world. A city on a hill cannot be hidden. Neither do people light (*kaio*) a lamp (*luchnos*) and put it under a bowl. Instead they put it on its stand, and it

> gives light (*lampo*) to everyone in the house. In the same way, let your light (*phos*) shine (*lampo*) before men, that they may see your good deeds and glorify your Father in heaven. (Matt. 5:14–16)

Light in ancient times was a symbol of strength, protection, happiness, glory, salvation, and knowledge.[2] We put our own Western rationalist spin on it, but our culture similarly uses light as a metaphor: people "see the light" or "become enlightened" when they understand something. Still, because we can flip a switch and have light, we tend to take it for granted.

Until the invention of the electric light bulb, the rhythms of human existence were dictated by the daily cycles of light and darkness. While a fire or candle could extend the working day by a few hours, mostly people slept when it was dark and worked while it was light. Planning and preparation were needed in order to have light when night came.

Today our world is so artificially lit that astronomers and casual stargazers have trouble finding places dark enough to view the night skies without the interference of what is called "ambient light." I'll never forget speaking at a camp in the north woods of Wisconsin. At night, we walked cautiously into a dark field with a hobby astronomer on the staff, and we could see the whole Milky Way lit up like a path across the night sky. Through a telescope, we were able to peer at Andromeda, the galaxy next door. We could see another galaxy! What's incredible is that those same stars and planets are above your head right now, but you cannot see them, ironically, because you have too much light. Likewise, our culture, distracted by the false light of celebrities and entertainment, or worries and cares, often cannot see the light of Christ.

Light is a dominant theme in Old Testament messianic prophesies, so imagine the Jews' reaction when Jesus declares, "I am the light (*phos*) of the world. Whoever follows me will never walk in darkness, but will have the light (*phos*) of life" (John 8:12). Certainly the familiar words of Isaiah 9 would have immediately come to mind: "The people walking in darkness have seen a great light" (v. 2).

LOVE

The Beatles famously sang that it was all you need. In 1967, hippies celebrated the summer of it, and chanted loudly that we should make it, rather than war. Love is, in our culture, a word often said but seldom understood; a word robbed of meaning, and yet one that can mean so many different things. It is the subject of everything from beer commercials to pop music, paperback novels to sappy Lifetime channel movies.

Anyone who grew up in church remembers hearing an explanation about Christian love, how it differs so greatly from our culture's definition. Biblical love is not about romantic love or popularity. We're called to love people even if we don't like them—which causes more confusion, I think. And while love in our culture is something you try to get, biblical love is something you're called to give, because God gave it to you.

Three ancient Greek words can be translated as "love" in English. The one likely most parallel to our secular culture's understanding of love is *eros*, from which we get the word *erotic*. Sexual or romantic love, even a crush, fits under the heading of *eros*. It is both self-seeking, and paradoxically, the conquest of another. The word *eros* is conspicuous by its absence in the New Testament.

The second word goes a little deeper. *Phileo,* often understood as loving in a brotherly way, is more accurately "to have tender affection for." We get our word *philanthropy* from its noun form *philanthropia*. It is not as self-seeking as *eros,* and in fact, is sometimes used to describe the love between the Father and the Son, or Jesus' love for his followers and friends. More often, however, that kind of love is typically the third word, *agapao*, or its noun form *agape*. This refers to the deeper love—the love of God, a spiritual, self-sacrificing love that doesn't depend on being reciprocated. It is God's love toward Jesus and human beings.

When the Bible says "God is love," the Greek word is *agape*. When Jesus says that the most important commandment is to love the Lord your God, the verb is *agapao*. And the second, to love your neighbor? Also *agapao*. *Agape* is the word used in 1 Corinthians 13, and in Romans 5:8: "But God demonstrates his own love for us in this: While we were still sinners, Christ died for us."

David Benner writes, "The Christian God is unlike any god humans could ever imagine. . . . The great distinctive of the love of the Christian God is that there are no strings attached to it. God simply loves humans. . . . The notion of God's loving us unconditionally is absolutely radical."[1]

To *agapao*, to love unselfishly, is ultimately the most satisfying love, both to give and receive. It requires not an emotional response, but an act of the will. But it is not without risk, and sometimes takes us through a valley of pain. But if we try to avoid the pain of love, we end up lonely, which is worse.

A contrast between *phileo* and *agapao* is seen in John 21:15–19, where Jesus asks, "Peter, do you love (*agapao*) me more than these?" And Peter, still living in the world of shame over his denial, knows he has not loved. His earlier boasts of not leaving Jesus were shown to be hollow. He did not love more than the other disciples. But he's still wrestling with pride, so he can't say no. So he replies, "Lord, you know that I love (*phileo*) you." Jesus asks again, "Do you *agapao* me?" And Peter says, "I *phileo* you." At first blush, it looks like Jesus is asking for self-sacrifice, and Peter's handing him a Hallmark card.

This is what shame and guilt and pride do to us—they hinder

our ability to love in the way God loves. I have a friend who likes to say, "You can't be anywhere except where you are." So finally Jesus asks, "Peter, do you love (*phileo*) me?" He seems to be lowering the bar. And Peter, humbled and hurt, says, "Yes, I *phileo* you." And then Jesus talks about what will happen when Peter is old. The statements are obscure enough that John feels compelled to explain them in verse 19. But I wonder if Jesus is still talking about love, and saying you can't be anywhere but where you are. You can give me *phileo* now, but someday, when you're old, you'll *agapao* me. You'll make sacrifices you never thought you could. You'll surrender your will, which is what *agape* is all about.

MERCY

Mercy is closely related to the word *compassion*, and the two are sometimes interchangeable. Their precise meanings, though, are slightly different, especially when you look at the Greek words. But while compassion is to "suffer with," mercy is to be so moved that we attempt to relieve that suffering. One who shows mercy must have, by definition, power to alleviate suffering.

So in a way, mercy depends on position. Say I have a friend who is in debt. I can have great compassion, even to the point of trying to help her pay off the debt. However, if she owes someone else the money, I cannot cancel her debt. Mercy is dependent in part upon position. For that reason, God is the ultimate mercy giver, because he is the one who can forgive our ultimate debt.

Mercy is not getting what we deserve. It is being let off the hook, so to speak, not because of what we have done but because of the desperation of our circumstances. (See ***Compassion*** and ***Grace***.) It is different from grace. While mercy is not getting what you deserve (especially the punishment or consequences you deserve), grace is getting what you don't deserve.

In the Greek, we encounter the words *eleeo* (to have mercy on) or *eleos*, which are often translated "mercy" but can mean either mercy or compassion. In ancient times, the secular meaning was more one of pity. While some Hellenistic philosophers (but certainly not all) thought feeling pity was acceptable, some, such as the Cynics and Stoics, saw pity as a weakness.

But in Judaism, and subsequently Christianity, the meaning of *eleos* shifted. It was an attribute ascribed to God, and one his people were to exhibit to their fellow human beings. In the New Testament, the ultimate symbol of mercy is the coming of Jesus, not as a king but as a servant, someone who identified with our weakness and suffered for our sins.

Spicq writes,

> St. Paul's innovation in the biblical theology of *eleos* is to locate God's mercy at the beginning and at the end of the plan of salvation: "Formerly you were disobedient to God; now you have obtained mercy. . . . God has consigned all people to disobedience so as to show mercy to all" (Rom. 11:30–32). Universal mercy extends to Gentiles as well as Jews (Rom. 15:9) and consists in the forgiveness of sins.[1]

One commentary notes: "*Eleos* is the free gift for the forgiveness of sins and is related to the misery that sin brings. . . . Grace removes guilt, mercy removes misery. *Eleos* is the outward manifestation of pity."[2]

Jesus taught, "Blessed are the merciful (*eleemon*), for they will be shown mercy (*eleeo*)" (Matt. 5:7). Again, both these words go beyond mere pity to merciful action.

Jesus also said, "Be merciful, just as your Father is merciful" (Luke 6:36). The Greek word for merciful in this verse is *oiktirmon*, a word that appears only three times in the New Testament. It means having compassion for the ills of others. It is also used in James 5:11 to describe God, who is full of compassion and mercy. It is part of another family of words that are all drawn from *oiktos*, meaning pity. The word *oiktirmos* is the strongest of this group, meaning a heart of mercy, a more deeply felt, tender compassion (Phil. 2:1; Rom. 12:1).

Paul describes God in Ephesians 2:4 as being "rich in mercy (*eleos*)," and Jesus uses it to describe God's mercy in Mark 5:19, and calls us to this sort of compassion through his parable of the unmerciful servant in Matthew 18.

In the parable of the Good Samaritan, the Samaritan stops to help his enemy because he is moved with compassion (*splagchnizomai*) by his plight. (See ***Compassion***.) After the story is told to answer a Pharisee's question ("Who is my neighbor?"), Jesus counters with a question of his own: Which man was a neighbor? The embarrassed Pharisee replies, "The one who had mercy (*eleos*)." And Jesus says to him (and to all of us), "Go and do likewise" (Luke 10:37). We are called not only to receive this kind of compassion—what an amazing gift—but to show it to others, even to our enemies.

MESSIAH

Depending on which theologian you consult, the Old Testament contains at least sixty direct prophesies of a coming Messiah, and nearly three hundred other references to him. The promise of deliverance for God's people is a pervasive Old Testament theme.

Still, after the prophet Malachi predicted that the "sun of righteousness will rise with healing in its wings" (4:2), the children of Israel heard absolutely nothing from God for four hundred years. An awkward four-century silence ensued. And while they continued to study the Torah, celebrate the festivals, and repeat the stories to offer sacrifices and teach their children, they had to have wondered—when? When will the Messiah come?

Meanwhile, the oppression of Rome continued to increase. The Jews were looking for a king from the line of David to rescue them from their oppressors and restore their earthly kingdom. They were straining to hear a word from God. Into this void comes John the Baptist, saying, "Here he comes!"

The Greek word *christos* means anointed. The Hebrew equivalent is *masiah*, and Aramaic is *mesiha*. All mean Messiah. Eventually *christos* was connected with Jesus to become not just a title but a name: Jesus Christ.

The word *Messiah* itself, a transliteration of the Hebrew word, is found only twice in the New Testament—in John 1:41 and John 4:25. But the word *Christ*, the Greek equivalent to *Messiah*, appears more than five hundred times, mostly in conjunction with the name *Jesus*.

Philip Yancey writes,

> It would be impossible to exaggerate the import of the word *Messiah* among the faithful Jews. The Dead Sea Scrolls discovered in 1947 confirm that the Qumran community imminently expected a Messiah-like figure, setting aside an empty seat for him each day at the sacred meal. . . . Every Hebrew prophet had taught that someday God would install his kingdom on earth, and that is why rumors about the "son of David" so inflamed Jewish hopes. . . . But let us be honest. When the one John pointed to arrived on the scene, neither the mountains trembled nor the nations quaked. Jesus did not come close to satisfying the lavish hopes of the Jews.[1]

People looked at Jesus and said, "Oh, really?" He was not what people expected. The *New Bible Dictionary* notes:

> While there were many strands to the Messianic expectation in 1st-Century Palestine, some of which find an echo in the NT, . . . the dominant popular hope was of a king like David, with a role of political liberation and conquest, and it seems clear that this would be the popular understanding of *christos*.[2]

Jesus himself sometimes seemed reticent. He'd often refer to himself as "the Son of Man" (see ***Son of Man***), which may have been a common way of speaking about himself in the third person, or could have been referring to a messianic prophesy in the Old Testament book of Daniel.

While he didn't walk around with a sign or tell everyone who he was, he was unafraid to claim divinity when asked. Still, he was so low-key about his mission that the religious leaders cornered him and asked him straight out whether he was the Messiah, the Christ. In John 10:23–26 we read,

> Jesus was in the temple area walking in Solomon's Colonnade. The Jews gathered around him, saying, "How long will you keep us in suspense? If you are the Christ, tell us plainly." Jesus answered, "I did tell you, but you do not believe. The miracles I do in my Father's name speak for me, but you do not believe because you are not my sheep."

By the end of the conversation, the Jewish leaders wanted to stone him for blasphemy.

Though he was a great and wise teacher, it was Jesus' radical actions of love that were the strongest proof of his identity. He didn't talk about himself, but he gave of himself. He chose to love and to suffer. He loved as only God could love.

John Ortberg wryly observes: "There was no grandiosity in Jesus at all. That is one reason that people had such a hard time recognizing him. . . . God's great, holy joke about the messiah complex is this: Every human being who has ever lived has suffered from it—except one. And he was the Messiah."[3]

MIRACLE

Miracles dance through the pages of Scripture: God speaks the universe into existence; sends plagues and parts seas to rescue his people from slavery; rains manna to quench grumbling; sends his son to be the Bread of Life.

In the Old Testament, miraculous events were ascribed to God, or happened when prophets prayed to God. But Jesus speaks miracles into existence. He heals lepers, gives sight to the blind, or even raises people from the dead not by chanting incantations or invoking magic, but on his own authority. After Jesus' resurrection, his followers continue to do miracles in his name.

There are two Greek words that are translated "miracle." First, *dunamis*, meaning force or miraculous power. It refers to power or ability residing in a person, especially when performing miracles. Second, *semeion*, which is most often translated "sign"—a deed that has within it a secret and mysterious power.

In Matthew 11 we read that John the Baptist, who had been imprisoned, sends some of his followers to ask Jesus a curious question. "Are you the one who was to come, or should we expect someone else?" (Matt. 11:3).

The question, if you think about it, is shocking. John is out there preaching repentance, saying the Messiah's here, and now he's asking if Jesus is the right guy? Was John just having a bad day? Was he discouraged? Was it perhaps John's way of saying, "Um, Jesus—a little help here?" Or did he honestly not know if Jesus was the Messiah or not? Matthew even editorializes a bit by prefacing the question from John with: "When John heard in prison what the Messiah was doing"—as if to say, "Hey, I know Jesus is the Messiah, but John doubted." What was going on?

Jesus does not answer directly. The text says, "Jesus replied, 'Go back and report to John what you hear and see: The blind receive sight, the lame walk, those who have leprosy are cured, the deaf hear, the dead are raised, and the good news is preached to the poor. Blessed is the man who does not fall away on account of me' " (Matt. 11:4–6).

Jesus points to his miracles as evidence that he is indeed the Messiah, which makes sense, then adds, "Blessed is anyone who does not stumble on account of me." Is he saying, "I hope John is not stumbling because I'm not the kind of Messiah he expected"?

And since we're asking questions, I have to wonder—why didn't Jesus do a miracle to keep John from getting beheaded?

Then again, why did Jesus do miracles at all? While they helped people, they had a greater purpose than making people feel better or improving their lot in life. Jesus didn't do a miracle for everyone he met. He seemed to avoid signs and wonders for their own sake—he was really about healing and restoring relationships, by miraculous means if necessary. He used miracles to point toward a larger reality—all of nature belongs to and is under the dominion of God.

A few verses later, in Matthew 11:20, we read, "Then Jesus began to denounce the towns in which most of his miracles had been performed, because they did not repent." He has harsh words for these cities because he expected a response to miracles: repentance. Miracles reveal God, and the proper response to truly seeing God is to repent, which means literally to turn away from sin and toward God.

Miracles reveal God's capabilities, focusing his power in a specific place and time. As C. S. Lewis wrote, "In all these miracles alike the incarnate God does suddenly or locally something that

God has done or will do in general. Each miracle writes for us in small letters something that God has already written, or will write, in letters almost too large to be noticed, across the whole canvas of Nature."[1]

Many people ask if miracles still happen today. Perhaps the more important question is whether those miracles (from the birth of a child to an answered prayer) lead us to repentance. Do they, as Lewis said, show us something God has already done on a grander scale, with the intent of drawing us toward him?

NEW

We call the book we're studying the *New* Testament, so it's not surprising that newness is a major theme throughout.

The word *testament* means covenant. The term "New Testament" comes from Jesus' words in Luke 22:20, which are quoted by Paul again in 1 Corinthians 11:25: "This cup is a new testament [in some versions, covenant] in my blood." (See ***Covenant***.)

So the Old Testament focuses on the old covenant (the Law), and the New Testament unpacks for us the story of the new covenant, in which we are saved by grace through faith. (Hebrews 9 and 10 is a great passage to study when comparing and contrasting the two covenants.)

In 2 Corinthians, Paul explains the implications of a new covenant—not only has everything around us changed, but faith in Christ has changed us. We are not just a party to a new covenant, we've become all new people. We're given a fresh start, a clean slate. We are changed and transformed.

The Message puts it this way: "Now we look inside, and what we see is that anyone united with the Messiah gets a fresh start, is created new. The old life is gone; a new life burgeons! Look at it!" (2 Cor. 5:17).

The Greek word in this passage is *kainos,* which is one of two words that express the idea of newness in ancient Greek. The second word is *neos*. *Neos* means new according to time, something or someone that is younger.

Kainos is used to describe the newness of that which is unused. Rather than describing something that is quantitatively new in time, *kainos* denotes newness of form or quality—a whole new perspective or innovation. *Kainos* is the adjective used to describe the new covenant and new commandment. The word is used eight times in the book of Revelation to describe things like a new heaven and earth or a new song. *Neos* does not appear in Revelation.

Throughout the New Testament, we see these two adjectives modifying the same noun, which results in different meanings. Vine's Dictionary notes:

> Thus the "new man" in Eph. 2:15 (*kainos*) is "new" in differing in character; . . . but the "new man" in Col. 3:10 (*neos*) stresses the fact of the believer's new experience, recently begun, and still proceeding. . . . The "New" Covenant in Heb. 12:24 is "new" (*neos*) compared with the Mosaic, nearly 1500 years before; it is "new" (*kainos*) compared with the Mosaic, which is old in character, ineffective.[1]

All three synoptic gospels record Jesus' conversation with John's disciples, who come to him to ask why Jesus' disciples did not fast—a common religious practice in that day that they and the Pharisees regularly engaged in. (See Matt. 9:16–18; Mark 2:21–22; Luke 5:36–39.) Jesus answers with parallel analogies, using what would have been familiar images to his listeners: patching clothes and making wine.

In Matthew and Mark, we see a third Greek word for new, *agnaphos*, which is used only there, to describe patching old garments with "new" cloth. It literally means uncarded (as in wool) or new cloth. Luke's rendering of Jesus' words is slightly different. Rather than just a "new cloth" used for a patch, he writes, "No one tears a patch from a *new* garment and sews it onto an old one. If he does, he will have torn the *new* garment, and the patch from the *new* will not match the old." All three times, the word is *kainos*.

In Jesus' day, new wine was put into animal hide containers to ferment. As it did so, it would expand, so it needed the elasticity of new wineskins. Wineskins that had already been used to hold wine had already been stretched to capacity and hardened. If you put new wine into old wineskins, the fermentation process would burst the skins. This passage highlights the difference between *neos* and *kainos*.

"Neither do people pour new (*neos*) wine into old wineskins. If they do, the skins will burst, the wine will run out and the wineskins will be ruined. No, they pour new (*neos*) wine into new (*kainos*) wineskins, and both are preserved" (Matt. 9:17)

The word *neos* describes Jesus' disciples who are new in their faith, immature. But his solution is not immature wineskins (or immature religion) but a whole new (*kainos*) approach.

ONE ANOTHER

The Greek word *allelon* appears one hundred times in the New Testament. Most often, it is translated "one another" or "each other." It expresses the mutuality and community that is an inextricable part of our faith.

The New Testament exhorts us to care for one another, serve one another, admonish one another, bear with one another, submit to one another, encourage one another, pray for one another. All of these and the many other "one another's" in the text are simply more specific ways to "love one another."

When we love one another, we benefit both others and ourselves. We experience community. In that fellowship, we experience God's love more fully.

We live in a culture that highly values independence and autonomy. We can't change that, but if we are to understand the Bible, we must recognize that the Bible was written to a culture completely opposite of ours in this regard. When we read the Bible, we tend to read the word *you* as singular, as if God were giving us individual instructions for our separate, private, custom relationship with him. While individual practices are important, they are incomplete. If we focus only on our private practices of faith, we will misinterpret the text.

The word *you* in the Bible is most frequently plural. If we had a "revised Southern version," it would translate the pronoun as "y'all." In the Old English of the oldest Bible translations, the plural *you* was "ye." The singular was "thou." The unfortunate problem with not using such archaic language is we aren't sure whether *you* means thou or y'all. So we have to look at the context.

For example, 1 Corinthians 15:2 says, "By this gospel you are saved, if you hold firmly to the word I preached to you. Otherwise, you have believed in vain." If any verse touches our individualistic Western sensibilities, this is one.

But look at the context: the prior verse begins, "Now, brothers . . ." Other versions say "brothers and sisters" (TNIV, NLT) or "Friends" (THE MESSAGE). In any case, the antecedent is plural. So Paul's instructions to hold firmly assume a context of community. And think of it—if you are a part of a fellowship that is exhorting one another, encouraging one another, praying for one another, and loving one another, doesn't that strengthen each person to "hold firmly" to their faith with more strength and conviction than if they were each doing it in isolation? In our weak moments, if those around us are holding firmly, we're supported and held up.

This assumption of community did not begin with the apostle Paul. Jesus gathered a group of disciples whom he taught and lived with for three years. They did everything together. Just look, for example, at how Jesus taught his disciples to pray: "Give *us* this day *our* daily bread, forgive *us* our debts as *we* forgive. . . ." The text does not say "Give *me* this day *my* daily bread." The teachings of Jesus recognize that Christianity is a one another faith.

Paul's letters to the churches were read out loud to groups, then discussed. Questions were posed, debated, discussed. They learned from one another. Each person may have thought and prayed individually after the discussion, but no one copied the text and took it home to study. They read and learned together.

While most world religions urge their followers to be charitable and kind to fellow human beings, Christianity elevates love of others as equally important to, and indeed an expression of, love for God himself. First John 4:12 says: "No one has ever seen God; but if we love one another, God lives in us and his love is made complete in us."[1]

God calls us to love him by loving one another. In this way, perhaps Jesus' prayer, that we might be "one" just as he and the Father are one, would be answered.[2]

PARABLE

As was predicted of him in the Old Testament, Jesus taught using parables. Matthew 13 contains eight parables, along with two conversations *about* parables. In verses 10–13, Jesus' disciples finally ask him why he's always speaking in parables. He replies:

> The knowledge of the secrets of the kingdom of heaven has been given to you, but not to them. Whoever has will be given more, and he will have an abundance. Whoever does not have, even what he has will be taken from him. This is why I speak to them in parables: Though seeing, they do not see; though hearing, they do not hear or understand.

Jesus quotes a passage from Isaiah that indicates that parables enlighten some people while hardening the hearts of others by their riddle-like quality.

After Matthew records a few more parables, we read: "Jesus spoke all these things to the crowd in parables; he did not say anything to them without using a parable. So was fulfilled what was spoken through the prophet: 'I will open my mouth in parables, I will utter things hidden since the creation of the world' " (Matt. 13:34–35).

Parables invited the poor and illiterate into the kingdom. Rather than highbrow discussions of theology and philosophy, Jesus talked about seeds and coins, weeds and fields. He translated the language of heaven into the common tongue. (See also ***Fruit*** and ***Harvest***.)

The Greek word *parabole* literally means to place one thing beside another. But a parable is much more than an analogy, and not quite as literarily complex as an allegory. Some parables were only a few words, a single sentence. Others were more complex stories. The parables were not always easily understood—especially by those who did not accept Jesus or want to know him. Parables were a litmus test of listeners' hearts, to determine if they were turned toward God.

Jesus called himself a vine, bread, a shepherd, and more.

Indeed, parables are themselves a parable for his favorite topic, the kingdom of God. For a parable is like the kingdom itself, at once puzzling and enlightening, both accessible and mysterious. Jesus himself could not be separated from his parables, for his very life was a parable. It was as if God said, "Do you want to know what I'm like?" And then answered that question with Jesus in the flesh, whose life story showed us the truth about God, because he was truth. It shed light on the nature of God, because he was light. It showed us the way to God, because he was the way.

Parables were meant to jolt people out of their complacency: "The parables were meant to force people to decide about their attitude to Jesus and his message . . . they are the form which the kingdom of God takes in the sphere of language."[1]

In John 6, Jesus has a lively discussion with a crowd of Jewish people who have been listening to his teaching. He calls himself "living bread that came down from heaven." And then tells the Jews they must eat his flesh and drink his blood in order to have eternal life (John 6:50). Not surprisingly, some of his listeners recoil. The text says many of his disciples said, "This is a hard teaching. Who can accept it?"

This crowd contains people who received a miraculous meal at the feeding of the five thousand, along with Jesus' disciples—not just the Twelve, but many more men and women who were following him, each with varying levels of commitment.

Jesus challenges them to understand the spiritual significance of this parable, then says, "This is why I told you that no one can come to me unless the Father has enabled him" (John 6:65). At this, the text says, "Many of his disciples turned back and no longer followed him." The Twelve, however, remained, believing that Jesus had "the words of eternal life." Those words, it seems, were woven into parables.

PATIENCE/PATIENT

What should a Christian look like? What virtues or character strengths ought they to have? If we are followers of Jesus, we ought to live and behave and even have the same attitude as Jesus. While we can never be God, we are called to seek godliness. Throughout the Bible, God is described as one who is "slow to anger, rich in love." Someone who is slow to anger is patient.

Jesus exhibited tremendous patience with his disciples, even as he occasionally expressed frustrations when they just didn't seem to get it. The New Testament teaches that patience is a Christian virtue. It is included in the description of the fruit of the Spirit in Galatians 5:22, and in other lists of the characteristics that should be the mark of a Christian, such as Colossians 3:12, which says, "Clothe yourselves with compassion, kindness, humility, gentleness and patience."

The Greek word in both these passages is *makrothumia*, which means patience or longsuffering, and is translated with either word depending on which version of the Bible you read. The related verb *makrothumeo* means to be patient.

A second Greek word translated "patience" is *hupomone*. It is also often, accurately, translated "endurance." Its verb form, *hupomeno*, means to bear patiently, to endure.

These words differ only subtly. *Hupomeno* is slightly more active. The exhortation in Hebrews 12:1, "Let us run with patience the race that is set before us" (KJV), which is sometimes translated "run with perseverance" or "run with endurance," uses the word *hupomone*—it is an active patience.

A number of scholars point out that *makrothumia* is used to describe patience with people, or the attitude or inner mindset we should have in the face of difficulties. *Hupomone* is the patience that is more active endurance or perseverance, and often refers to having patience with things or circumstances, which then translates into outer actions. It is often connected to the idea of hope. Strong's concordance adds: "*Hupomone* is the temper which does not easily succumb under suffering, *makrothumia* is the self-restraint which does not hastily retaliate a wrong."[1]

The oft-quoted 1 Corinthians 13 begins, "Love is patient (*makrothumeo*)." Our inner attitude toward others should be one of patience. The text goes on to say, "Love is kind." This points to the outer action, in which that patient love manifests itself.

In contrast, Romans 12:12 talks about how we should act in the face of trying circumstances: "Be joyful in hope, patient (*hupomeno*) in affliction, faithful in prayer." We must actively choose joy, endure affliction, engage in prayer, and so on.

Both nouns are found in Colossians 1:11–12, where Paul tells the church of his prayer for them: "[Be] strengthened with all power according to his glorious might so that you may have great endurance (*hupomone*) and patience (*makrothumia*), and joyfully giving thanks to the Father . . ."

The goal of the Christian faith is that our character is formed into the image of Christ. God is patient (see 2 Peter 3:9), so we should seek to be patient. How can we develop this trait? Simply trying to be patient by gritting our teeth will not get us very far. Rather, patience naturally occurs when we ask God for help and engage in practices that stretch our capacities—caring for a two-year-old will help you become patient, for example. Author and pastor John Ortberg suggests we can grow in patience by engaging in the practice of "slowing." It involves deliberately doing things like eating slowly and actually chewing your food, or choosing the longest line at the grocery store, and so on.[2]

The book of James opens with an exhortation to embrace our trials as a means of developing patience or perseverance (*hupomone*): "The testing of your faith produces perseverance. Let perseverance finish its work so that you may be mature and complete, not lacking anything" (James 1:3–4). Other versions use the word *endurance* instead.

A few verses later it says, "Everyone should be quick to listen, slow to speak and slow to become angry" (1:19). Again, the phrase "slow to anger" is used most frequently of God. If we obey this command of Scripture to be eager listeners who think before we speak, we will grow in patience—that is, we will grow spiritually. We will become godly people who live as Jesus would if he were in our place.

PEACE

I grew up during the waning years of the Cold War, fearing the Communists and nuclear war with them. But our enemy of that day, the Soviet Union, is now broken up into many independent countries, and the U.S. seems to be "at peace" with all of them—meaning we're not at war with them at the moment. In other areas of the world, former allies have become enemies. This is the kind of peace the world gives—unstable, shifting, uncertain.

War and conflict have always been a part of the human story. As a result, peace has always been tenuous. But Jesus offers a different sort of peace.

Peace that passes understanding (see Phil. 4:7) goes beyond the absence of conflict. It is not dependent on treaties or negotiation. Jesus told his disciples that they could have peace even as they faced his imminent death. "Peace I leave with you; my peace I give you. I do not give to you as the world gives. Do not let your hearts be troubled and do not be afraid," he told them (John 14:27). Had I been in that little group of followers, I think I would have simply felt sorrowful and scared, not peaceful.

God's peace is a deeply abiding assurance in spite of difficulties that "all shall be well, and all manner of things shall be well."[1] It's a peace in spite of circumstances, not because of them. It's a peace that comes from the indwelling of the Holy Spirit (see John 14:26; 16:6–7). We cannot manufacture it on our own through positive thinking or therapy, only receive it as a gift. Jesus himself is our peace (see Eph. 2:14).

All of Paul's epistles open with the greeting, "Grace and peace to you from God our Father and the Lord Jesus Christ," or some only slight variation on that (he adds "mercy" to his letters to Timothy). The peace God gives is intimately connected to God's grace—when our sins are forgiven and we are in right relationship with God through grace, we will be at peace. While Paul used this word as a greeting, it was also a way of affirming this theological truth.

Many of the early churches receiving his letters faced persecution and struggle. Their lives were anything but peaceful. In a single sentence, Paul's greeting reminds them of Jesus' promise of grace and peace through faith.

In all these cases, the Greek word for peace is *eirene*. This noun occurs in each of the books of the New Testament, except for 1 John, for a total of ninety times. It means harmonious relationships between people or nations, friendliness, freedom, order, and even harmony between God and people. This word corresponds to the Hebrew word *shalom*, which is not just peace but wholeness. The same word is used in phrases like "the God of peace" and "the gospel of peace."

The Bible tells us to "Let the peace of Christ rule in your hearts" (Col. 3:15). To allow peace to reign, we must be willing to trust. While we cannot make ourselves feel peaceful by simply trying really hard, we can find peace by choosing to trust. Peace is one of the characteristics of the fruit of the Spirit, and again, it flourishes in our hearts when we allow the Spirit to have access to our hearts.

A few Greek verbs relating to peace appear in the gospels. Several, such as *siopao, phimoo, sigao*, and *hesuchazo*, mean to be quiet or to hold one's peace, and occur only rarely.

In Matthew 5:9, Jesus says, "Blessed are the peacemakers (*eirenopoios*), for they will be called children of God." When we choose actions like forgiveness and kindness, which bring peace rather than conflict, we show our "family resemblance" to God.

The *Expository Dictionary of Bible Words* notes, "In the New Testament it is clear that 'peace' finds its ultimate expression in an intimate relationship with God, made possible by the saving work of Christ. Indeed, the person of Christ is declared as the embodiment of peace, bringing about the eternally permanent reconciliation between humankind and God."[2] His exhortation to be a peacemaker is a call to put on his character, which we can only do with his help.

PERSECUTE/PERSECUTION

Christians in North Korea have reportedly been tortured and even killed for simply being believers. In Iran, anyone who leaves the Muslim faith can be sentenced to death, and so Christians there are often arrested for talking publicly about their faith. In Saudi Arabia, public practice of any kind of worship other than Islam is against the law, and violators can be arrested, beaten, or deported. If you live in a country where religious freedom is a given, you may think these sorts of things happened decades or centuries ago—but they are happening now, and not just in those three countries but all over the world.[1]

The early church faced persecution of all kinds. The Greek word *dioko* means persecute (and sometimes to follow or to pursue) and is found in the New Testament about fifty times. The related noun *diogmos* means persecution and is found ten times. Jesus seemed to assume that persecution was not only a given for anyone who followed him, but was to be considered a blessing. While this seems counterintuitive, we must understand some important truth when thinking about persecution.

First, history shows that the most robust growth of the church and of the Christian faith occurred during seasons of persecution. This does not mean we ought to seek out persecution as a strategy for church growth, of course, but rather, that we should be unafraid to face struggles related to our faith and its free expression, knowing that God will use it for good both now and in the life to come.

Jesus said, "Blessed are those who are persecuted because of righteousness, for theirs is the kingdom of heaven. Blessed are you when people insult you, persecute you and falsely say all kinds of evil against you because of me. Rejoice and be glad, because great is your reward in heaven, for in the same way they persecuted the prophets who were before you" (Matt. 5:10–12).

Romans 12:4 has a similar message, but takes it a step further. Rather than simply rejoicing in sufferings, we should bless those who persecute us, echoing Jesus' teachings to love your enemies and pray for them

The word *dioko* means literally to pursue. Because it can also mean to pursue good things (1 Tim. 6:11; 2 Tim. 2:22), it is critical to look at the context to determine which meaning the author intends. In Matthew 23, Jesus rants against the Pharisees, saying to them, "You snakes, you brood of vipers! How can you escape being sentenced to hell? Therefore I send you prophets, sages, and scribes, some of whom you will kill and crucify, and some you will flog in your synagogues and pursue from town to town" (vv. 33–34 NRSV). In other versions, the word *pursue* is translated "persecute." The idea is the kind of persecution that hunts down or drives someone away. It is obvious from Jesus' tone and words that this is a hostile pursuit.

Even if we live in a place where Christians are free from the threat of physical martyrdom for our faith, we can still sometimes face discrimination or scorn. In cases where we seem to be excluded or ridiculed, we often feel hurt or wonder why.

Paul's words can be of comfort to us: "We are afflicted in every way, but not crushed; perplexed, but not driven to despair; *persecuted, but not forsaken;* struck down, but not destroyed" (2 Cor. 4:8–9 NRSV, emphasis mine). We are *dioko*, but not *egkataleipo*. While *dioko* has a connotation of being driven away or pursued, *egkataleipo* means abandoned, with the connotation of being left behind. Throughout Scripture, God promises never to leave or forsake (*egkataleipo*) us. (See Heb. 13:5, also Josh. 1:5.) Both words give a picture of running and movement. When we are pursued and driven away, God goes with us. Even when someone is after us for our faith, driving us away, God never leaves us behind.

PERSEVERANCE

In some versions of the Bible, the word *perseverance* is translated "patience," a word we've studied previously. Perseverance is also related to *persecute*. We are called to endure persecution with perseverance. But it goes beyond merely enduring suffering. Perseverance in the New Testament is something that develops in our character when we are intentional about our pursuit of growth.

Perseverance is a character trait that seems to be in short supply in our culture. We tap our foot impatiently waiting for the microwave to cook our dinner. If we cannot persevere enough to wait five minutes for a fully-cooked meal, how will we be able to persevere through actual struggles and trials?

A synonym for perseverance, both in the Bible and today, is endurance. We get stronger physically by pushing ourselves to run another lap when we're tired or lift that weight one more time when we think we can't. We get stronger relationally by sitting down, with a counselor if necessary, to work out messy, confusing conflicts with our family or friends. And we build spiritual endurance by continuing to seek God even when it's difficult or he seems distant or life is just plain hard and we want to give up. As Bill Hybels wrote, "You build endurance by learning how to crash through quitting points."[1]

Spiritual growth happens as a result of our cooperation with God. We cannot make ourselves grow without the Spirit's help any more than a child can make himself grow by hanging from the monkey bars in an effort to "stretch" himself. But neither is our growth purely up to God. Several passages list perseverance as a part of the logical progression of spiritual growth. It does require some effort.

For example, 2 Peter 1:5–7 says, "For this very reason, make every effort to add to your faith goodness; and to goodness, knowledge; and to knowledge, self-control; and to self-control, perseverance; and to perseverance, godliness; and to godliness, brotherly kindness; and to brotherly kindness, love." Notice the logical progression. We can't just start with perseverance—we need to begin with the foundation of faith. From there we build a spiritual life with goodness, then knowledge, and then self-control. Again, we do these things with God's help, but we cannot afford to be passive in them. Nor is perseverance the highest value. As we can see, love (*agape*) is the ultimate goal of our growth.

Similarly, Romans 5:3–4 notes, "Not only so, but we also rejoice in our sufferings, because we know that suffering produces perseverance; perseverance, character; and character, hope." Here again we see a progression, as well as the important truth that perseverance is forged in the crucible of suffering.

James, whose words we have studied in previous entries, again connects for us trials and persecution with perseverance. "Consider it pure joy, my brothers, whenever you face trials of many kinds, because you know that the testing of your faith develops perseverance. Perseverance must finish its work so that you may be mature and complete, not lacking anything" (James 1:2–4).

The Greek word that is translated "perseverance" in modern translations is one we have studied earlier: *hupomone*, which means endurance, constancy, patience. It comes from two Greek words: *hupo*, meaning under, and *meno*, to abide. So it means literally an abiding under. It is a patience that perfects our character. It was modeled by Jesus. (See ***Patience***.)

Perseverance is an active patience that refuses to give up or despair in the face of difficulty. Hebrews 12:1 exhorts us to "throw off everything that hinders and the sin that so easily entangles, and let us run with perseverance the race marked out for us." This is obviously not merely "hanging in there" or just putting up with difficulty. Rather, it involves "throwing off sin," which means seeing and dealing with our own faults and acknowledging the role such flaws might play in our life's struggles, and then moving forward in forgiveness and confidence to follow hard after God.

PHARISEE

The word *Pharisee* in English has come to be a synonym for hypocrisy. But in the first century, the Pharisees were one of the most influential sects within Judaism, known for their careful study of the Torah and their desire to live according to God's laws.

First-century Jewish culture differed from ours in many ways, but two are essential for us to understand. First, the Torah was revered. The Jews talked about and memorized the Scriptures—often committing the entire Old Testament, word for word, to memory. Second, to learn, they argued. Their teaching method consisted of questioning. Students were expected to debate, even by answering with another question. And while all Jews believed that the Scriptures were true, they differed greatly on the interpretation of those Scriptures.

Those different interpretations gave rise to several religious factions, including the Pharisees, Sadducees, Essenes, and Zealots. Pharisees believed in a bodily resurrection of the dead, as did Jesus; the Sadducees did not. The Pharisees had elevated the oral tradition of Jewish laws to be as important as the Scriptures themselves, which is something Jesus took them to task for. The Sadducees were the high priests, often wealthy men more concerned with politics than religion, and capitulated to Rome. Both parties made up the Sanhedrin, "the full assembly of the elders of Israel" (Acts 5:21). A third group, the Essenes, were isolationists, recommending asceticism as a path to God. At the same time, they were expecting a Messiah who would go to war with Rome. The Zealots (also called the Iscariots—yes, Judas Iscariot was one of them) were in favor of a violent revolution against the Roman government and were also hoping for a military Messiah. When the apostle Paul says he was a Pharisee, he's not pointing to his own hypocrisy but rather his theology (Acts 23:1–11).

Within the Pharisees, there were two major schools of thought, stemming from two rabbis who came before the time of Jesus. Shammai, who taught about 100 BC, was legalistic and strict. Hillel, who taught between about 30 BC and AD 10, was more liberal. When the Pharisees would ask "by whose authority" Jesus taught, they were asking whether he was passing on the teachings of Hillel or Shammai, or perhaps someone else. That's one reason they were infuriated when he claimed his own authority.

While Jesus did sometimes call the Pharisees hypocrites and vipers, he had much in common, philosophically and theologically, with them. He talked with them and ate with them (Luke 7:36). Pharisees were not priests, but typically common laborers (like Jesus) who simply wanted to live out God's law. They often taught using parables, and they had groups of followers (see ***Disciple***) as Jesus did. There are a number of scholars who suggest that Jesus actually was a Pharisee, at least in his philosophies and teaching methods. Orthodox Rabbi Harvey Falk, for example, argues that Jesus was a part of the Hillel school, and his scathing criticisms were directed at those in the Shammai group, not against all Pharisees.[1]

All of Matthew 23 is devoted to Jesus' critique (seven woes) of the Pharisees, even though he prefaces his words by affirming their authority.

"You may be surprised to learn that the rabbis themselves had formulated a nearly identical list," write Anne Spangler and Lois Tverberg. "Their list included seven types of Pharisees, each one caricatured as falling into an error: legalism, pride, hypocrisy, and so on. Only the last Pharisee, who serves God out of love, escapes criticism. Obviously, the Pharisees weren't afraid to recognize the flaws in their own movement."[2]

Jesus' words "You must be born again" (John 3:7) are spoken to a Pharisee, Nicodemus, who comes to Jesus under the cover of night. In John 7:50, Nicodemus makes a feeble attempt to defend Jesus to the other Pharisees. It is not until Jesus dies that Nicodemus has the courage to step out of the shadows and ask that he be allowed to bury Jesus' body.

To look down our noses at the Pharisees is to commit the same sin they did. The Pharisees' story is our own story—in our zeal to follow God, we can easily elevate human tradition and rules over the supreme value of love.

POWER

Whether we are aware of it or not, we are engaged in a power struggle. The battle between good and evil goes on around us and within us constantly. Jesus has broken the power of sin, yet still we struggle. The Bible speaks of the power of God, the power we receive through him. But it also clearly states that there are powers of darkness, with which we do battle.

The most common Greek word for power is *dunamis,* which refers to miraculous power, power that God has, or that he gives to us through the Holy Spirit (see Acts 10:38). It is used to describe the power and authority Jesus gave to the Twelve when they went out in his name. It describes the power of the Apostles' teaching in Acts 4:33, and the power of the resurrection in Philippians 3:10. *Dunamis* is sometimes translated "miracle" or "mighty work."

Dunamis power, according to the Bible, is paradoxical. It comes not from ourselves but from God—but only if we are humble (in other words, powerless) enough to receive it. The apostle Paul asked God to remove an affliction, but God refused. Paul wrote in 2 Corinthians 12:9, "But he said to me, 'My grace is sufficient for you, for my power (*dunamis*) is made perfect in weakness.' Therefore I will boast all the more gladly about my weaknesses, so that Christ's power (*dunamis*) may rest on me." When we are weak, we're strong. When we acknowledge our lack of power, God brings forth power in our lives—power by God's grace to do God's will.

Another key word is *exousia,* which means "liberty of action," then authority, privilege, force, capacity. When *exousia* refers to

God, it refers to ultimate authority. When it refers to people, it refers to an authority that is given by God. Jesus claims this authority in Luke 5:24 when he heals a paralytic to show not only his power to heal but also to forgive sins.

Jesus understood power, while many around him did not. In John 19, we read this conversation:

> "Do you refuse to speak to me?" Pilate said. "Don't you realize I have power (*exousia*) either to free you or to crucify you?"
>
> Jesus answered, "You would have no power (*exousia*) over me if it were not given to you from above. Therefore the one who handed me over to you is guilty of a greater sin" (vv. 10–11).

Like so many of us, Pilate misunderstood power. His authority was given to him by God (whether he acknowledged God or not). Pilate can't find any guilt in Jesus, but he clearly demonstrates his own lack of power, ironically, in that he cannot convince the people to let an innocent man go free.

We find three different words for *power* or *rule* in Ephesians 6:12: "For our struggle is not against flesh and blood, but against the rulers (*arche*), against the authorities (*exousia*), against the powers (*kosmokrator*) of this dark world and against the spiritual forces of evil in the heavenly realms."

Arche means beginning, implying a ruler who is the origin, the cause. Then there is this curious word *kosmokrator*, which appears only here in the entire New Testament. It's a compound word, assembled from *kosmos,* meaning the world, and *krateo*, to use strength or seize; therefore, it means a world-ruler (by implication, Satan). It refers to demonic, antagonistic spiritual powers.

While this verse and others like it acknowledge the power of evil, the power of God is greater than any other power on earth or in heaven. Ultimately we know the victory will belong to Jesus, but in the meantime, we must find a way to "plug in" to the power of God that flows abundantly, to let it flow through us.

Second Thessalonians 1:11 says, "With this in mind, we constantly pray for you, that our God may count you worthy of his calling, and that by his power (*dunamis*) he may fulfill every good purpose of yours and every act prompted by your faith."

Power is not something we can create within ourselves, but rather, by God's power, he brings forth greater amounts of goodness and faith within us.

PRAY

In his book *Whole Prayer*, Walter Wangerin Jr. writes that prayer is communication, so it has, like all communication, four parts: "First, we speak—while, second, God listens. Third, God speaks—while, fourth, we listen. . . . Without our truly listening, prayer will seem to have failed because communication, remaining incomplete, *did* in fact fail. The circle stayed broken, and love was left unknown."[1] He writes that our words to God are "empowered" by God's attentiveness to them. He adds, "How much love God lavishes on each particular heart when he murmurs words intended for that heart alone! How much love the lonely heart misses if it will not hear the personal word."[2]

We sometimes avoid listening to God because we know that if, for example, we pray a prayer of intercession for someone, God may prompt us to actually do something for that person, and it may cost us time, effort, money, or convenience. We may bravely pray prayers of confession, but if we stop before we listen, we might miss God's instructions on how to avoid that sin in the future.

In spite of this, we sometimes feel compelled to pray. We hunger for intimacy with God. Marjorie Thompson argues that what we think of as our desire to pray actually comes from God. "Like the spiritual life itself, prayer is initiated by God," she writes. "No matter what we think about the origin of our prayers, they are all a response to the hidden workings of the Spirit within."[3]

Throughout the gospels we read that Jesus would go away to "lonely places" to pray. He modeled the spiritual practices of solitude and prayer. Before key decisions or particularly challenging ministry tasks, Jesus sometimes spent entire nights praying. We must assume that he not only spoke to his Father but listened, seeking guidance and wisdom.

Luke 11 tells us about a time Jesus was praying. His disciples waited until he had finished, then asked for instructions. He responded by teaching them what we now call the Lord's Prayer.

According to Matthew, he prefaced the prayer with instructions to pray "in secret" and without mindless repetition (Matt. 6:5–13). The Lord's Prayer is not meant to just be recited, but to serve as a model for how to approach God—in love and intimacy, with simple, heartfelt requests.

Prayer was of course familiar to Jesus' disciples, who were raised in the Jewish community. Every day, twice a day, pious Jews prayed the Shema, a prayer that began, "Hear, O Israel: The Lord our God, the Lord is one." They recited Deuteronomy 6:4–9; 11:13–21; and Numbers 15:37–41, passages that included the exhortation to love God with all your heart and soul and might. In the synagogue, they would offer prayers as well.

As an observant Jew, Jesus would have prayed the Shema each day, but he also connected with his heavenly Father in a much more intimate way, which the disciples wanted to emulate.

In his book *Prayer: Does It Make Any Difference?* Philip Yancey writes, "Prayer invites me to lower defenses and present the self that no other person fully knows to a God who already knows."[4] Yancey wisely points out that prayer is not merely talking to God, or even talking and listening. Our resulting action to further God's kingdom is also an essential component of prayer. "We are God's fellow workers, and as such we turn to prayer to equip us for the partnership," he writes.[5]

Richard Foster writes, "Real prayer comes not from gritting our teeth but from falling in love."[6]

The Greek word *proseuchomai* means to pray to God, and is the most common of several words used to describe prayer in the New Testament. Its noun form, *proseuche*, means prayer, and always refers to prayer to God, where the noun *deesis* means a petition or prayer, either to God or to a person.

PREACH

I am a journalist by trade. For years I was a newspaper reporter, making my living proclaiming the news from the pages of a local paper, covering the corruption and scandal of local politics, announcing tax increases or plane crashes. But such news is often bad news, and by the next day, yesterday's news and not new at all.

Journalists learn to write tightly, packing as much information as they can into small amounts of space. The essential questions—who, what, where, why, when, and how—have to be answered up front, as succinctly and compellingly as possible.

Matthew announces at the opening of his third chapter (having dispensed with genealogies and a quick summary of Jesus' birth), "In those days John the Baptist came, preaching in the wilderness of Judea and saying, 'Repent . . .'" In half a sentence, we learn who, what, when, how, and where. John preached to prepare the way (see ***Way***) for Jesus. His message was urgent and confrontational. The word *preach* in the Greek is *kerusso,* meaning to proclaim.

Jesus launched his ministry, according to Luke, by announcing that God had anointed him to preach the gospel to the poor and deliverance to the captives. Most modern translations use the word *proclaim* rather than *preach*, so in the NIV, the phrase in Luke 4:18 is rendered, "to preach good news to the poor . . . proclaim freedom for the prisoners." In the Greek, however, this verse contains two different verbs: "to *euaggelizo* to the poor . . . and *kerusso* freedom for the prisoners and recovery of sight for the blind." The NRSV acknowledges this difference by translating the phrases as "bring good news to the poor . . . and proclaim release to the captives and recovery of sight to the blind." And what is this good news, this gospel? That the kingdom was at hand, right now. As you can see, some English versions don't differentiate between these two words. But the two words in the original language were chosen for a reason. *Kerusso* means to proclaim or preach, and can be used to describe the preaching or announcing of a variety of messages. In this verse, what is being proclaimed is release and recovery. *Euaggelizo* means to preach the good news, or the gospel.

Kerusso is used to describe the preaching of the apostles when Jesus sends them out to preach, and it is also used in the book of Acts. Matthew and Mark say Jesus picked up where John the Baptist left off, starting his public ministry by preaching repentance.

Mark 1:14–15 says, "After John was put in prison, Jesus went into Galilee, proclaiming (*kerusso*) the good news (*euaggelion*) of God. 'The time has come,' he said. 'The kingdom of God has come near. Repent and believe the good news (*euaggelion*)!' "

Matthew 4:17 and 23 says, "From that time on Jesus began to preach (*kerusso*), 'Repent, for the kingdom of heaven is near.' . . . Jesus went throughout Galilee, teaching in their synagogues, preaching (*kerusso*) the good news (*euaggelion*) of the kingdom, and healing every disease and sickness among the people."

What exactly did Jesus proclaim? Jesus' Sermon on the Mount, recorded in Matthew 5–7, offered an incredible amount of profound truth packed into very few simple words. Still, his preaching at times inflamed or infuriated the people around him: the Pharisees he lambasted, for example.

But what about the Jewish peasants who listened to his words? They may have appreciated "blessed are the poor in spirit," or "blessed are the meek." But they may not have been quite so open to hearing that persecution was a blessing. The land they considered their homeland was occupied by Rome, which kept the peace by means of military intimidation. Imagine being a woman in the crowd, who'd perhaps been sexually harassed or even raped by Roman soldiers. She hears Jesus say, "Love your enemies, pray for those who persecute you." This is good news? To her it may have felt like hurtful news, impossible instruction. Especially to people who were looking for a political messiah.

Jesus' preaching sometimes irked his listeners, sat uncomfortably on their expectations. The Bible tells us that at various times, his followers became disenchanted with his teaching and gave up (John 6:60–68). But Jesus strove not just to impart information, but to effect transformation in the hearts and minds and actions of his listeners. At the end of both Matthew's and Mark's gospels, Jesus asked his followers to continue his ministry of preaching and proclamation. Those who kept listening to his preaching and let that word dwell richly in their hearts not only changed themselves, they changed the world.

PREPARE

Have you ever been a guest in the home of someone who truly has the gift of hospitality? When you walk in, the house is welcoming. It may be simple, even stark, but you can see evidence of effort and attention. It may not be fancy, but the table is set, the food is simmering on the stove. If you are staying overnight, your bed has been made up with clean sheets, there's a towel set out for you in the bathroom. Perhaps there are flowers on the nightstand or even a basket with a few snacks, or a stack of books or magazines set in your room. Your host *prepared* for your visit, and that preparation and forethought welcomes you. It loves you.

Jesus told his followers: "In my Father's house are many rooms; if it were not so, I would have told you. I am going there to prepare a place for you. And if I go and prepare a place for you, I will come back and take you to be with me that you also may be where I am. You know the way to the place where I am going" (John 14:2–4).

And of course his disciples wonder how they will know the way to this place, and Jesus replies not that he will show them the way or reveal the way, but simply, "I am the way."

The Greek verb in this passage, *hetoimazo,* means to prepare or make ready, and is used in a variety of contexts, including the preparation of a meal (including the Passover meal), and is used about forty times in the New Testament.

The gospel writers describe John the Baptist as the one who fulfills this prophesy from Isaiah 40:3 (NKJV): "The voice of one crying in the wilderness: 'Prepare the way of the Lord; make straight in the desert a highway for our God.'" (See Matt. 3:3; Mark 1:3; Luke 3:4.) It is also used to describe God's preparations of blessing for his people.

A second Greek word, *kataskeuazo*, is also used to describe John's mission of preparing the way of the Lord. It can mean to prepare or build. (See Matt. 11:10.) Throughout Scripture, we see these two words, *prepare* and *way*, used together. God's preparations have purpose. They usher us into a specific place; they make a way for us to be in his presence.

A third Greek word appears only twice in the New Testament, but carries much weight theologically. *Proetoimazo* means to prepare beforehand, and refers to the preparations God has made for our salvation long before he spoke the universe into being.

In Romans 9:23, this word metaphorically describes God's chosen people (alluding to the doctrine of predestination). It's also used in Ephesians 2:10, which says: "For we are God's workmanship, created in Christ Jesus to do good works, which God prepared in advance for us to do."

What a picture of our sanctification—which happens not as a result of our efforts alone, nor of God's manipulation, but when we cooperate with the Spirit. God did the work of preparing things for us to do, even before he created the world, but we must agree to submit our will to God's, and simply do them. Our obedient actions further God's work in the world and also transform us into his likeness, so that people will see that we are his workmanship, that we have been formed and made by him.

Another word, *paraskeue*, means preparation, and is used only to describe Preparation Day, the day before the Sabbath. Because the Jews did not work on the Sabbath, the day of preparation was a day to get things done, to prepare the meals that would be eaten on the Sabbath, to finish other weekly chores in anticipation of the day of rest.

Preparation Day also just happens to be the day of the week on which Jesus was crucified. In many ways, Jesus' work on the cross was what made him the way, what enabled him to prepare a place of eternal rest for us. As he did the gracious work of dying for our sins, he opened the way for us to experience the ultimate hospitality of heaven.

PROMISE

In the New Testament, the word *promise* (*epaggelia* in Greek) almost always refers to the promises of God, not people. A promise, in this context, is not just a pledge or contractual agreement to do something. God's promises, which he is not slow in keeping (see 2 Peter 3:9), are embodied in their own fulfillment.

God's promise is not something we earn or can make him fulfill through our hard work or law keeping. We do not hold God's feet to the fire, demanding, "You promised!" Rather, we humbly receive the promise by faith. It is far better than anything we could demand. This theme is carefully explored in Romans 4, Galatians 3, and Hebrews 6 and 11.

The Greek word in all of these passages is *epaggelia*. It was a legal term that meant a summons, but it also meant a promise. The verb form, *epaggello*, which means to announce or proclaim, means to profess or to promise. William Barclay notes that in the secular realm, the word *hyposchesis* meant a promise based on a mutual agreement, but "*epaggelia* is characteristically a promise freely made and freely given. It has in it far more of a free offer than a conditioned promise."[1] Thus the promises of God differ greatly from the promises of people, because they are unconditional.

Mostly, the word *promise* refers to Jesus, the Messiah, who was promised in God's original covenant with Abraham. This brings up an important point. God's promise was given first to the Jews, through Abraham, in a specific time and place. They were his chosen people, through whom he would eventually redeem all people, everywhere.

God does not just make an idle promise of redeeming his people; he sends the promised one to be the means of that redemption. God's promise is not just about a Messiah; the Messiah is God's promise in the flesh.

In Romans 4, Paul writes that "the promise comes by faith, so that it may be by grace" (v. 16). As his philosophical argument unfolds in the next chapter, he talks about the free gift (see ***Gift***), the *charisma*, of God. Again, he is talking not about God saying he'll send Jesus, but about Jesus himself. We don't just have the promise *of* Jesus, we have Jesus, who is the promise. God's promise is not something we negotiate, it's a gift we receive. God's promises are unchanging and not dependent on us. But for the promise (of salvation) to be appropriated in our lives, we must receive it with faith.

The third chapter in Paul's letter to the Galatians discusses the promise of God in a similar way, building a case that God's promise was given in the original covenant with Abraham. Paul clearly points out that God's promise is embodied not in the law, but in Christ (see Gal. 3:16). God also gave the law, many years after making his promise. But the law does not save us, nor was it the promise itself, though the law is not opposed to the promise (see Gal. 3:21). Righteousness in God's eyes is a gift.

Paul's purpose in writing these letters, especially Galatians, was to refute false teachers, Judaizers, who were trying to demand that Christians keep all of the Jewish law (see Gal. 3:1–3). Paul builds a strong logical argument that we are saved only by grace through faith in God's promise.

Galatians 3:14, for example, says that "we might receive the promise of the Spirit." But we receive more than just a promise—we receive the Spirit himself. The promise is embodied, and is "given through faith in Jesus Christ" (Gal. 3:22). It is not something we can earn or force God to give us—we don't extract a promise from him through bargaining. Rather, we freely receive that which is promised by a God who is rich in mercy and love.

Through the promise (or gift) of Jesus, God promises us forgiveness for our sin, God's presence through the Holy Spirit, eternal life, and more.

PROUD/PRIDE

Pride is the first and foremost of the traditional seven deadly sins, perhaps because it is in many ways the root of other sins. Even the "original sin" of Adam and Eve was not mere disobedience, but at the heart of it, pride—Adam and Eve wanted to "be like God" (Gen. 3:5). Ironically, the fruit that opened their eyes (Gen. 3:7) actually turned their perspective inward, a fatal selfishness that has plagued the human race ever since.

While the words *proud* and *pride* occur more frequently in the Old Testament than the New, Jesus often spoke against pride by telling stories that, ironically, did not contain the word *pride* itself. His critiques of the Pharisees and other religious leaders of his day were aimed primarily at their pride.

Pastor and author Jeff Cook writes,

> Pride is the natural love for myself magnified and perverted into disdain for others. Augustine called pride the foundation of sin, for "pride made the soul desert God, to whom it should cling as the source of life, and to imagine itself instead as the source of its own life." . . . Obsession with self is the defining mark of a disintegrating soul. Unlike other sins, pride usually appears when I am at my best. Pride capitalizes not just on my failures but even more so on my successes. When I choose to abstain from base desires, gluttony and lust may be defeated, but not pride. Pride tells me what a fine person I am for resisting such rubbish—and my eyes turn inward.[1]

The Bible says that God scatters the proud (Luke 1:51), and resists them (James 4:6 and 1 Peter 5:5). The Greek word in these verses is *huperephanos*, which refers to a person who considers himself to be better than others. For example, in Jesus' parable in Luke 18 about a Pharisee who thanks God that he is not like other people, especially sinners like tax collectors, the Pharisee is *huperephanos*. His pride causes him to compare himself with other people and find himself superior.

Barclay observes of this word and the related *huperephania* (pride): "It does not so much mean the man who is conspicuous and to whom others look up, as the man who stands on his own little self-created pedestal and looks down."[2]

Pride (sometimes translated "arrogance") is listed among vices in Mark 7:21–22, Romans 1:30, and 2 Timothy 3:2. Conversely, humility is listed among virtues we are to cultivate. (See ***Humble***.) Our goal, then, ought to be like Paul, who boasted of Christ, not himself.

The word *pride* can also have a positive connotation, as it does several times in 2 Corinthians, for example. In these verses, the word *pride* (in other versions it is translated "boasting," "glorying," or "rejoicing"), is a translation of *kauchaomai*, which can mean to boast or glory in either a good sense ("valid glorying") or a negative sense ("vainglorying"), or its noun form *kauchesis*, meaning boasting. These verses from 2 Corinthians help us understand this word.

> We are not trying to commend ourselves to you again, but are giving you an opportunity to take pride (*kauchaomai*) in us, so that you can answer those who take pride (*kauchaomai*) in what is seen rather than in what is in the heart. (5:12)

> I have great confidence in you; I take great pride (*kauchesis*) in you. I am greatly encouraged; in all our troubles my joy knows no bounds. (7:4)

> Therefore show these men the proof of your love and the reason for our pride (*kauchesis*) in you, so that the churches can see it. (8:24)

We can see from the context that Paul intends a positive meaning in these verses. However, it's important to realize that Paul is speaking not about self-promotion, but commending others. Primarily, pride is a sin that we should seek to avoid.

QUIET

In the midst of a busy time of ministry and teaching, Jesus turned to his disciples and said, "Come with me by yourselves to a quiet place and get some rest" (Mark 6:31).

The Greek word in this verse, *eremos*, is one of several words that is translated "quiet" in some versions of the New Testament, each with different shades of meaning. *Eremos* in other versions is translated with the more stark, but perhaps more accurate, "desert." It implies a lonesome, solitary, or wilderness place. In other verses and contexts, it is most frequently translated "wilderness."

Jesus would often rise early and go out to pray in the wilderness or a solitary place. (See Luke 4:42 and Mark 1:35; in both verses the word is *eremos*.) But because the crowds often followed him, he frequently taught in these quiet, wilderness, *eremos* places as well. The feeding of the five thousand occurred in such a place, for example.

The invitation to follow Jesus is, at its heart, an invitation into a wilderness. When we give him our lives, the things that we once worshiped, needed, or wanted are slowly stripped away. Following Jesus to a wilderness sounds somehow less inviting than following him to a quiet place. A wilderness seems harsh, whereas a "quiet place" I imagine as lush and green, perhaps with a brook or fountain babbling through it. But we must remember that Jesus walked the earth in a desert region. There were towns and villages surrounded by a lot of desert. If you wanted to get away from people, you had to go into the wilderness. And sometimes people followed you to the wilderness, so it became a place of ministry.

To respond to Jesus' invitation today, we must be willing to brave the spiritual desert, devoid of the distractions of entertainment and stimulation that we've become addicted to. At first it may feel quite desolate. When we are willing to go to a quiet place, we can pray, we can rest. The external quiet can create a quietness within us. *Eremos* means a quiet from outside the self, a quiet environment. It contrasts with, and complements, a more commonly used word, *hesuchios*, which means a tranquility from within, peaceful. *Eremos* is outer; *hesuchios* is inner.

Paul urges Timothy to pray for government leaders in 1 Timothy 2:1–2, so that "we may live peaceful and quiet lives in all godliness and holiness." The word *peaceful* is *hesuchios;* but the word *quiet* is a Greek word so similar to the "wilderness *eremos*" that its English transliteration is the same. In Greek, however, just two letters are transposed. Rather than wilderness or desert, it refers simply to a tranquility that comes from without.

First Thessalonians 4:11 exhorts us to "make it your ambition to live a quiet life," and uses the verb *hesuchazo,* which means to be still or live quietly. Like the related *hesuchios*, it refers to an inner quiet. We cannot always control our circumstances, but we can choose how we respond to them in our spirit.

When we purposefully seek out external quiet, and in that place learn to live with a quiet spirit, we will find that like Jesus, we have opportunity to minister. The wilderness becomes a place of fruitfulness, our quietness a gift to others.

There are several words that mean quiet in the sense of holding one's peace, being silent. For example, in Mark 4, when Jesus calms the storm and says "Quiet! Be still!" to the wind and waves, and in Luke 18:39, when the crowd tries to quiet a blind man (or in Matthew 20:31, where two loud blind men cry out to Jesus), we see the word *siopao*. This word is used to describe an involuntary stillness or the inability to speak. This contrasts with *sigao*, which is a voluntary keeping of one's peace, or silence. (See Luke 20:26 and Acts 15:12, for example.)

In the case of the blind men who won't be quiet, Jesus hears and heeds their request for healing. In both accounts, after they are healed, it says, the blind men got up and followed Jesus. Their healing quieted their hearts, and then they were able to follow him. Ironically, they still did not know where they were going, but that didn't matter, because now they could see the one they were following.

RECONCILIATION

When my friends who don't know God yet ask me what the Bible's about, in a nutshell, this is what I tell them: The Bible is the true story of God seeking a people to call his own, a God crazy in love with people who, despite their best intentions, often wander away from that love. It's about the great lengths to which God is willing to go to reconcile people to himself—to bridge the gap and restore broken relationships.

Despite its centrality as a theme, the word *reconcile* (in its various forms, e.g., reconciliation, etc.) appears only a handful of times in the Bible. The Greek word is *katallasso* (verb) or *katallage* (noun), which means an exchange, i.e., restoration to divine favor. It can also mean atonement.

But the phrase "a sacrifice of atonement" (or "propitiation" in some versions) is a different Greek word: *hilasterion*, a derivative of *hilasmos*, which refers specifically to the mercy seat, or lid of the ark of the Covenant. Propitiation means to appease or conciliate. It is the way by which we get right with God, or are reconciled to him, the method by which God's justice is satisfied. But even this word appears only three times in the New Testament (Romans 3:25; 1 John 2:2; 1 John 4:10). In contrast, the Old Testament uses the word *atonement* dozens of times.

Read the gospels—they do not contain the words *katallage* or *hilasmos*. And yet the story of Jesus' life, his parables, his death, and most important, his resurrection, all paint a picture of God's persistent efforts to reconcile us to himself. It is arguably the subtext for the whole gospel. Jesus fulfilled the Old Testament laws for atonement in a once-for-all sacrifice. But he did more than save us. His life and death call us to live differently. The few verses that speak directly about reconciliation are powerful nuggets of theology that explain the meaning of Christ's death and its implication for us.

> Since we have now been justified by his blood, how much more shall we be saved from God's wrath through him! For if, while we were God's enemies, we were reconciled (*katallasso*) to him through the death of his Son, how much more, having been reconciled (*katallasso*), shall we be saved through his life! Not only is this so, but we also boast in God through our Lord Jesus Christ, through whom we have now received reconciliation (*katallage*). (Rom. 5:9–11)

Furthermore, with salvation comes a heavy yet beautiful gift: the ministry of reconciliation.

> Therefore, if anyone is in Christ, he is a new creation; the old has gone, the new has come! All this is from God, who reconciled (*katallasso*) us to himself through Christ and gave us the *ministry of reconciliation*. (*katallage*) that God was reconciling (*katallasso*) the world to himself in Christ, not counting men's sins against them. And he has committed to us the message of reconciliation (*katallage*). We are therefore Christ's ambassadors, as though God were making his appeal through us. We implore you on Christ's behalf: Be reconciled (*katallasso*) to God. God made him who had no sin to be sin for us, so that in him we might become the righteousness of God. (2 Cor. 5:17–21)

Reconciliation is good news—not just for you. It's good news for the people you've been living estranged from, or even the people in your own home that you're holding a grudge against, because it calls you to take the first step to reconcile relationships. It calls you to that messy and painful *agape* we talked about in a previous chapter. And if you are trusting Christ as your Savior, you are reconciled to God, but you've also been given a message and ministry of reconciliation. You are Christ's ambassador, called to invite others to be reconciled to God.

RELIGION/RELIGIOUS

It's odd. Even though most people believe the Bible to be a religious book, the words *religion* and *religious* appear only a handful of times, and in only one is there a positive connotation. Yet even in that passage (James 1:26–27 TNIV) religion is contrasted with false religion:

> Those who consider themselves religious and yet do not keep a tight rein on their tongues deceive themselves, and their religion is worthless. Religion that God our Father accepts as pure and faultless is this: to look after orphans and widows in their distress and to keep oneself from being polluted by the world.

The word *religion* is *threskeia*, which refers to the external aspect of religion. In other words, James seems to be saying, live out your faith—act justly and love mercy (Mic. 6:8). And don't gossip. James is expounding on his thought from a few verses earlier, where he writes, "Do not merely listen to the word, and so deceive yourselves. Do what it says" (v. 22 TNIV).

Religion has a connotation of rules and legalism, so many Christians will not describe themselves as religious. Our faith is based not on religion, but on a relationship with Jesus. As I heard in so many evangelical sermons growing up, religion is spelled D-O because it's about what you have to do, but relationship with Jesus is spelled D-O-N-E because it's based on what Jesus has done for us. The term *religious* had a negative connotation in many ways.

Genuine *threskeia* is the external expression of an internal quality mentioned far more frequently: godliness. This trait has to do with our actions. Do we extend grace, forgive, love? In other words, godliness is living out our religion. And true religion, James seems to be saying, requires some doing. Not to earn God's favor, but to proclaim him, to respond to his love for us.

The tension lies, of course, in how to engage in social justice (the "doing" of the word, which James seems to be encouraging) and yet to keep yourself unspotted or unstained (the Greek word is *aspilos*, without spot) by the world. *Aspilos* is used only three other times in the New Testament. Looking at these other passages can give us insight into the meaning of this word, which is crucial for our understanding of the word *religion*.

Aspilos is used to describe Jesus as an unblemished sacrificial lamb in 1 Peter 1:19 and to express the idea of being free from defilement in 2 Peter 3:14.

The other use of *aspilos* gives us a glimpse into what true religion is. Paul writes to his protégé Timothy with these stirring words:

> But you, man of God, flee from all this, and pursue righteousness, godliness, faith, love, endurance and gentleness. Fight the good fight of the faith. Take hold of the eternal life to which you were called. . . . I charge you to keep this command without spot or blame (*aspilos*) until the appearing of our Lord Jesus Christ. (1 Tim. 6:11–14)

Paul tells Timothy to "flee from all this." All *what*? If you look at the context, "this" refers to the prior verse, where Paul condemns the love of money as "the root of all evil." To be unspotted is to be free from the clutches of the pursuit of wealth. It is to put God first.

True religion fights the good fight, pursues godliness, and yet shows compassion. Someone who loves money cannot care for widows in their distress, because he will want to keep his wealth for himself.

In Paul's famous address on Mars Hill, he says to the crowd: "Men of Athens! I see that in every way you are very religious" (Acts 17:22), but he is not paying them a compliment.

The word rendered *religious* is a long Greek word that appears only once in the Bible: *deisidaimonesteros*, which is a combination of *deilos*, which means faithless, or fearful; and *daimon*, which means a demon, devil, or supernatural spirit. The KJV translates the phrase "too superstitious." Paul then goes on to explain why the many idols in the city are not true gods, and shares the gospel with them. In other words, he explains true religion, by which they can actually be saved.

REMAIN

In his famous teaching that begins "I am the true vine," Jesus exhorts his disciples (including us) to remain in his love. He gave them a word picture of a vine and branches to explain what he meant—staying with him in deep, life-giving connection that is focused on love. As *The Message* translation puts it:

> I've loved you the way my Father has loved me. Make yourselves at home in my love. If you keep my commands, you'll remain intimately at home in my love. That's what I've done—kept my Father's commands and made myself at home in his love. (John 15:9–10)

The KJV says, "Abide in my love." But how, exactly, do we do that?

The word *remain* can mean to stay, to continue on, or to be left over. In modern translations of the Bible, the word *remain* is often the translation of a Greek word, *meno*, which means to abide or stay, which is used both literally and metaphorically. Five other words, created by adding prefixes to *meno*, are used to convey various shades of meaning. For example, *epimeno* means to remain in or continue in, while *parameno* means to remain beside.

Jesus said he was the vine, which is the main "trunk" of a grapevine. And we are branches, the offshoots of that vine—and the place where fruit grows. What does that look like in our daily lives? A branch doesn't actually have to work to cling to the vine—it merely exists that way. It is fed only by its connection to the vine; it can't go elsewhere. A branch does not have a choice.

We, on the other hand, must make choices every day to remain in Christ or go our own way. We must consciously decide that we will be like a branch is to a vine. We must choose to remain. We must use Jesus' metaphor to frame our lives.

We can understand what Jesus meant by "remain" if we look at other verses that contain the same word. We see the word *remain* several times in 1 Corinthians 7, with verses like this one: "Brothers and sisters, all of you, as responsible to God, should remain in the situation in which God called you" (v. 24 TNIV).

This letter was apparently addressing how to respond to a certain situation, and Paul was advising people in that church to maintain their marital status: "Because of the present crisis, I think that it is good for a man to remain as he is. Are you pledged to a woman? Do not seek to be released. Are you free from such a commitment? Do not look for a wife" (1 Cor. 7:26–27 TNIV). Whether the crisis was persecution or some other problem, the Corinthians had apparently asked Paul some questions about marriage and social standing.

The word *remain* can also refer to staying in a place, as it does in Acts 15:35, which tells us that at a certain time, Paul and Barnabas remained in Antioch.

Later in the same letter, Paul writes, "And now these three remain: faith, hope and love. But the greatest of these is love" (1 Cor. 13:13). Again, the verb in Greek is *meno*, which can also mean to continue, endure, or dwell. This verse is a call to cling to the things that endure—primarily, it is a call to love.

Jesus says that if we remain in him, his joy will remain in us, and we'll bear fruit, which will also remain (John 15:11, 16). John repeats this teaching in his later epistles. He writes:

> As for you, the anointing you received from him remains in you, and you do not need anyone to teach you. But as his anointing teaches you about all things and as that anointing is real, not counterfeit—just as it has taught you, remain in him. (1 John 2:27)

To remain is to be steadfast, something that is not valued in our rapidly changing world. But as Jesus promised, if we remain in him, he will remain in us—an intimacy that will never change.

REPENT

We first hear the word *repent* from the lips of John the Baptist. He is preparing the way. As the gospel story unfolds, and Herod manages to silence John the Baptist by slaying him, Jesus picks up the cry, again saying, "Repent!" (Matt. 4:17). A few years later, Peter preaches and three thousand are converted in a day—that was a powerful sermon! (Acts 2:14–31). But what did he say, and who were these people, their hearts so plowed and ready to receive the Word?

His message echoed his rabbi's: "Repent!"

Jesus taught on repentance by telling stories. In a poignant parable, Jesus tells of a poor man named Lazarus who goes to "Abraham's side" when he dies, while a rich man who ignored his plight goes to hell. The rich man asks Abraham to send Lazarus with a drop of water to cool his tongue, "because I am in agony in this fire" (see Luke 16:19–31). Abraham refuses, saying the gap is too wide. It's interesting that the rich man, even in the fires of hell, still has the attitude that he expects Lazarus to serve him. He's unrepentant, even as he's burning.

In our day, the command to "Repent!" sometimes feels like a judgment: guilty! But repent means to feel sorry for a past action, and even to be inspired to change once we realize the error of our ways. "Pent" comes from the same Latin root as the word *penitent*, meaning to feel sorry or sorrow. However, this etymology confuses us in English. We think that repentance involves doing penance—trying to balance out our sins with good deeds, or by repeating certain prayers. Such an undertaking is impossible. Biblical repentance means not trying to earn God's favor, but throwing yourself on God's mercy, knowing his favor cannot be earned and is certainly not deserved.

In Greek, the word is *metanoeo*, which means literally to perceive afterwards. *Meta* means after, but implies in that meaning to change, *noeo* means to perceive. So *metanoeo* is to change our perception. It happens when we are perhaps confronted—by a person or our conscience or the Holy Spirit—and think again about what we have done. We feel regret, but we don't stop there. We seek forgiveness, but also, we change our actions. We decide to go a new way, and then—and this is absolutely key—we actually go that new way. We make it right. To repent is not just to feel guilty over our mistakes, but to choose a new path. It is to make a 180-degree turn, to turn around and walk in a new direction.

Another word that is sometimes translated "repent" (in other versions, "regret") is *metamellomai*. *Metamellomai* appears only six times in the New Testament, and means to feel regret or compunction. Its meaning does not extend to action. *Metanoeo* is used much more frequently (thirty-four times) and implies a change in direction, away from sin and toward God. It always includes the action that is missing from *metamellomai*.

Another Greek word, *lupeo*, means godly sorrow—grieving over our sin. It is one of the steps we must take in order to move toward repentance, but in itself it is not repentance. In 2 Corinthians 7:8–10, we see these three words compared and contrasted:

> Even if I caused you sorrow (*lupeo*) by my letter, I do not regret (*metamellomai*) it. Though I did regret (*metamellomai*) it—I see that my letter hurt (*lupeo*) you, but only for a little while—yet now I am happy, not because you were made sorry (*lupeo*), but because your sorrow (*lupeo*) led you to repentance (*metanoia*). For you became sorrowful (*lupeo*) as God intended and so were not harmed in any way by us. Godly sorrow (*lupeo*) brings repentance (*metanoia*) that leads to salvation and leaves no regret, but worldly sorrow (*lupeo*) brings death.

Because sin ultimately leads to death, when we truly repent (*metanoeo*), we find freedom. We are helped by the Spirit to truly change our ways, and that change does not bring regret or guilt, but joy.

REST

In his brilliant book *The Rest of God*, Mark Buchanan argues compellingly that when we ignore the gift of God's rest—the practice of Sabbath—our experience of God is incomplete. In order to experience the rest of God (the part we're missing), we need to engage in the rest (stopping work) that he offers us.

He writes: "Get this straight: The rest of God—the rest God

gladly gives so that we might discover that part of God we're missing—is not a reward for finishing. It's not a bonus for work well done. It's sheer gift."[1]

The New Testament contains several different Greek words that can be translated "rest." Some are only translated "rest" once or twice, like *eirene*, which in almost every other instance means peace.

Jesus said, "Come to me, all you who are weary and burdened, and I will give you rest" (Matthew 11:28). In this verse, the Greek word for rest is *anapauo*, meaning to give intermission from labor, or to refresh in order to recover strength. Unlike the Pharisees, whom Jesus accused of burdening people with heavy rules, Jesus offered an easier way—even though it required everything of those who followed him. This word is used only five times in the New Testament. (The same word is used in Mark 6:31, when Jesus invites his disciples to come to a quiet place and get some rest.)

But in the next verse from Matthew 11, Jesus said, "You will find rest for your souls." In this case, the word is *anapausis*, meaning cessation or refreshment. Only someone who has been working previously can *anapauo*, as it means to stop the work you are doing so that you can recover. So "rest for souls" would seem to imply that previously, people had been making some sort of spiritual effort—perhaps again referring to the legalistic requirements of the Pharisees.

Jesus offers his disciples rest, even as we are about his work in the world. There is an assumption of a rhythm of work and rest. Our labor, however, is not an attempt to earn his favor, but rather cooperation with him and through him. When we rest in him we are strengthened and refreshed. Then we can accomplish much and love well, because it is he who is yoked to us, sharing our burdens and helping us to be more than we thought possible.

Sometimes in English, the word *rest* means the remaining ones, a remnant of things or people. In these cases (see Luke 24:9 NASB, for example), the Greek word is *loipoi*.

Paul says in 2 Corinthians 2:13 that he had no rest in his spirit. The word in this and four other verses is *anesis*, which means relief. It refers not to a rest from ordinary daily work, but a rest from suffering or struggle.

The word *rest* appears nine times in the fourth chapter of Hebrews, where the writer draws the parallel between the Old Testament Sabbath commandment and the ultimate rest of intimacy with God.

Most of these are the noun *katapausis*, meaning a causing to cease, rest, or repose, often referring to God's rest, i.e., his dwelling place (see Acts 7:49), where we will eventually be with him. It can also refer to our confident assurance of his provision and peace in our lives right now. The related verb, *katapauo*, appears three times in the chapter, and it means to cause to cease, or to restrain.

In Hebrews 4, we also find another word for rest (translated "Sabbath-rest"), which is *sabbatismos*, the repose of Christianity. It refers to our ultimate rest in heaven, although the text says we enter it now, even if not fully. God's rest is a hope within us.

In Hebrews 4:9–10 we see the subtle differences between these words as they are in context with one another. "There remains, then, a Sabbath-rest (*sabbatismos*) for the people of God; for those who enter God's rest (*katapausis*) also rest (*katapauo*) from their own work, just as God did from his." (See ***Sabbath***.)

RESURRECTION

Way before Jesus rose from the grave, Jews were arguing about whether there would be a resurrection of the dead. Pharisees and Essenes believed firmly in an afterlife. The Sadducees, another party within the religious leadership at the time of Jesus, did not believe in a resurrection of the dead. (See ***Pharisee***.) It is the Saduccees who pose a riddle to him about whose wife a woman will be in the resurrection (Matt. 22:28; Mark 12:23; Luke 20:33). They don't really care about his answer; their point is to show their opinion about how absurd belief in a resurrection is.

The *IVP Bible Commentary* notes: "The Sadducees borrow the story line of a woman with seven husbands from the popular Jewish folktale in Tobit 3:8; they want to illustrate the impossible dilemmas they believe the doctrine of *resurrection* creates."[1]

Jesus refutes them by saying that there will indeed be a resurrection and an afterlife, but marriage will not be a part of that life. Little did they know that when he died and rose again, Jesus would forever alter the debate about resurrection.

Pagan religions also had myths about various gods who died and were resurrected (commonly known as Corn King myths, sometimes used to explain the rebirth of plants in the spring). The most well-known was that of the Egyptian god Osiris. However, Osiris, according to most stories, was brought back to life by his wife, Isis, and soon died again. The stories pale in comparison to the resurrection of Jesus, which was documented by eyewitnesses and historians who were outside the faith.

Many modern scholars have pointed to these myths as so called proof that Jesus' resurrection was yet another myth. Christian scholars argue that these myths only point to humanity's longing for God, who ultimately is the only one who can overcome death completely.

When a group of women go to the tomb where Jesus was hastily buried, they find the tomb empty. An angel tells them, "He is not here, he is risen, just as he said." (See Matt. 28:5–7; Mark 16:5–7; and Luke 24:5–7.) Later, the resurrected Christ appears to the women, his disciples, and larger crowds of people.

Christianity preaches not only that Jesus was resurrected, but that eventually he will return to earth. When he returns, all who have died will rise again as well. The Greek word translated "resurrection" is *anastasis,* which means literally "to cause to stand up on one's feet again." It can mean a resurrection from physical death, or a recovery of spiritual truth.

Simeon, the old priest, uses this word when he tells Mary that "this child is destined to cause the falling and rising (*anastasis*) of many in Israel, and to be a sign that will be spoken against" (Luke 2:34). Imagine young Mary, clutching the baby Jesus in wonder, trying to understand what he means.

Only once is *exanastasis* used, in Philippians 3:10–11 (TNIV), which says, "I want to know Christ—yes, to know the power of his resurrection (*anastasis*) and participation in his sufferings, becoming like him in his death, and so, somehow, attaining to the resurrection from the dead (*exanastasis*)."

First Corinthians 15 provides a summary of Christ's resurrection and its theological implications. We see the phrase "resurrection of the dead" (*anastasis*) four times. We also see the word *raised* ten times. The verb in Greek is *egeiro*. This word has a broader meaning: It can mean to rouse from sleep, to raise up, to rise up against someone or something, or even to raise a building, and of course, to raise from the dead. It is sometimes translated "risen," as in Luke 24:34, "the Lord is risen indeed" (NKJV).

This chapter in 1 Corinthians is pivotal to the Christian faith. The chapter begins, "I want to remind you of the gospel I preached to you." The gospel, *euaggelion,* hinges on the resurrection. As Paul writes: "And if Christ has not been raised, our preaching is useless and so is your faith" (v. 14). Everything depends on the truth of the resurrection. Otherwise, Jesus was just another rabbi, and our hope is in vain.

RIGHTEOUSNESS

In many religious contexts, righteousness is understood to be piety or living according to the rules. For many Christians, righteousness is unfortunately limited to avoiding bad behavior. While moral behavior is commendable, that is only a fraction of the meaning of the word *righteousness* in the Bible.

The Greek word *dikaiosune* is most often translated "righteousness" in the New Testament. This rich word refers to righteousness that is proactive, that pursues not only holiness but justice. God's righteousness and his justice are inseparable. If you live rightly, you will live justly—you will seek out justice not just for yourself but for the oppressed. You will not only love God but love your neighbor as yourself. Your choices in life will reflect this.

Dikaiosune implies a concern for fairness and fair treatment of all people. It is so much more than sin avoidance. It is often used to describe the righteousness of God. We attain it only by faith, not by our own efforts. However, once we have been justified by faith, we seek out justice for others.

Jesus said, "Blessed are those who are persecuted because of righteousness, for theirs is the kingdom of heaven" (Matt. 5:10). Again the Greek word is *dikaiosune*. It is unlikely that anyone would be persecuted for simply trying to avoid moral transgressions. While in some places people are persecuted for their beliefs, this is not what Jesus is referring to. But if we understand that *dikaiosune* means fighting injustice, then the possibility of persecution becomes very real.

This is one of a family of words that have to do with righteousness or justice, which in the Bible are two sides of the same coin. *Dikaios* means righteous or just; *dikaioo* means to justify. To do what is right means to do what is fair.

When Jesus said our *dikaiosune* should exceed that of the Pharisees (Matt. 5:20), he was not telling us we ought to be even more legalistic than they. It's unfortunate that the word is translated "righteousness," when it could just as accurately be translated "justice." For though the Pharisees loved the law and strove mightily to obey it, they had lost sight of the heart of it. They did not think about justice for others, which, at the heart of it, is what truly righteous behavior will always encompass. These concepts are inseparable and come together in the word *dikaiosune*.

This word appears throughout the New Testament, including thirty-seven mentions in the book of Romans. In this book, we read of God's righteous judgment. The word *dikaios*, righteous, appears four times. The word *dikaioo*, which is sometimes translated "justify," and sometimes "righteous," appears ten times. For example, Romans 3:20: "No one will be declared righteous (*dikaioo*) in his sight by observing the law; rather, through the law we become conscious of sin." In Romans 6, Paul writes that believers are "instruments of righteousness" and "slaves of righteousness." We are the means by which God carries out justice and righteousness in the world. And yet there is a tension: While we are commanded to live righteously and justly, we cannot justify ourselves by our actions. Rather, we are justified by grace (Rom. 3:24) and by faith (3:28). But we have been justified in order that we might live as "slaves to righteousness" (6:18), meaning we will seek justice for others and "live in accordance with the Spirit" (8:5).

Pastor and author Mae Cannon writes,

> Christians believe that justice is ultimately the manifestation of the righteousness of God. God is the source of justice. The laws and will of Yahweh, the God of Israel, defines what is right and what is wrong. His laws are expressed throughout the Old and New Testaments. God is the defining source of virtue, truth and justice. The source of justice is divine.[1]

ROCK

In English, *rock* is a solid word—implying steadfastness, immovability. It can also imply movement—when someone rocks your world, when you dance to rock and roll, when your path through life seems rocky.

The Old Testament, especially the Psalms, talks about God as a rock, a safe place, a firm foundation.

In the New Testament, the word *rock* appears less frequently, but it is nonetheless an important word theologically, used to describe obedience to the Word of God (Matt. 7:24–27), Jesus himself (1 Cor. 10:4), and of course the disciple whose name was "Rocky"—Peter (Matt. 16:18). But as it does in English, *rock* can have a negative connotation as well.

The word *petra*, the feminine of *petros*, means a mass of rock. *Petros*, the masculine, means a piece of rock, a boulder, or a stone that might be thrown.

Petros or *Petrus* (in Aramaic, *Cephas*) was the name of the apostle who was originally called Simon, son of Jonah. The word means rock or stone.

In Matthew 16, Jesus asks his disciples, "Who do you say that I am?" The text then continues:

> Simon Peter answered, "You are the Christ, the Son of the living God."
>
> Jesus replied, "Blessed are you, Simon son of Jonah, for this was not revealed to you by man, but by my Father in heaven. And I tell you that you are Peter, and on this rock I will build my church, and the gates of Hades will not overcome it" (vv. 16–18).

Jesus is playing with words—prior to this event in the text, Simon was referred to as Peter. One commentary notes, "The play on words would be brought out even better in Aramaic where one word *kepha* lies behind *Petros* and *petra*."[1] It's likely that the other disciples may have been scratching their heads. Peter, if we look at his actions and words as recorded in the gospels, was known to be impetuous—his name didn't fit. But Jesus gave him a name to grow into.

Because Jesus was sometimes referred to as the stumbling stone or cornerstone (Rom. 9:33; 1 Peter 2:6), "Some interpreters have therefore referred to Jesus as the rock here, but the context is against this. Nor is it likely that Peter's faith or Peter's confession is meant. It is undoubtedly Peter himself who is to be the rock, but Peter confessing, faithful and obedient."[2]

Rock is not always a positive term in the New Testament. For example, the word *rock* in Jesus' parable of the sower refers to a hardened heart. Some of the seed falls on rock and sprouts but dies for lack of moisture (see Luke 8:1–15). The rock keeps the seed from developing roots. The rock, Jesus says, represents a heart that does not have the depth to endure a time of testing.

Petra also is the word used to describe the place where Jesus was buried, in "a tomb cut out of rock." The opening to this man-made cave was covered with a large stone. Certainly the symbolism would not have been lost on Jesus' Jewish followers, who remembered the story of Moses standing in a cleft in the rock on Mt. Horeb as the presence of the Lord passed by him, and the prophesy from Isaiah 8:14, "He will be a sanctuary; but for both houses of Israel he will be a stone that causes men to stumble and a rock that makes them fall."

Both Romans 9:33 and 1 Peter 2:4–8 quote that prophesy. Peter notes that Jesus is the Living Stone, and we are living stones. Obviously, again, a rock or stone can be a refuge of safety, or something to stumble over, depending on our approach.

Stone in Greek is a different word, *lithos*, which can refer to stones on the ground, tombstones, a millstone, stone tables, and so on. The verb *lithazo* means to stone, meaning to kill by throwing stones—an unfortunately common occurrence in biblical times.

First Corinthians 10:3–4 refers to the Old Testament story of Israel's exodus from Egypt. When the people complained of thirst, God gave them water from a rock in the middle of the desert. Moses hit a rock with his staff and water gushed forth (see Ex. 17:1–6). The New Testament explains the symbolism: "For they drank from the spiritual rock that accompanied them, and that rock was Christ" (1 Cor. 10:4). This rock was a symbol of the presence of Christ, who was with the Israelites in the desert.

How fitting that Jesus referred to himself not only as the cornerstone and a rock, but as the source of living water (Matt. 21:42; John 4). As always, the Old Testament prophesies, stories, and festivals are fulfilled and come together in the person of Jesus.

SABBATH

"Remember the Sabbath day, and keep it holy" (Ex. 20:8 NRSV). Thus reads the fourth commandment of the ten. And yet so many Christians I meet seem to think that the New Testament teaches that this command no longer applies, that it may be discarded or ignored; if you're too busy, you can skip it.

I would argue that if you consider yourself too busy, treating Sabbath as optional will do you more spiritual harm than good.

The English word *Sabbath* and Greek *Sabbaton* both derive from the Hebrew word *Shabbat*, which means simply to cease or stop. We don't rest when we're done with our work, but rather, we obediently set our endless work aside, whether we have completed it or not. We cease, out of pure obedience.

It is to our own detriment that we choose to use our freedom in Christ to discard the gifts of God, including Sabbath. The Sabbath was *made* for people—a custom gift, crafted in the heart of God. And yet we leave it, like an unopened package, stowed away. When things settle down, we think, we'll perhaps open that box and poke around in it. Except that things don't. Ever. Settle. Down.

The New Testament teaches us that in Jesus' day, Jews gathered for teaching and worship in the synagogue on the Sabbath. It was a day in which no work was done. The Pharisees abided by this rule of course, except that they worked very hard to catch Jesus breaking it. They plotted and spied on the Sabbath, but missed the irony of that.

Jesus often taught by saying, "You've heard it said . . . but I say . . ." He'd then give a new interpretation of the Torah, calling people to embrace the spirit of the law rather than just the letter.

Oddly, he never used the "You've heard it said, but I say" formula to teach about Sabbath. Still, he taught all the time about Sabbath with his actions and with his own defense of those actions. (See Luke 13:10–16.)

Pastor and author Mark Buchanan writes: "When Jesus broke man-made Sabbath regulations, he always went in this direction: he healed, he fed, he claimed the right to rescue creatures fallen into wells or to lead to wells creatures falling down with thirst. Jesus pursued those things that give life."[1]

In Mark 2, the Pharisees accuse Jesus of breaking the Sabbath when his disciples grab some grain and snack on it as they walk through a field. He responds by saying, "The Sabbath was made for people, not people for the Sabbath" (see v. 27).

"And that, actually, is all we need to know to keep the Sabbath holy," Mark Buchanan comments on this verse. "This day was made for us. God gave it to you and me for our sake, for our benefit, for our strengthening and our replenishment."[2]

Jesus set us free, not from keeping the Sabbath at all, but from the legalism that was associated with it.

Colossians 2:16–17 says, "Therefore do not let anyone judge you by what you eat or drink, or with regard to a religious festival, a New Moon celebration or a Sabbath day. These are a shadow of the things that were to come; the reality, however, is found in Christ."

This verse echoes several Old Testament passages that name the Sabbath Day and the Day of the New Moon as special worship days (see Ezek. 46:1–3; Isa. 66:23, etc.). This passage offers us freedom in the way that we worship and keep Sabbath. Our salvation is not dependent upon religious festivals or rules. And we are not to judge each other.

Some Christians have argued that this passage means that we no longer have to keep the Sabbath. I disagree. The Sabbath, like other ancient practices, is a symbol of things to come—of our ultimate Sabbath rest with God (see Heb. 4). But it is still a valid spiritual practice, and a gift to embrace. When we take a day each week to rest, we get to experience God in fresh ways. (See ***Rest***.)

SACRIFICE

Romans 12:1 reads: "I appeal to you therefore, brothers and sisters, by the mercies of God, to present your bodies as a living sacrifice, holy and acceptable to God, which is your spiritual worship" (NRSV). God's mercy should evoke a response of worship—and not just the worship of our words or songs, but with our bodies. How do we worship with our bodies? How is it that we can offer them as "living sacrifices"?

Although we are spiritual beings, we live this life in a body. And the things we choose to do, to think about, will affect our spiritual life. Our spirits are contained in a body, and as Dallas Willard says,

"The spiritual and the bodily are by no means opposed in human life—they are complementary."[1] As Romans 12 continues: "Do not conform any longer to the pattern of this world, but be transformed by the renewing of your mind. Then you will be able to test and approve what God's will is—his good, pleasing and perfect will" (v. 2). Paul then goes on to describe spiritual gifts—things we can do with our bodies in order to serve God, in order to worship him.

Part of how we offer our body as a sacrifice is to move it in a different direction than "the pattern of this world" and to "renew our minds"—to choose to think and act differently. The Greek word for sacrifice in this verse is *thusia*, a noun that means both the act of offering and the thing that is offered.

To understand the word *sacrifice* in the New Testament, we must of course look to the Old Testament, where it describes an elaborate system of offerings required to atone for sin. These requirements were, as we have said before, symbols of the ultimate sacrifice, which would be Jesus. It was all a setup so that God could show us the extent of his love.

The book of Hebrews compares the Old Testament and New Testament sacrifices.[2] Jesus was both the sacrificial lamb and the high priest, "once for all" (see Heb. 7:27).

Now, we no longer sacrifice animals, but we are still called to sacrifice: "Through Jesus, therefore, let us continually offer to God a sacrifice of praise—the fruit of lips that confess his name" (Heb. 13:15).

The Old Testament laws were not meant to be empty ritual, but an expression of a contrite spirit (see Ps. 51:17). It is notable that the first occurrence of the word *sacrifice* in the New Testament is when Jesus quotes the Old Testament, saying, "I desire mercy, not sacrifice."

Jesus utters these words in Matthew 9:13 and Matthew 12:7 in the midst of heated discussions with the Pharisees. He tells them to go and learn what this means. In other words, go study this section of the Torah again, because I don't think you get it. Jesus was employing a common method of rabbinical teaching—alluding to an entire section of Scripture by quoting one short phrase from it. All of his audience, not just the Pharisees, would have had the Torah memorized. They would immediately know that the context of "mercy, not sacrifice" in Hosea 6 says things like "I killed you with the words of my mouth," and "Like Adam, they have broken the covenant—they were unfaithful to me." Jesus was, to put it in our vernacular, talking smack to the Pharisees. No wonder their response was to plot to kill him.

As Luke describes the day of Jesus' death, he writes, "Then came the day of Unleavened Bread on which the Passover lamb had to be sacrificed" (Luke 22:7). Indeed, in the Jewish calendar, that day was Passover, when devout Jews literally sacrificed lambs and ate ritual meals, as they had for centuries. But it was also the day upon which the ultimate Passover lamb, Jesus, would be sacrificed, to atone for the sins of all people, once and for all.

First John 4:10 says, "This is love: not that we loved God, but that he loved us and sent his Son as an atoning sacrifice for our sins." The Greek in this verse (sometimes translated "propitiation") is *hilasmos*, a word connected to both atonement and mercy—that once for all sacrifice that demonstrated God's love, allows us to be in right relationship with him, and inspires us to offer a sacrifice of praise. (See ***Reconciliation***.)

SALT

Salt was used in ancient days, as it is now, for seasoning food. But the word had a far more complex flavor than that. Without refrigeration, people used it to preserve food as well as to flavor it. Salt was sometimes added to manure to form fertilizer. It was required to be thrown on the altar with sacrifices, and newborn babies were sometimes rubbed down with it. Despite the fact that it was abundant, it had great value. In ancient Rome, salt was used as currency.

Salt was part of the sacrificial system. The Old Testament offerings were all to contain salt—because the meat and grain offered was typically eaten by the priests, but also because salt symbolized permanence and holiness. Particularly important covenants were called "salt covenants." (See Lev. 2:13; Num. 18:19; 2 Chron. 13:5.)

So when Jesus says, "You are the salt of the earth" (Matt. 5:13), what is he saying about his followers? He is calling us to have the characteristics that salt has. Salt makes food savory or palatable; it can enhance flavor, purify, and change that which it comes in contact with. It can induce thirst. It is a symbol of holiness, permanence, covenant. "Being possessed of purifying, perpetuating and antiseptic qualities, 'salt' became emblematic of fidelity and friendship among Eastern nations. To eat of a person's 'salt' and so to share his hospitality is still regarded thus among the Arabs."[1] An Arab who shared salt with someone shared a meal with him, and by that intimate act was pledging his allegiance to that person.

This is a high calling—to be the salt of the earth meant to be all of these things. But then Jesus goes on to ask: "What good is salt that loses its flavor?" He's continuing to build on this metaphor, but also alluding to the sacrifices his Jewish listeners would have made on a regular basis. The layers of meaning would be obvious to his audience. A salt covenant is inviolable, serious. Further, the word *moraino*, which is translated "tasteless" or "loses its flavor," can also mean to become foolish, which provides a bit of a play on words. If you act foolishly, you cannot have a positive impact for the kingdom. Salt that has lost its flavor has "lost the ability to make thirsty for spiritual truth and to preserve from further corruption."[2]

One commentary offers this insight:

> A disciple of the kingdom who does not live like a disciple of the kingdom is worth about as much as tasteless salt or invisible light. . . . The point here is closer to that expressed by a rabbi at the end of the first century. When asked how one could make saltless salt salty again, he replied that one should salt it with the afterbirth of a mule. Being sterile, mules have no afterbirth, and he was saying that those who ask a stupid question receive a stupid answer. Real salt does not lose its saltiness; but if it did, what would you do to restore its salty flavor—salt it? Unsalty salt was worthless.[3]

The Greek words *halas* and *hals* mean salt, and can be used literally or metaphorically (typically as a metaphor for a person's character). Jesus' multifaceted metaphor communicated to his disciples his view of the importance of their ministry and his vision for their potential to change the world.

In Matthew, Jesus' teachings on saltiness are fairly straightforward, even though they are metaphorical. But in a parallel passage in Mark 9:49–50, his words are a bit more obtuse: "Everyone will be salted with fire. Salt is good, but if it loses its saltiness, how can you make it salty again? Have salt in yourselves, and be at peace with each other."

The term *salted with fire* may have been another allusion to the salt used in sacrifices, which was burned on an altar. It also may be alluding to the coming of Pentecost, where the Holy Spirit came in the form of tongues of fire resting on the head of each person.

SALVATION

The words *salvation* and *saved* appear frequently throughout the New Testament, and many verses that talk about repentance, eternal life, and so forth are about the idea of salvation even if they do not use that exact word.

The Greek word *sozo*, which means to save or deliver, appears 110 times in the text and can mean both physical saving from danger, but also spiritual salvation that comes through faith in Jesus. *Soteria,* meaning salvation or deliverance, appears forty-five times. The related *soter* means deliverer or savior.

New Testament scholar Ceslas Spicq writes that the words *sozo* and *soteria,* when used in secular texts contemporary to the New Testament, mean "to deliver when there is a particularly perilous situation, a mortal danger. . . . the most common usage . . . is medical: to save means to heal a disease; remedies are saviors . . . physicians are saviors. In the second century BC, a decree of Samos honors the physician Diodorus, who cared for and restored many patients and 'was the cause of their salvation' . . ."[1]

He goes on to note that the New Testament writers used the secular definition, but also used the word *soteria* to mean "deliverance from sins and the wrath to come."[2]

One of the greatest hurdles in the way of anyone finding salvation, or "getting saved," is the fact that they don't believe they are in need of saving, because they consider themselves a "good person" who mostly does what is right. They may ask, "Saved from what?" Blindness to sin and its consequences keeps us from being desperate about our need to be rescued from it.

Often we are also blind to the power of God. Contrast that to the story of the jailer in Acts 16, who sees God send an earthquake to free Paul and Silas. The jailer's first question when he gets a glimpse of God's power is, "What must I do to be saved?" The apostles reply simply, "Believe in the Lord Jesus, and you will be saved—you and your household" (v. 31).

Likewise, 1 Thessalonians 5:9 says, "For God did not appoint us to suffer wrath but to receive salvation through our Lord Jesus Christ."

Ephesians 2:1–9 explains that while we must believe in order to be saved, salvation cannot be earned, as it is a gift from a loving God. It brings us back to life after we are dead in sin: "But because of his great love for us, God, who is rich in mercy, made us alive with Christ even when we were dead in transgressions—it is by grace you have been saved . . . through faith—and this is not from yourselves, it is the gift of God—not by works, so that no one can boast" (Eph. 2:4–9).

In some ways, salvation is incomplete until we are actually rescued from the wages of sin, which is death. For example, in Philippians 2:12–13, Paul writes: "Therefore, my dear friends, as you have always obeyed—not only in my presence, but now much more in my absence—continue to work out your salvation with fear and trembling, for it is God who works in you to will and to act according to his good purpose."

What does that mean, to work out salvation? Isn't it a free gift, as we saw in the passage above from Ephesians? And even in these two verses, Paul says that we should work out our salvation, but also that it is God who works in us. So is it us, or God? The answer to that is "yes." It is our humble asking for mercy that God responds to, but it is his offer of grace that we respond to. We seek God because he first loved us and sought us. As we respond to him, he continues to work in us. Even after we "get saved," the process of our salvation continues until we get to heaven.

SEEK

To seek means to look for, to search. In my particular church subculture, someone who has not yet decided to follow Jesus is known as "a seeker," which is better than what I grew up with.

Back then we called such people "non-Christians," which is a rather negative term.

Seeking, though, is a lifelong process. While we may find new life in Jesus, we must daily decide to follow him and seek to know him more fully. Further, the Bible says that we should seek God, but also that he seeks us out. A beautiful interplay exists, where God seeks us, stirring and whispering in a voice we may not yet recognize. And so begins a search for the God who longs to be found (Jer. 29:13–14).

Jesus said, "Ask and it will be given to you; seek and you will find; knock and the door will be opened to you. For everyone who asks receives; those who seek find; and to those who knock, the door will be opened" (Luke 11:9–10; see also Matt. 7). The implication in the text is this: Keep on asking, keep on seeking, keep on knocking. Even after we find, if we keep seeking, we'll keep discovering new things about God and about ourselves in light of our relationship with God. Knowing God is like peeling an infinite onion. Just when we think we're done, we realize there's another layer to peel back, more to discover.

Jesus also said, "Seek first his kingdom and his righteousness" (Matt. 6:33). This too is an ongoing seeking, with a bit of urgency associated with it.

The Greek verb translated "seek" in this and many other passages is *zeteo*. Like the English word *seek*, it has several different meanings. *Zeteo* means to seek to worship God, but it also means to seek knowledge or meaning, often by asking questions. In John 16:19 Jesus says, "Are you asking one another (*zeteo*) what I meant when I said, 'In a little while you will see me no more, and then after a little while you will see me'?"

Zeteo can also mean a negative seeking. In Matthew 2:20, Herod plotted to kill Jesus (sought his life), and in Mark 11:8 and Luke 12:29, the religious leaders were seeking the same thing.

In Acts 17, we read that Paul reasoned with the philosophers in Athens by quoting their own philosophers. He urged those who sought truth to keep seeking, and that their search would lead them to God. The text says:

> From one man he made every nation of men, that they should inhabit the whole earth; and he determined the times set for them and the exact places where they should live. God did this so that men would seek (*zeteo*) him and perhaps reach out for him and find him, though he is not far from each one of us. (vv. 26–27)

Lost people are not the only ones who seek. Jesus was a seeker who sought us out. His goal was to draw all people to himself. In Luke 19:10 Jesus says, "For the Son of Man came to seek and to save what was lost."

In some verses, the prefix *ek-* is added to *zeteo*. This prefix (or *ex-*) denotes origin, but can mean from, out of, of, and so forth. The resulting word, *ekzeteo*, means to seek out, search after, search for. It implies a greater urgency, sometimes meaning "to require." We find it in Romans 3:11 in a negative sense, saying that none seek after God, and in a positive sense in Hebrews 11:6, where we read: "And without faith it is impossible to please God, because anyone who comes to him must believe that he exists and that he rewards those who earnestly seek (*ekzeteo*) him." This earnest seeking is a response of faith to the stirrings in our heart that come from God, who seeks and saves.

SELF-CONTROL

Ironically, self-control for the Christian is only possible when we give God control of our lives. In surrendering our will to the divine will, we gain the power to resist temptation and live according to the Spirit, rather than the flesh. Rather than being controlled by what is around us, we are controlled by what is inside us—the very spirit of God.

The late pastor and theologian J. Hampton Keathley III wrote, "Fundamentally, self-control is the ability or power to rule or regulate one's personal life so that we are neither driven nor dominated, as the apostle John puts it, by the desires of the flesh, the desires of the eyes, or the pride of life (1 John 2:16)."[1]

The word most frequently translated "self-control" is the Greek word *enkrateia*. A similar Greek word, *akrasia*, means the opposite, a lack of self-control. Unlike our culture, which lives by a "if it feels good, do it" rubric, the Greeks highly valued self-control as a virtue. Socrates saw it as the basis for all other virtues.

Scholar Ceslas Spicq writes about *akrasia* (lack of self-control) and *enkrateia* (self-control): "Both of these terms derive from *kratos*, 'force'; the *enkrates* is the person who is master of himself; the *a-krates* is the one who cannot contain himself, who is lacking in power."[2] The verb *enkrateuomai* means to be disciplined, to be self-controlled, or to abstain. The root *kratos* means strength.

Keathley points out that in addition to the "kratos" family of words, two other word families have to do with the virtue of self-control.

The first is made up of the various forms of the word *sophos*, which means wisdom or wise. This group of words, which all focus on mental soundness, being thoughtful, or having good judgment, includes *sophroneo*, *sophronismos*, *sophrosune*, *sophronos*, and *sophron*.

For example, 2 Timothy 1:7 says, "For the Spirit God gave us does not make us timid, but gives us power, love, and self-discipline." Other versions say "a sound mind." The adjective is *sophronismos*—it implies an admonishment to self-control.

Keathley adds:

> A third important word group is *nepho* and *nephalios*. The verb *nepho* basically means "be sober." In the New Testament, however, it is only used figuratively in the sense of "be free from every form of mental and spiritual drunkenness." In 1 Peter 1:13, Peter wrote, "Therefore, get your minds ready for action, by being fully sober, and set your hope completely . . ." The verb means, "free from excess, passion, rashness, confusion, i.e., *be well-balanced, self-controlled, be self-possessed under all circumstances*."[3]

Self-control is included in the description of the fruit of the Spirit in Galatians 5:23, although some versions translate the word *egkrateia* as "temperance." In 1 Thessalonians 5:6, Paul urges Christians to be "alert and self-controlled (*nepho*)."

In his advice to married couples about how to balance their sex lives and their prayer lives, Paul writes: "Do not deprive each other except perhaps by mutual consent and for a time, so that you may devote yourselves to prayer. Then come together again so that Satan will not tempt you because of your lack of self-control" (1 Cor. 7:5). In this verse, one word, *akrasai*, means lack of self-control.

Self-control is a required character trait for those who are put in position of authority in the church as an overseer or elder:

> Since an overseer is trusted with God's work, he must be blameless—not overbearing, not quick-tempered, not given to drunkenness, not violent, not pursuing dishonest gain. Rather he must be hospitable, one who loves what is good, who is self-controlled (*egkrates*), upright, holy and disciplined. He must hold firmly to the trustworthy message as it has been taught, so that he can encourage others by sound doctrine and refute those who oppose it. (Titus 1:7–9; see also 1 Tim. 3:2)

It is notable that almost all of these qualifications have to do with some aspect of self-control. It is certainly the mark of a mature Christian, and as we said, only possible when we submit our will to God's.

SERVE/SERVICE

For the Christian, service is not an occasional activity, somehow separate from the rest of our life. Rather, it is how we live. Whom or what we serve colors all of our lives. As Bob Dylan famously sang, "You gotta serve somebody." Whether we're aware of it or not, each of us has decided to orient our life around someone or something. That decision colors all our other choices.

Jesus said, "Whoever serves me must follow me; and where I am, my servant also will be. My Father will honor the one who serves me" (John 12:26). Serving and following are connected. The verb translated "serve" in this verse is *diakoneo*, which can also mean to minister. (See ***Deacon***.) And following is not simply registering as a member of a church or praying a prayer when given the invitation. Following is a lifestyle. Those who followed Jesus when he walked this earth gave up all other ambition save that to be with their rabbi.

The verb translated "follow" in this verse is *akoloutheo*. It is a rich word implying union and companionship. It comes from the root *keleuthos*, which means a road or a way, so it literally means to go the same way as. In other words, when you follow someone, you do as they do, and do it with them.

Jesus also said it was impossible to serve two masters (Matt. 6:24; Luke 16:13). In our multitasking culture, I wonder if we believe that. We strive so hard to balance endless commitments. We juggle things, keep the plates spinning. Even though we know we can't have it all, we keep trying.

The verb for serve in this verse is *douleuo*, which means to serve as a *doulos* (slave), but it is often used without an association of slavery. His point was not that it is impossible to multitask. He was talking specifically about money and its power to enslave us. Our choices will be oriented around either God or money. We must choose which will be our top priority. This same verb is also used in the New Testament when we are told to serve one another. (See, for example, Gal. 5:13.)

Perhaps we think of service as doing acts of charity or volunteering at church. While those are important, Jesus is talking about having a servant's attitude toward every task and every relationship in our lives. To serve Jesus is to follow him, to walk along the way with him. It is also to eschew promotion and status. Jesus told his followers that in his kingdom, the last would be first. He also told them, "Not so with you. Instead, whoever wants to become great among you must be your servant (*diakonos*), and whoever wants to be first must be slave (*doulos*) of all. For even the Son of Man did not come to be served (*diakoneo*), but to serve (*diakoneo*), and to give his life as a ransom for many" (Mark 10:43–45).

We are clearly called to serve. This word is connected with the idea of fellowship and church—each member of the body has a function and is meant to serve in some way. However, service goes beyond just *what* we do, but also asks us to consider the way in which we do it. When we take the time to encourage a co-worker, we are serving Jesus. When we wipe away the tears or the crumbs from a child's face, we are serving Jesus. When we do our work "heartily, as to the Lord," we are serving Jesus.

In the midst of a tale of his adventures in the book of Acts, Paul tells of a dream or vision he had. He describes it in this way: "Last night an angel of the God whose I am and whom I serve stood beside me" (27:23). The word in Greek for serve is *latreuo*, which literally means to work for hire (akin to *latris*, a hired servant). However, the primary meaning of this word is to worship (in some verses and versions, it is translated "worship"). Again, service is a lifestyle because of whom we follow and worship.

SHEEP/SHEPHERD

In an earlier chapter, we considered the word *lamb*. While lamb often describes Jesus as the ultimate sacrifice, the word *sheep* often refers to his followers. While much has been made of the low intelligence and general helplessness of sheep, they were also of great value in biblical times. Wealth was often measured by the size of one's herds and flocks. Sheep were raised not only for wool, meat, and milk; they were also considered worthy of being sacrificed to the Lord, often on special occasions (most notably, the Passover).

While most Americans have never met a shepherd or encountered sheep outside a petting zoo, that was not the case for most of the people in ancient Palestine. Sheep were an integral part of most people's lives. Many of the patriarchs of the Old Testament, including David, were shepherds or owned flocks. The word *shepherd* was used metaphorically to describe a leader's relationship with his subjects.

In the first century, being a shepherd was a lowly occupation. However, the first people outside of Jesus' family to hear about his birth and to visit him were shepherds (in Greek, *poimen*). These may have been young boys or even girls. They may have been hired hands, people near the bottom of the social hierarchy of their day. The text doesn't tell us the age, gender, or race of these shepherds. Their very anonymity reflects a truth that is repeated in the angel's words to them. The Savior was born "for all people" (see Luke 2:10). Jesus' proclamation that the last would be first was lived out even as lowly shepherds were invited to be the first witnesses to the incarnation.

This value permeated Jesus' ministry. In Luke 15:1–7, Jesus defended his radically inclusive ministry by comparing a sinner who repents to a sheep that is found by a shepherd who goes searching for it.

In John 10, we read these words of Jesus: "I am the good shepherd; I know my sheep and my sheep know me—just as the Father knows me and I know the Father—and I lay down my life for the sheep" (vv. 14–15). These words, now so familiar, came in the middle of a long teaching comparing false teachers to thieves and Jesus proclaiming himself to be the shepherd (again, *poimen*). His claims shocked Jesus' listeners, some of whom proclaimed him to be mad (v. 20).

Why? It's such a lovely metaphor—and so accurate, knowing what we know now. But the Pharisees (who likely didn't appreciate being referred to as thieves), would hear Jesus' words and immediately think of Old Testament verses like Genesis 49:24, which alludes to God as the shepherd of Israel, or Psalm 78:52, which says of God, "But he brought his people out like a flock; he led them like sheep through the desert." And Isaiah 40:11: "He tends his flock like a shepherd: He gathers the lambs in his arms . . ." Again, this verse is talking about God and prophesying the coming Messiah. Jesus, much to the Pharisees' consternation, was claiming to be the Messiah (see also all of Ezek. 34).

He also said, in the same breath, "I know the Father"— claiming an unprecedented intimacy with Yahweh. To add insult to injury, he claimed to have authority that no one else had—to lay down his life, but then to take it up again. He also claimed to be both the shepherd and the gate for the sheep pen. No wonder people questioned his sanity but were also furious with him. He didn't fit their picture of what the Messiah ought to look like; his words sounded like blasphemy.

If Jesus is the Good Shepherd, what does it mean to be a sheep? John 10 gives us some guidance: Sheep listen and respond to the Shepherd's voice. We must also realize that the sheepfold is not an exclusive club. Rather, Jesus said, "I have other sheep that are not of this sheep pen. I must bring them also. They too will listen to my voice, and there shall be one flock and one shepherd" (v. 16). The idea of those outside the "fold" coming under the care of "one shepherd" was also offensive to the Jews—and may be discomfiting to some Christians today. But Jesus invites all to follow him.

SIN

Jesus, it may surprise you to learn, didn't use the word *sin* very often. He talked about specific sins, like greed or hypocrisy, quite a bit. In fact, two of the four gospels don't contain the word *sin* at all. However, the rest of the New Testament contains plenty of exposition on this term. The book of Romans, for example, delves into our "sin nature" at great length. It reminds us that all of us have sinned and fall short of God's glory (3:23), and the wages of that sin is death, but the free gift of God is eternal life (6:23). Despite our sinful nature, we are not condemned, because Jesus has set us free from the law of sin and death (8:1–2). Even in the midst of a discourse on sin, the Bible is hopeful.

Once, when a blind man came to Jesus asking for healing, the disciples asked a question that reflected the common theology of the day: "Who sinned, this man or his parents?" Physical affliction was punishment for sin, in their minds. Jesus corrected their theology by saying it was neither. His temporary affliction had occurred "so that the work of God might be displayed in his life" (John 9:3).

When the Pharisees try to trap Jesus by bringing a woman

caught in adultery, Jesus tells them that anyone who had no sin of his own could cast the first stone at her. When her accusers slink off, Jesus kindly but firmly tells her that he does not condemn her, but that she must leave her life of sin. (See ***Repent***.)

Hamartia, the word translated "sin" in the New Testament, comes from a term used in the sport of archery, meaning to miss the target. William Barclay notes,

> In classical Greek, *hamartia* has as its basic meaning the idea of "failure." *Hamartanein* began by meaning "to miss the mark" as when a spear is thrown at a target. It can be used for missing a road, for failure in one's plan or hope or purpose. In classical Greek these words are always connected with some kind of negative failure rather than with some kind of positive transgression, but in the New Testament they come to describe something which is very much more serious. It is to be noted that in the New Testament *hamartia* does not describe a definite act of sin; it describes the state of sin, from which acts of sin come.[1]

Hamartia, or its verb form *hamartano*, describes our general tendency or nature, or a power, not specific acts that are sinful.

Sin is missing the mark, falling short like an arrow that does not reach the target, failing to follow God as we ought to, making the wrong choice. There are times we do this willfully, but often our sin flows out of our brokenness—our sin nature. This does not excuse it, but helps us to understand it. Even the apostle Paul wrestled with this sin nature (see Rom. 7:14–25). We often do this because, as Barclay has said, we are ruled by our sin nature—the state we are in as human beings.

The Bible, as we said earlier, is mostly hopeful when it speaks of sin. That hope lies not in sweeping our wrongdoing under the carpet, but in courageously admitting the specific ways in which we have missed the mark of his perfect will. When we are willing to name our sin, rather than deny it, the Bible promises forgiveness:

> If we claim to be without sin, we deceive ourselves and the truth is not in us. If we confess our sins, he is faithful and just and will forgive us our sins and purify us from all unrighteousness. If we claim we have not sinned, we make him out to be a liar and his word has no place in our lives. (1 John 1:8–10)

The secret, then, to dealing with sin and our sinful nature is not denial, but confession. It is there that we find freedom, purity, and joy.

SON OF MAN

One of the greatest mysteries of the Christian faith is the belief that Jesus was fully human, yet fully man. As John 1:14 declares, "The Word became flesh and made his dwelling among us."

This mystery is captured in the phrase *Son of Man*, or *huios tou anthropou* in Greek, *bar enos* in Aramaic, which Jesus used to refer to himself.

Theologians have debated for centuries what this meant, exactly. Was Jesus emphasizing his humanity and humility? Or was he pointing to his Messianic role?

One commentary notes: "The term itself obviously speaks of a human, perhaps even of a representative human . . . yet because the Son of Man comes from heaven and exercises divine prerogatives, he also shares in divinity. Thus the term is a complex one, speaking to Jesus' deity and his humanity."[1]

Some scholars argue that because Jesus did not come as a revolutionary or military messiah, he chose a more subtle title. He was not denying his own Messiahship, simply pointing out that his kingdom was nothing like what they were expecting. When Peter proclaims Jesus as "the Christ," Jesus tells his disciples not to tell anyone (see Mark 8:27–30). In the very next verse, Jesus began to "teach them that the Son of Man must suffer many things. . . ." The *New Bible Dictionary* notes: "Jesus' conception of his Messianic role was so much at variance with the popular connotations of Christos that he preferred to avoid the title."[2]

Instead, Jesus often referred to himself as *bar enos*, which some scholars say was simply an Aramaic idiomatic way of referring to one's self in the third person. Others argue that the term was even more strongly messianic than the word *Christos*. (See ***Messiah***.)

Merrill Unger notes,

> The term "son of man" occurs conspicuously in the book of Ezekiel, being used ninety-two times in addressing the prophet. . . . As used of Ezekiel, the expression "the son of man" suggests what the prophet is to God, not what he is to himself. As "the son of man" the prophet is chosen, spiritually endowed, and delegated by God. These factors are also true of the Messiah as the Representative Man, the new Head of regenerated humanity.[3]

The term *Son of Man* also appears in a messianic prophesy in the book of Daniel, where Daniel describes a vision in which he sees "one like a son of man, coming with the clouds," who approaches the throne of God and is given authority, glory and power. (See Dan. 7:13–14.)

"In the first century, this passage was universally understood as a reference to the coming Messiah," write Ann Spangler and Lois Tverberg. "This passage from Daniel was considered the most potent messianic prophecy in all of Scripture. . . . Jesus also speaks about himself as the Son of Man who will come in glory on the clouds (Mark 13:26; 14:62; Luke 21:27), a clear reference to this passage from Daniel. His audience would know exactly what he is saying."[4]

And what his audience would surmise, these writers argue, is that he was indeed claiming to be the Messiah. Especially when he said things like "the Son of Man who came from heaven" and "the Son of Man must be lifted up" (see John 3:13–14).

The first instance of this phrase in the New Testament is in Matthew 8:20, where Jesus identifies not only with the human race, but with the poor, as he says, "Foxes have holes and birds have nests, but the Son of Man has no place to lay his head." As an itinerant rabbi, Jesus was essentially homeless, depending on the hospitality of strangers.

And yet, just a few pages later, Jesus seems to be pointing to his divine power as he heals a paralytic: "Know that the Son of Man has authority on earth to forgive sins" (Matt. 9:6). This is an unmistakably clear reference to his divine authority.

Thus the term *Son of Man* is an expression of the mystery of Christ: divinity wrapped in the role of a servant and a sacrifice. As he said, "The Son of Man did not come to be served, but to serve, and to give his life as a ransom for many" (Matt. 20:28). In this verse he is telling his disciples to be like him, to serve.

SOUL

In modern English, the terms *soul* and *spirit* are often used interchangeably, if they are used much at all. We are, as the song says, living in a material world, with an emphasis on the empirically provable and physically tangible. We don't make any distinctions between spiritual realities, if we acknowledge them at all.

However, in the minds of the writers of Scripture, as well as the philosophers of that time, the two terms were used to describe different aspects of the immaterial nature. The soul, *psyche* (some translators, *psuche*), was "that immaterial part of man held in common with animals."[1]

Some philosophers saw the *psyche* as the "lower" part of our immaterial nature—where our desires and passions were held. They contrasted it with *pneuma*, spirit (see ***Spirit***), which designated the loftier or higher aspects of the immaterial self—which were unique to human beings. Animals, they thought, had a soul but not a spirit. It was through the *pneuma* that human beings could connect with God.

This was not to say the *psyche*, or soul, did not have value—quite the opposite. The word was sometimes used to describe life itself. It can mean a person, or the life-force within a person, or the part of them that will live on after death. In Matthew 16:24–26 we read:

> Then Jesus said to his disciples, "Whoever wants to be my disciple must deny themselves and take up their cross and follow me. For whoever wants to save their life (*psyche*) will lose it, but whoever loses their life (*psyche*) for me will find it. What good will it be for you to gain the whole world, yet forfeit your soul (*psyche*)? Or what can you give in exchange for your soul (*psyche*)?" (TNIV)

Note that the word for life and soul is the same word, but because of the context, has a slightly different meaning. This verse echoes Matthew 10:39, where Jesus asks similar questions. While the translation is accurate, because *psyche* can mean both things, in the Greek it is a play on words. One commentary notes: "A clear choice is thus offered between self-preservation at all costs and the risky business of following Jesus. But the self that is preserved by such a 'safe' option is not worth preserving since the *true* self is lost. By contrast, the loss of *psyche* (in the sense of physical life) is the way to find *psyche* (in the contrasting sense of the true life which transcends death)."[2]

Jesus' question "simply underlines the supreme importance of the *psyche*; nothing else compares with its value."[3]

The word *soul* is also used to describe the immaterial part of people that is uniquely them. It is the place within us where we have nothing but ourselves. Jesus, on his knees in the Garden of Gethsemane, was deeply troubled, and said, "My soul (*psyche*) is overwhelmed with sorrow to the point of death" (Mark 14:34). He was, in that moment, not only facing physical death, but identifying with human beings and our loneliness and pain.

The soul (like the spirit) is distinct from the body, and lives on after physical death. As Jesus said, "Do not be afraid of those who can kill the body but cannot kill the soul" (Matt. 10:28).

The related adjective *psuchikos*, or *psuchikon*, also means soul, with an emphasis on the animal or natural aspect of this part of us.

In 1 Corinthians 15:44, we read: "If there is a natural body, there is also a spiritual body." But in the Greek, the distinction is not between the physical and spiritual, but between soul and spirit. The verse "refers to a body *psuchikon*, a body governed by the soul or natural and fallen instinct of man, and a body *pneumatikon*, spiritual, governed by the divine quality in man, the spirit."[4]

For more on this difference between soul and spirit, see the next entry.

SPIRIT

As we discussed in the previous entry, the Greek word for spirit is *pnuema*, which also means breath or wind (see ***Holy Spirit***). Of the 375 times this word occurs in the New Testament, 250 refer to the Holy Spirit.

In most English translations, *spirit* is sometimes rendered with a capital S, other times not. The capitalized version is similar to a proper noun, shorthand for the Holy Spirit or the Spirit of God. The lowercase is reserved for phrases like "a gentle spirit" or "I had no rest in my spirit," which describe the spiritual dimension of a person, or a temporary spiritual condition. It's also used to describe an evil or unclean spirit, which must be cast out of a person.

Biblical writers and their contemporaries thought of the spirit of a person as the part of them that was uniquely human (rather than animistic) and could therefore connect with God. While animals were considered to have a soul, they did not have a spirit. A person was thought to have both. Their soul was forever changed when they were spiritually reborn (see John 3).

Theologians have debated the exact nature of soul and spirit for centuries. Despite the distinction between *psyche* and *pnuema*, they are closely connected. As it says in Hebrews 4:12: "For the word of God is living and active. Sharper than any double-edged sword, it penetrates even to dividing soul (*psyche*) and spirit (*pnuema*), joints and marrow; it judges the thoughts and attitudes of the heart."

Can we, from this verse, draw an analogy—that soul is to spirit as joints are to marrow, or thoughts are to attitude? Not precisely. First of all, the three pairs are not set up in exact parallel. But it does seem to be saying that the soul and spirit are distinct, yet as closely connected as joints and marrow—each is a part of the other.

Another verse that mentions both soul and spirit (thus indicating that they are not the same thing) is 1 Thessalonians 5:23. "May God himself, the God of peace, sanctify you through and through. May your whole spirit, soul and body be kept blameless at the coming of our Lord Jesus Christ." Some Christians have used this verse to argue that people are tripartite, that is, having three parts: body, spirit, and soul. However, others argue that this theology is incorrect.

When God breathed life into creatures, they became living souls, according to Genesis. While soul describes the life-force that is in all beings, spirit describes the life that God breathes into each of us when we are spiritually reborn. In fact, both words can also mean breath—in the case of soul, it is that life breath that animates the body; in the case of spirit, it is a life-force that connects us with God.

We also see the adjective "spiritual" (*pneumatikos*), which is used both metaphorically (spiritual meat in 1 Cor. 10:3) and literally (spiritual songs, for example, in Eph. 5:19). This word appears only in the New Testament after Pentecost, because it describes the influence of the Holy Spirit.

While each person has a spirit and is a spiritual being, numerous verses that mention spirit also include the idea of community—starting with, of course, Pentecost—when the Holy Spirit was given to the group of disciples gathered together. Spiritual gifts are not given to us for our own pleasure or pride, but so that we may serve the body of Christ.

So the Spirit, and our spirits, unify us with one another and with God. As it says in Ephesians 4:3–6, "Make every effort to keep the unity of the Spirit through the bond of peace. There is one body and one Spirit—just as you were called to one hope when you were called—one Lord, one faith, one baptism; one God and Father of all, who is over all and through all and in all."

While our spirit is that part of us that connects with God, it is also the part of us that connects us with other believers. Our spirits, and the Spirit, are what make unity possible.

STRENGTH

God's strength is infinite, yet it's never used for evil. Better yet, God imparts his strength to believers when they trust in him. We are at our strongest when we are putting our strength into loving God. Then God's strength flows through us.

Every day, twice a day, devout Jews prayed the *Shema* (Deut. 6:4–9; 11:13–21; Num. 15:37–41), which declared "Hear, O Israel: The Lord our God, the Lord is one. Love the Lord your God with all your heart and with all your soul and with all your strength." (See ***Pray***.) Jesus and the people he spoke to would have grown up with this prayer woven into the fabric of their daily lives. When asked what the most important command is, he quotes this prayer. (See Matt. 22:36–39; Mark 12:30.)

It is one thing to say you love God with all your strength; it is another to actually do it. Perhaps that is why Jesus said that the second, but equally important, command was to love your neighbor. It requires a certain strength to love a neighbor who can be hard to love.

The Greek word in these verses is *ischus,* which means ability, force, strength. To love God with all your strength is to love him with your whole being—heart, soul, mind, and body. The same word is used in Ephesians 1:19 and 6:10, which speak of the power God gives us, "the power of his might" (6:10 NKJV). (See also 1 Peter 4:11 and 2 Peter 2:11.) (See ***Power***.)

There are many other Greek words that convey the idea of strength. Some are more accurately translated "power," and we dealt with those earlier. But let's look at three others, which are all in Acts 9.

Saul, who had been fasting since his encounter with the risen Christ on the road to Damascus, broke his fast and thus "regained his strength" (v. 19). The Greek word in this verse is *enischuo*, which means to invigorate or strengthen. The text then tells of the preaching of the newly converted Saul, and the amazement of those who heard him, describing him as "more and more powerful" (v. 22). The NKJV says Saul "increased all the more in strength." The word in this verse is *endunamoo,* a combination of the words *en* and *dunamis*, meaning literally in power. This word is a prevalent theme in Paul's writings: a strength that comes from God. We find this same word in 1 Timothy

1:12, which says, "I thank Christ Jesus our Lord, who has given me strength," and Philippians 4:13, "I can do everything through him who gives me strength." (See also 2 Tim. 4:17; Rom. 4:20.)

A few verses later in Acts 9, we see another word: "Then the church throughout Judea, Galilee and Samaria enjoyed a time of peace. It was strengthened; and encouraged by the Holy Spirit, it grew in numbers, living in the fear of the Lord" (v. 31). The word *strengthened* in this verse is *oikodomeo*, which means literally to build a house.[1] It is used to describe building anything. In this verse, it conveys the idea of spiritual development and growth.

Acts 15:41 says of the apostle Paul, "He went through Syria and Cilicia, strengthening the churches." A similar verse, in Acts 18:23, says he strengthened the disciples. Although it seems to be talking about the same thing as Acts 9:31, the Greek in these two verses is *episterizo*, which means to lean upon. Paul strengthened the churches by supporting them, allowing them to lean on him.

Ephesians 3:16 says, "I pray that out of his glorious riches he may strengthen you with power through his Spirit in your inner being . . ." The verb in this sentence is *krataioo*, which is used only three other places. In Luke 1:30 and 2:40 it means to wax strong—this strength comes over time, not suddenly.

While many New Testament words can mean strength, the vast majority of them have this in common—the most potent strength we can access comes not from ourselves, but from God.

TEMPTATION

Jesus came to our planet to live as a man, facing the same struggles and temptations we face. Unlike us, though, he never succumbed to sin's enticement. After his baptism, Jesus retreated to the wilderness, where Satan tempted him, trying to pull him off task.

All three Synoptics mention this event. Matthew 4:1–11 offers the most detail.

Satan tempted Jesus to turn stones to bread, to test God by throwing himself off the highest point of the temple, and to rule the world if he would only bow down and worship him. He appealed to Jesus' humanity (physical hunger), tried to cast doubt on his identity as the Son of God, and tempted him to forgo the cross, to obtain power without having to suffer. Whole sermons have been preached on the significance of these temptations. Jesus calmly answered each test with Scripture, even when Satan twisted the Word of God to try to make his point.

But that was not the end of his temptations. Certainly, we should assume that Satan tried to whisper in Jesus' ear at other times as well. One of those times Jesus responded by saying to Peter, "Get behind me, Satan!" (Matt. 16:23). Surely in the Garden of Gethsemane Satan again tried to tempt him.

Throughout his ministry, religious leaders tried to trap Jesus into saying something that would prove him a heretic. For example, in Matthew 16:1 we read, "The Pharisees and Sadducees came to Jesus and tested him by asking him to show them a sign from heaven."

The word translated "tested" is *peirazo*, which means to tempt or to put to the test. It is the same word used to describe what Satan did during his wilderness encounter with Jesus. It is used frequently to describe the harassment the Pharisees inflicted upon Jesus.

Temptation is an urge to sin. But *peirazo* also means to test. A test determines what you know, what you are made of. We often test things like water to be sure they are pure. A test determines the quality of something—so when we are tested, or tempted, we will see clearly the quality, the purity of our faith.

This same word also occurs in 1 Corinthians 7:5 of couples tempted to violate their marriage vow, and in 1 Thessalonians 3:5 it refers to Satan tempting believers generally.

Jesus knew that his followers would face temptations, so he taught them to pray against it. (See Matt. 6:13 and 26:41.)

Unger's Bible Dictionary defines temptation as "the enticement of a person to commit sin by offering some seeming advantage. The sources of temptation are Satan, the world, and the flesh."[1]

Another word meaning to tempt or put to the test is *ekpeirazo*. We see this word only four times in the New Testament, twice in Jesus' rebuke when Satan tries to tempt him, telling him you should not put God to the test (see Matt. 4:7 and Luke 4:12).

The noun *peirasmos* also means temptation or trial, with the focus on the testing of our integrity. This word occurs in 1 Corinthians 10:13, which says, "No temptation (*peirasmos*) has overtaken you except what is common to us all. And God is faithful; he will not let you be tempted (*peirazo*) beyond what you can bear. But when you are tempted (*peirasmos*), he will also provide a way out so that you can endure it" (TNIV). Such trials are common not only to all people, but they were also endured by Jesus himself when he walked this earth as a man.

This same word occurs in James 1:2: "Consider it pure joy, my brothers and sisters, whenever you face trials (*peirasmos*) of many kinds . . ." (TNIV). We may think of trials as those times when things do not go our way, times when we face hardship or difficulty. Such struggles often tempt us to doubt, to not trust God. They are both trials and temptations, which test the quality of our faith. God has given us the means to overcome temptation and to use trials as a means of purifying our faith.

THIRST/THIRSTY

Jesus chose to visit our planet not in a forest, a polar cap, or a lush plain, but in a desert. Those who lived in such a climate understood thirst. While Palestine has a rainy season, it also has a long dry season, and its land is mostly porous limestone, so it does not retain water.

When someone is thirsty, the longing for water is all-consuming. The Bible uses the word thirst, *dipsao*, to describe both physical thirst and the deep spiritual longing that is in every heart.

Jesus said that his followers would be known by their actions: "For I was hungry and you gave me something to eat, I was thirsty and you gave me something to drink. . . ." (see Matt. 25:35–36).

It is clear from the context, which lists practical forms of helping the needy, that Jesus is not using the word *thirsty* in a purely metaphorical sense. The human kindness of giving an actual drink to a thirsty person often has a spiritual effect, of course.

In John 4, Jesus initiated a conversation with a Samaritan woman at a well, asking her for a drink. We can easily miss how radical this was. In his culture, rabbis did not talk to women—especially women with this one's reputation. Jews did not talk to Samaritans and certainly would not drink from their water jugs. Jesus plowed through racial and ethnic and gender barriers to offer this woman life.

Not surprisingly, she was shocked by his request. But he turned the conversation around and offered her "living water." Eventually he revealed to her that he knew her story—she'd had five husbands and was living with a man not her husband. If ever a person was thirsty, spiritually speaking, this woman was.

As he often did, Jesus used the situation at hand—drawing water—to illustrate spiritual reality. He said to the woman, "Everyone who drinks this water will be thirsty again, but whoever drinks the water I give him will never thirst. Indeed, the water I give him will become in him a spring of water welling up to eternal life" (John 4:13–14).

As they talked, Jesus also revealed to her his story—that he was the Messiah. And this sinful woman not only quenched her thirst by believing in him, she led others in her village to do the same.

In John 6, Jesus spoke to the crowd of Jews who'd just listened to his teaching and been fed miraculously: "Then Jesus declared, 'I am the bread of life. He who comes to me will never go hungry, and he who believes in me will never be thirsty. But as I told you, you have seen me and still you do not believe' " (vv. 35–36). Their disbelief stood in contrast to the response of the Samaritans.

One chapter later, Jesus and his disciples are in Jerusalem for the Feast of the Tabernacles, also known as Sukkot. A key part of this festival, which occurred at the end of the dry season, was to pray for rain. Spangler and Tverberg write,

> On the last day of that feast, the priests performed a water libation ceremony accompanied by impassioned prayers for life-giving water in the form of rain. At that point the joyful voices of thousands of worshipers reached a thunderous intensity. . . . It was on this last and greatest day of Sukkot that Jesus stood up in the midst of the clamorous crowds and shouted: "Let anyone who is thirsty come to me and drink. Whoever believes in me, as Scripture has said, rivers of living water will flow from within them" (John 7:37–38).[1]

Even if we rarely experience extreme physical thirst or drought, every human soul is parched. Our deep longings, which we may not be able to articulate, are actually a thirst for the living water Jesus offers. When we believe in him, we don't just satisfy our own thirst, but as this verse attests, our lives will overflow.

TRUTH

Jesus said, "I am the way and the truth and the life" (John 14:6). He also said, "You will know the truth, and the truth will set you free"

(John 8:32). He told Pontius Pilate, "For this I came into the world, to testify to the truth. Everyone on the side of truth listens to me." And Pilate responded cynically, "What is truth?" (John 18:37–38).

People continue today to ask Pilate's question, but they often believe the answer is that there is no such thing. In the second half of the twentieth century, it became fashionable to talk about "your truth and my truth" as pop culture embraced moral relativism, not seeing the dangers in that sort of philosophy. The Bible was written in a cultural context where philosophers debated and studied to try and understand lofty concepts like truth—and they had a lot of different ideas. So in some ways, the New Testament is a response to that discussion.

The Bible talks about truth as reality, actual physical things that you can see and touch. This stood in contrast to Greek philosophers like Plato, who thought of truth as metaphysical, something beyond the physical realm. But the Bible also acknowledges spiritual truth.

Truth can also mean honesty, which is always how Paul uses the word. His focus is on telling the truth or speaking truth rather than lies.

The most common Greek word used in the New Testament to mean truth is *aletheia*. As we've said, secular Greek philosophers differed in their understanding of that word, but for New Testament writers, truth was the truth of God, the truth of his Word. It was not "a truth" among many but "the truth"—objective and absolute reality.

We also see the related adjective *alethes*, meaning truthful when it describes a person (Matt. 22:16; Mark 12:14) or truly (John 4:18).

We're exhorted to "speak the truth in love" in Ephesians 4:15. The verb is *aletheuo*, which means to deal faithfully or truly with someone. The challenge is to find that balance between truth and love, because sometimes the truth is harsh, and it hurts. How can we tell the truth without damaging people? By looking to Jesus' example—for as John says, he was "full of grace and truth" (John

1:14). He didn't just speak truth, he embodied it in a way no one else ever had or has since.

Many of Paul's letters were written to set various churches straight on the truth, to refute heresy that distorted the truth of the gospel. He chastised the Galatians, "I am astonished that you are so quickly deserting the one who called you by the grace of Christ and are turning to a different gospel—which is really no gospel at all. Evidently some people are throwing you into confusion and are trying to pervert the gospel of Christ" (Gal. 1:6–7). In other words, this fledgling church had been led away from the truth, and Paul was determined to bring them back to it. A different truth is no truth at all.

Similarly, in 2 Thessalonians 2, he contrasts the truth of the gospel with the lies of Satan. Always, the New Testament points to the truth of God and his Word. In 2 Timothy 2, Paul also refutes false teachers who have "walked away from the truth" (v. 18).

Scholar Ceslas Spicq writes, "St. Paul uses the term *aletheia* in a way that agrees with its Greek etymology (that which may be seen in the open, as it is) but also takes account of OT usage . . . Salvation depends first of all on the adherence and submission of the heart to objective truth. . . ."[1] In a word, the Christian religion is a cult of truth.

To be a Christian, at the heart of it, is to accept and live by God's truth. Truth is what we believe, what we put our faith in, what we have knowledge about, what our relationship with Jesus is based on.

UNDERSTAND

The opening chapter of the gospel of John makes these statements about Jesus:

> "The light shines in the darkness, but the darkness has not *understood* it" (v. 5). The verb in Greek is *katalambano*, which means to take eagerly, seize or possess. It also means to appropriate, to lay hold of with the mind, to understand or perceive. (From *lambano,* to take or receive.)
>
> "He was in the world, and though the world was made through him, the world did not *recognize* him" (v. 10). The verb is *ginosko*: to know absolutely, to understand completely, be sure of.
>
> "He came to that which was his own, but his own did not *receive* him" (v. 11). This word in Greek is *paralambano,* to receive from another, to associate with, to learn.

All three words have to do with understanding or perception. And all three verses point to a central theme in the life of Jesus—that of being misunderstood. Even though God became flesh and was right there in front of us, we didn't realize it. We didn't understand. In the words of the old spiritual, "Sweet little Jesus boy. We didn't know who you was."

A recurring lament in the text is that people are "hearing but not understanding." Jesus and others quote from the prophet Isaiah: You will "Be ever hearing, but never understanding; be ever seeing, but never perceiving" (Isa. 6:9; see also Mark 4:12).

The Greeks highly valued the intellect, and so had several words that express various nuances of understanding. The Greek verb in these verses is *suniemi*, which means to bring or set together, to put together mentally, to unite the perception with what is perceived. We find this word on the lips of Jesus when he asked his disciples, "Do you still not see or understand?" (Mark 8:17; see also 7:14; 8:21). Jesus did not long for his disciples to blindly follow him, but rather, to sharpen their perception, comprehend what was going on as the kingdom was arriving right at their doorstep. He was often frustrated with their lack of comprehension.

In Hebrews 11:3 we read, "By faith we understand that the universe was formed at God's command, so that what is seen was not made out of what was visible." We may think that something we understand by faith is something we know intuitively, or just trust without knowing why. But the text tells us just the opposite. The word in this verse is *noeo*, which means to perceive with the mind (rather than the feelings), understand by thinking. Literally, it means to exercise the mind. It is found fourteen times in the New Testament, including Matthew 15:17; 16:9, 11; 24:15.

A couple of words, *epistamai* and *ginosko*, mean to know, or to understand completely, and are sometimes translated "to understand," but usually translated "to know."

Jesus and then the writers of the epistles urge believers to engage their minds, to test the truth, to seek wisdom. All of this requires understanding. The key to faith is not blind acceptance, but seeing clearly.

In Colossians 2:2–3 Paul writes, "My purpose is that they may be encouraged in heart and united in love, so that they may have the full riches of complete understanding, in order that they may know the mystery of God, namely, Christ, in whom are hidden all the treasures of wisdom and knowledge." The word translated "understanding" in this text is *sunesis*, which means to apprehend or consider quickly and thoroughly. We find the same noun in Colossians 1:9 and 2 Timothy 2:7.

In Philippians 4:7 we read, "And the peace of God, which transcends all understanding, will guard your hearts and your minds in Christ Jesus." The word for understanding in this text is *nous* (the root of the verb *noeo*, above). While our faith grows deeper with intellectual understanding, the peace that it provides transcends, or goes beyond, that understanding. Peace that passes understanding is peace that we have in spite of our circumstances, even though we know them full well.

VINE/VINEYARD

In the book of Isaiah, the fifth chapter describes a vineyard, *kerem* in Hebrew, which is a metaphor for the nation of Israel. Grapes and olives were two mainstay crops in ancient Israel, from which they derived two sacred symbolic foods—wine and olive oil. These were used not only for food but for other purposes, including medicine.

So imagine the surprise of the Jews, who saw themselves as the vineyard, when Jesus said that his Father was the gardener, but that Jesus himself was the vine! In John 15:1–3 we read,

> I am the true vine, and my Father is the vine-grower. He removes every branch in me that bears no fruit. Every branch that bears fruit he prunes to make it bear more fruit. You have already been cleansed by the word that I have spoken to you. (NRSV)

The words translated "removes" in verse 2 are sometimes translated "cuts off," but in other versions "takes away." The word in Greek is *airo*. It can mean to take up or away, to raise up. Some scholars believe that *airo* refers to a common practice with tending vines, in which the gardener will lift up branches that are lying on the ground and prop them up with rocks or trellises so that the fruit does not lie in the dirt and rot. It's an image of nurture rather than destruction. *Strong's Concordance* notes: "Airo here indicates those branches which are on the ground, hence unable to bear fruit, God raises up so the branch can be fruitful."[1]

The words for *prunes* and *cleansed* are very similar. Prune or purge in verse 2 is *kathairo*, which can also mean to cleanse. It is only used twice in the New Testament. In Hebrews 10:2 it speaks of purging worshipers from guilt. It is a derivative of the word we find in verse 3, *katharos*, which means clean or pure, where it says "you have already been cleansed." John 15 continues:

> I am the vine, you are the branches. Those who abide in me and I in them bear much fruit, because apart from me you can do nothing. Whoever does not abide in me is thrown away like a branch and withers; such branches are gathered, thrown into the fire, and burned. (vv. 5–6 NRSV)

The word for branch and branches, *klema* (from *klao*, broken), is unique to this passage. "*Klema* denotes a tender, flexible branch, especially the shoot of a vine, a vine sprout."[2]

With the vine imagery comes a promise of both union with God and judgment. The Greek word for vine is *ampelos*, which appears eight times in the New Testament. The word for vineyard, *ampelon,* is more common, appearing twenty-two times in the synoptic gospels and in only one other verse, 1 Corinthians 9:7.

In Revelation 14, instead of Jesus being the vine, his enemies are "the vine of the earth." An avenging angel harvests this vine and puts its grapes into the "great winepress of God's wrath." When trampled, blood flows from the grapes and floods the land. This symbolism alludes to Isaiah 63, where God's judgment is likened to treading of grapes.

Matthew 20 and 21 contain three parables, all set in a vineyard—a setting very familiar to the audience. The parable of the workers (where those hired last were paid the same as those who worked all day), the parable of the two sons (one who says he'll work in the vineyard but doesn't, one who says he won't but does), and the parable of the evil tenant farmers.

In this last parable (which is also told in Mark 12 and Luke 20), the hired farmers stage a coup and kill the servants and even the son of the landowner. It is a parable obvious even to the Pharisees, who "knew he was talking about them" (Matt. 21:45). How did they know? Because they were the ones entrusted with the care of the vineyard (Israel), and because they had rejected Jesus.

The metaphor of the vine shows us how spiritual growth can occur: not through our striving, but by staying connected to Jesus and allowing the Father to raise us up and gently prune away the things that keep us from living fruitful lives. Our job, as the branches, is to abide in the vine and trust the Gardener.

WATER

For his first miracle, Jesus turned water into wine. John baptized with water but told people Jesus would baptize with fire and with the Spirit. Jesus walked on water, and Peter, who wanted to follow him everywhere, did too. Jesus told Nicodemus that to enter the kingdom you must be "born of water and of the Spirit" (John 3:5).

The Greek word for water is *hudor*. It is used both literally and metaphorically in the New Testament, where it appears some seventy-nine times. Just as all life on earth depends on water biologically and physically, living water is essential for spiritual life.

Water is, not surprisingly, a symbol of purity. The sacrament of baptism (being born of water) symbolizes both cleansing and rebirth. It's also a symbol of fulfillment, as Jesus offers us the living water of a relationship with him that satisfies as nothing else can.

Ephesians 5:26 tells husbands to love their wives just as Christ loves the church, "cleansing her by the washing with water through the word."

Hebrews 10:22 says, "Let us draw near to God with a sincere

heart in full assurance of faith, having our hearts sprinkled to cleanse us from a guilty conscience and having our bodies washed with pure water."

First John 5:6–8 says, "This is the one who came by water and blood—Jesus Christ. He did not come by water only, but by water and blood. And it is the Spirit who testifies, because the Spirit is the truth. For there are three that testify: the Spirit, the water and the blood; and the three are in agreement."

One commentary on this passage notes, "Some think that the two sacraments are here meant: baptism with water, as the outward sign of regeneration, and purifying from the pollution of sin by the Holy Spirit; and the Lord's supper, as the outward sign of the shedding Christ's blood, and the receiving him by faith for pardon and justification."[1]

The word *water* or *waters* appears more than a dozen times in the book of Revelation, often as a symbol for life or purity or holiness—as in the crystal sea, or the river of the water of life.

In the chapter on thirst, we looked briefly at John 4. Let's return to that text.

In his extraordinary conversation with the woman at the well, Jesus asked her for water (breaking all kinds of taboos by doing so), then told her that he had "living water." Scholar W. Hall Harris III notes that John 4:10–11 "serves as a perfect example of John's use of misunderstanding as a literary technique. Jesus is speaking of 'living water' which is spiritual (ultimately this is a Johannine figure for the Holy Spirit, cf. 7:38–39) while the woman thinks he means physical water of some sort which will satisfy thirst."[2]

Hall notes that John uses two different words for *well* in verses 6–14 to make a play on words. In verse 6, he uses the word *pege* for Jacob's well. *Pege* means a fountain, coming from a spring. But in verse 11, John switches to the word *phrear*, which can mean a cistern, a pit dug for water, or even a pit leading to the abyss! (In other words, a lifeless well.) Then when Jesus describes the spring of living water, he again uses the word *pege*, and modifies the word *water* with the word *hallomai*, which means to jump or leap (v. 14).

Even a sacred well, when compared to the living water of Jesus, becomes a mere cistern. The things we think will bring us life are dry and lifeless in comparison to the wellspring of life that we can find in relationship with him.

WAY

Matthew 3:3 quotes Isaiah 40:3, "Prepare the way for the Lord." Jesus tells his followers, "Narrow is the gate and difficult is the way which leads to life, and there are few who find it" (Matt. 7:14 NKJV). In a key conversation with his disciples, Jesus says, "I am the way and the truth and the life. No one comes to the Father except through me" (John 14:6).

As we pointed out in the introduction, this was a radical statement. To say he was the way, the truth, and the life was to allude to being the personification of the Torah, the living Word of God. For devout Jews in the first century, the Torah was the Way. How could Jesus be the Torah? Was he claiming to be the Messiah? Was he claiming to be God?

Jesus is that narrow gate, that way to God. In the vast majority of verses containing the word *way*, the Greek is *hodos*, which is often used literally, meaning a path or road, or the way a person travels "on his way." It also serves as a metaphor for behavior or thinking, or a way of life.

We use the word *way* in English to describe the method for doing something, saying, "This is the way you do it." This is true in Greek as well. For example, in Acts 16:17 and elsewhere we see "the way to be saved."

Hodos refers to an actual path or roadway when it describes blind men "sitting by the way side" in Matthew 20:30 (KJV), or seed that "fell by the way side" in Jesus' parable in Matthew 13:4 (KJV). Sometimes it means where you are going literally, physically; and at other times, it means where you're headed philosophically or in life.

In Luke 20, we read of the religious leaders trying to trap Jesus. They send spies to ask him questions. In verse 21, these spies say to him, "Teacher, we know that you speak and teach what is right, and that you do not show partiality but teach the way of God in accordance with the truth. Is it right for us to pay taxes to Caesar or not?"

Jesus casually asks to see a coin and gives them a brilliant answer. But we mustn't miss the spies' attempt at flattery: they use "the way" and "the truth" when describing Jesus' teaching. They were giving him a high compliment—that he taught Torah and taught it well. They were saying he was highly orthodox—exactly the opposite of what they truly thought of him. Those words, "the way" and "the truth," were words the Jews used to describe the Torah. But Jesus sees through their false flattery.

The first-century believers, before they became known as Christians, were known simply as "followers of the Way" (see Acts 22:4). In Acts 24, Paul is accused of being a "ringleader of the Nazarene sect" (v. 5)—which referred to the first Christians, of which Paul had become a part (Jesus was a Nazarene). He says, in his own defense: "I admit that I worship the God of our ancestors as a follower of the Way, which they call a sect. I believe everything that is in accordance with the Law and that is written in the Prophets, and I have the same hope in God as these people themselves have, that there will be a resurrection of both the righteous and the wicked" (vv. 14–15 TNIV).

Here Paul says he is a part of the Way. That means, he explains, that he is thoroughly Jewish, believes in resurrection, and is also a follower of Jesus. They didn't only follow Jesus, but also believed in the sanctity of the Scriptures—not the New Testament, because it wasn't written yet. They were living out the Torah in the way they had been taught by their rabbi, Jesus.

We often misunderstand Jesus as "the way," thinking it means simply that he is the only path to God, the way to get to heaven. While this is true, we must, like those early Christians, walk in the Way of his Word and live as part of the kingdom of God here and now.

WISE/WISDOM

In order to understand Jesus' teachings and actions, it is helpful to know a bit about the people he spoke to. What did the average person in the crowd know or think about? What were the popular philosophies of the day? What stories did they share—what ideas shaped their thinking?

As we've said before, first-century Jews were intimately acquainted with the Old Testament, as well as other writings that are not part of our Bible. These texts had much to say about wisdom.

Proverbs 8 depicts wisdom as a woman who was present at God's side "from the beginning, before the world began" (Prov. 8:23) and all during the creation (see Prov. 8:23–31). The entire book of Proverbs was understood to contain wisdom.

Similarly, the Apocrypha (books not included in the Protestant canon) included books like the Wisdom of Solomon and the Book of Sirach. These writings "develop the motif with the imagery of wisdom present at God's side, active in creation and taking up residence in Israel . . ."[1] While not all Christians today accept these books as Scripture, Jesus' contemporaries would have been intimately familiar with them. Understanding this background helps us to understand Jesus and his words to that particular people.

Into this tradition walks Jesus, whom John declares is the *Logos*, the word, who "was in the beginning with God" (1:2 KJV). One commentary observes: "For those attuned to the imagery of wisdom, the evocation could not be more forthright, and the well-known scene of wisdom choosing Israel from among all of the nations as her dwelling place is replayed as 'the Word became flesh and dwelt among us.' "[2]

Many scholars argue that the gospel writers, steeped in this Jewish tradition, presented Jesus not just as a wise person, but as the Wisdom of God personified.

The Greek word for wisdom is *sophia*, and its New Testament meaning included both the apocryphal imagery and the common sense necessary for daily living.

Jesus talks about how both he and John the Baptist were not accepted by their generation, then adds, "But wisdom is proved right by her actions," or in the KJV, "Wisdom is justified of her children" (Matt. 11:19; Luke 7:35). Notice Jesus personifies wisdom as a female—again alluding to the ancient Jewish texts.

Sophia is used to describe every sort of wisdom, from scientific knowledge to the mysterious omniscience of God, so we must look at the context to understand what is meant. A similar noun, *sophos*, means one who is wise, skilled, or an expert.

The first two chapters of 1 Corinthians compare worldy wisdom with God's wisdom:

> Where is the wise man? Where is the scholar? Where is the philosopher of this age? Has not God made foolish the wisdom of the world? For since in the wisdom of God the world through its wisdom did not know him, God was pleased through the foolishness of what was preached to save those who believe. (1 Cor. 1:20–21)

Paul uses hyperbole and irony to compare the wisdom of God to that of man. "The foolishness of what was preached" was not foolish at all, but only appeared to be so to those who did not understand God's wisdom. As he writes just a few verses later: "But God chose the foolish things of the world to shame the wise (*sophos*); God chose the weak things of the world to shame the strong" (1 Cor. 1:27).

How can we access God's wisdom? Through the Holy Spirit (see 1 Cor. 2:7–14).

The book of James exhorts us to ask God for wisdom (James 1:5). James expounds on that theme in his third chapter: "Who is wise (*sophos*) and understanding among you? Let him show it by his good life, by deeds done in the humility that comes from wisdom." James goes on to compare the purity and goodness of godly wisdom with the selfishness of worldly wisdom (3:13–17).

The Greek word *phronimos* appears fourteen times in the New Testament and means wise, thoughtful, practical, prudent. We see it in Romans 12:16, "Be of the same mind toward one another. Do not set your mind on high things, but associate with the humble. Do not be wise (*phronimos*) in your own opinion" (NKJV). Again, the prevailing theme is that God's wisdom is higher than human wisdom.

WITNESS

The New Testament opens with five books that bear witness to the life of Jesus. Matthew begins his gospel with the evidence of a genealogy, then jumps into the story of Jesus' birth, life, and death. Mark cites an Old Testament prophesy and then jumps, with characteristic forthrightness, into the story itself. But Luke, who loves detail, explains that he has conducted an investigation and written an "orderly account"—like a lawyer in a courtroom, drawing out the facts from the witnesses in order to get at the truth. His book of Acts also presents the accounts of eyewitnesses to the birth of the church. Likewise, the language and style of the gospel of John is presented like a case in a courtroom, in which he argues that Jesus is God. The idea of witness is again a major theme.

Indeed, in the gospel of John, it says of John the Baptist, "There came a man who was sent from God; his name was John. He came as a witness to testify concerning that light, so that through him all might believe. He himself was not the light; he came only as a witness to the light" (John 1:6–8). John the Baptist came as a *marturia*, a witness. A witness does not speak on his own behalf, though he will often share his own experience, but it is for the purpose of telling about another. When I give my testimony, I tell my story, but for the purpose of showing God's work and intervention in that story.

The Greek verb translated "witness" or "testify" is *martureo*, which comes from the root *martus*, a noun meaning a witness or martyr. We get our English word *martyr* (a person who bears witness with his death) from this word. In fact, the Greek is often transliterated as *martyreo*. *Martureo* "means to affirm that one has seen or heard or experienced something or that he knows it because taught by divine revelation or inspiration."[1]

The word *pseudomartureo* means to bear false witness, or to lie, which is of course a vice that breaks the ninth commandment.

The *Dictionary of Jesus and the Gospels* notes that Luke uses the word *witness* or related terms thirty-nine times in the book of Acts. "Jesus had prepared his disciples for their future role as witnesses (Luke 24:44–49). He had told them: 'you will receive power when the Holy Spirit comes on you; and you will be my witnesses in Jerusalem, and in all Judea and Samaria, and to the ends of the earth' (Acts 1:8). This verse summarizes the thrust of Acts."[2]

For many people, this verse constitutes a call to missions. It is also a call to live every moment of our lives as his disciples, bearing witness to his power and love.

The Bible is a true story—the gospels are not just a collection of the wise sayings of Jesus but an account of his life, death, and resurrection. The Bible, in a way, witnesses to us about God. Further, "It is the Spirit who testifies (*martureo*), because the Spirit is the truth" (1 John 5:6). The Spirit and the Word are corroborating witnesses.

The eleventh chapter of Hebrews catalogs the heroes (and a few heroines) of the faith, summarizing the high points of the Old Testament story. What conclusion may we draw from the story of God's people? "Therefore, since we are surrounded by such a great cloud of witnesses, let us throw off everything that hinders and the sin that so easily entangles. And let us run with perseverance the race marked out for us" (Hebrews 12:1). Because of the witness of all these people, we too can walk (or run) by faith.

WONDER/WONDERS

A typical response to Jesus is wonder or amazement. People marvel at him. And sometimes he marvels back at them—as he does in the case of a heathen Roman centurion who understands and exhibits faith better than "anyone in Israel." (See Matt. 8:10 and Luke 7:9.)

The word in these passages is *thaumazo* and means to wonder or marvel at. People marveled at Jesus' power and his words at his birth and later at his resurrection. Pilate was amazed how quickly Jesus died on the cross (Mark 15:44).

The New Testament contains several words that convey the idea of wonder, amazement, or marvel, most of them forms of *thaumazo*. Many marveled or wondered at Jesus' miracles and at his wisdom. For example, there are two words that mean wonderful: *thaumasios* (only in Matt. 21:15, to describe the wonderful things Jesus did) and *thaumastos* (only in Matt. 21:42, where Jesus quotes the Old Testament: "It is marvelous in our eyes"). The word *megaleios*, meaning wonderful things, is found in Acts 2:11 and Luke 1:49.

The words *wonder* and *wonderful* are worn out and overused in English. We are rarely filled with wonder, desensitized to special effects and indifferent to power. Consequently, we sometimes miss the tinge of fear that biblical wonder includes.

When Peter heals a lame man and people see him walk, the text says they were "filled with wonder (*thambos*) and amazement (*ekstasis*) at what had happened to him" (Acts 3:10). The word *ekstasis*, the root of the English *ecstasy*, means being thrown into a state of surprise or fear. *Thambos* means amazement, but is again connected with fear or terror as well. Miracles like this didn't just pique people's interest. In the vernacular of today, we might say signs and wonders freaked people out.

Jesus' miracles had this effect at times as well. When he sends demons into a herd of pigs, and the pigs stampede into a lake and drown, people are amazed. Matthew 8:34 tells us, "Then the whole town went out to meet Jesus. And when they saw him, they pleaded with him to leave their region." Their response to this strange miracle was, understandably, fear.

The word *teras* is a noun typically translated "wonder" or "miracle." It is always used in the plural, and almost always coupled with the word *semeia*, which means signs. Hence, we find the term "signs and wonders," most often in the book of Acts, used to describe the miraculous work of God in and through the apostles. These were considered evidence of the power of the Holy Spirit in the early church, and a sign of God's power.

Vine's Concise Dictionary of the Bible notes: "A sign is intended to appeal to the understanding, a 'wonder' appeals to the imagination."[1]

Wonders are signs of God's power and authority. For example, in the second chapter of Acts we read Peter's sermon. In it, he quotes the prophet Joel, saying: "I will show wonders (*teras*) in the heaven above and signs on the earth below" (v. 19).

He goes on to mention wonders and signs as evidence of Jesus' authority: "People of Israel, listen to this: Jesus of Nazareth was a man accredited by God to you by miracles, wonders (*teras*) and signs, which God did among you through him, as you yourselves know" (v. 22 TNIV).

The chapter concludes with a description of the community and sharing of the first church, and says: "Everyone was filled with awe (*phobos*) at the many wonders (*teras*) and signs performed by the apostles" (v. 43 TNIV).

The other words in this verse help us understand the significance of wonders and signs. The word modern translations render "awe," but the KJV renders this verse, "fear came upon every soul." The Greek, *phobos*, means fear with the idea of being scared, not just respect or wonderment. The wonders the apostles did were no small things. People, despite their joy at the fellowship, were amazed and frightened by the sheer power of these miracles.

The question for us is, are we filled with a fearful wonder at the things God has done and continues to do? Can we set aside our modern cynicism to experience that wonder?

WORD

The word *word* is surprisingly controversial. There are two words in the Greek text that mean word: *logos* and *rhema*. As we have seen, Greek has more words to express nuance than English does. Where English has just "love," Greek has *agape, phileo,* and *eros*, for example.

Some argue that *logos* is a written word and *rhema* is a spoken word, although that is not exactly clear from the text in all cases. Others say they are interchangeable synonyms.

Within the charismatic movement, some preachers emphasize the difference between these two words. *Logos* is the word that we have in the Bible, but *rhema* is a revelation of the Holy Spirit given directly to a person to give specific direction or truth.[1]

Critics of the charismatic position seem to be concerned that more weight would be given to a *rhema* than to the *logos*, the written biblical record. And that anyone can claim to have a "*rhema*" from God that may or may not be correct. To counteract this, they teach that *logos* and *rhema* mean exactly the same thing.

For example, in Matthew 26:75, Mark 14:72, and Luke 22:61, we read: "Then Peter remembered the word Jesus had spoken: 'Before the rooster crows, you will disown me three times.'" The verses are almost identical, and "word" refers to a spoken word. In Matthew and Mark, the Greek is *rhema*, but in Luke it is *logos*.[2]

Another possibility is that a *rhema* is a specific verse that God brings to mind in a particular situation. The only way a verse can come to mind is if you memorize it. So if you memorize the *logos*, you're more apt to receive a *rhema*. You could say that *rhema* is *a* word that comes to us from God, *logos* is *the* Word, God's transcendent truth. (See, for example, Luke 3:2, which says the word [*rhema*] of God came to John the Baptist, or Romans 10:8, which says, "The word [*rhema*] is near you.")

Most scholars agree that *logos* had an evolving meaning with Greek philosophers way before John declared, "In the beginning was the Word (*logos*)" and that in fact, John chose this word so that he could enter into the philosophical discussion of the day.

The philosopher Heraclitus suggested that there was a universal power he called the *logos*. One Web site notes that he coined the term around 600 BC "to designate the divine reason or plan which coordinates the entire universe."[3] Aristotle defined *logos* as a mode of persuasion: *Logos* was an argument from reason.

The Stoics, starting around 300 BC, understood *logos* as "the organizing, integrating, and energizing principle of the whole universe." In other words, a Higher Power, i.e., God. The Stoics believed each person had a bit of the divine *logos* within them.[4] Think of the ancient secular view of *logos* as similar to "the Force" in the *Star Wars* movies.

So into this centuries-long discussion comes the apostle John, who says that before time began, the *Logos* existed. The philosophers would agree. But then he says, at a particular time in history, the *Logos* (life-force of the universe) put on flesh and became a man—Jesus of Nazareth. This was startling, to say the least.

Logos means not just a word, but the embodiment of a concept or idea. It is often used in the New Testament to speak about the revealed will of God, particularly Jesus as the revealed Truth.

Rhema meant an utterance or a topic, but is also used twice to describe the gospel in Romans 10:8: " 'The word (*rhema*) is near you; it is in your mouth and in your heart,' that is, the word (*rhema*) of faith we are proclaiming." When Jesus is tempted by Satan to turn stones into bread, he quotes Deuteronomy 8:3: "People do not live on bread alone, but on every word (*rhema*) that comes from the mouth of God." (See Matt. 4:4 and Luke 4:4.)

Both words are found in John 15. Jesus says, "You are already clean because of the word (*logos*) I have spoken to you" (v. 3). But then in verse 7 he says, "If you remain in me and my words (*rhema*) remain in you, ask whatever you wish, and it will be given you."

RK/WORKS

rk, both of God and of people, is an important theme in the ew Testament. The work that Jesus did on the cross by dying r our sins, the work of the Holy Spirit in our hearts, the works f faith that we engage in, prompted by our love for God and for people—these are all essential components of our theology and our faith practice.

The Greek noun *ergon* means work, employment, or toil, and appears in the text 176 times. The related word *ergasia* indicates the process of working, or diligence. The verb *ergazomai* describes manual labor, and occasionally, the good deeds of a believer. One dictionary notes: "*Ergazomai* also indicates the work of God in the hearts of human beings, illuminating their hearts (cf. John 5:17), and 'performing' miraculous deeds (cf. Acts 13:41). Similarly, in John 6:30; 9:4, Christ is said 'to perform' a miraculous sign in order to fulfill the purposes of God."[1]

The New Testament holds two seemingly paradoxical ideas in tension: first, that our works of righteousness do not earn our salvation (see Eph. 2:8–10), and second, that the life of faith includes doing the work God has called us to do.

The book of James explores the tension between faith and action (works) in great detail, using the word *ergon* thirteen times in the second chapter alone. James contends that works of righteousness are the result of a living faith, the natural outcome of it.

Many verses explore the idea of a "work of faith"—such as 1 Thessalonians 1:3: "We continually remember before our God and Father your work (*ergon*) produced by faith, your labor (*kopos*) prompted by love, and your endurance inspired by hope in our Lord Jesus Christ."

The work of faith is initially just turning our lives over to God. *Kopos* means toil that leads to weariness, laborious work. This does not earn our salvation or even God's love, which we alrea[dy] have in infinite measure; our work and toil is a response to th[e] love of Jesus.

Philippians 2:12 uses a more emphatic form of the verb, *katergazomai*, when it urges believers to "continue to work out your salvation with fear and trembling." Again we see the tension between God's work in us and our godly response of work, because the very next verse says, "for it is God who works (*energeo*) in you to will and to act in order to fulfill his good purpose." *Energeo* means to work actively in.

The prefix *sun-* is occasionally added to form *sunergeo*, the verb we find in Mark 16:20 to describe God's help for those doing his work: "Then the disciples went out and preached everywhere, and the Lord worked with them and confirmed his word by the signs that accompanied it."

John 6:27–29 records what Jesus says about work:

> "Do not work (*ergazomai*) for food that spoils, but for food that endures to eternal life, which the Son of Man will give you. On him God the Father has placed his seal of approval." Then they asked him, "What must we do to do the works (*ergazomai*) God requires?" Jesus answered, "The work (*ergon*) of God is this: to believe in the one he has sent."

The only work that God requires, when it comes to being saved, is to believe. While it sounds too simple, anyone who has wrestled with doubt knows that the work of belief can be arduous. And once we have been saved, God invites us to join him in his work: "For it is by grace you have been saved, through faith—and this not from yourselves, it is the gift of God—not by works (*ergon*), so that no one can boast. For we are God's workmanship (*poiema*), created in Christ Jesus to do good works (*ergon*), which God prepared in advance for us to do" (Eph. 2:8–10). *Poiema* means product, thing that is made. Again we see the cooperation we have with God that allows us to engage in his work in the world.

YOKE

Jesus issues this invitation: "Come to me, all you who are weary and burdened, and I will give you rest. Take my yoke upon you and learn from me, for I am gentle and humble in heart, and you will find rest for your souls. For my yoke is easy and my burden is light" (Matt. 11:28–30).

It might seem a contradiction or paradox. A yoke, used to harness beasts of burden to pull a plow or wagon, was easy? How can a burden be light, especially to someone who is already burdened? But Jesus' listeners would have heard this in a very different way.

First, the word *zugos*, translated "yoke," comes from the root *zeugnumi*, to join, especially by a yoke. *Zugos* also means a beam of balance, which connected scales. A *zugos* connected two things together. So to take on Christ's yoke is to be linked with him, to have his help, rather than shouldering burdens alone.

Second, those listening to Jesus had recently heard him criticize the Pharisees because of the burdens they put on people. A few chapters earlier, Jesus had told his followers that they should obey the law, but not act like Pharisees, because "they do not practice what they preach. They tie up heavy loads and put them on men's shoulders, but they themselves are not willing to lift a finger to move them" (Matt. 23:3–4). Jesus was contrasting his yoke with the repressive and hypocritical one of the Pharisees.

Third, Jesus was a Jewish rabbi, whose goal was to teach people how to live out God's law. Rob Bell offers this insight:

> A rabbi's set of rules and lists, which was really that rabbi's

> interpretation of how to live the Torah, was called that rabbi's yoke. When you followed a certain rabbi, you were following him because you believed that rabbi's set of interpretations were the closest to what God intended through the Scriptures. And when you followed that rabbi, you were taking up that rabbi's yoke.[1]

Finally, Jesus' listeners would have been intimately familiar with the Book of Sirach, part of the Jewish wisdom literature. "In Jesus' beckoning to the weary and heavy laden to come and take his yoke upon them, the imagery of wisdom lies close to the surface. The book of Sirach closes with wisdom beckoning the 'uneducated' to 'draw near to me . . . acquire wisdom . . . Put your neck under her yoke and let your souls receive instruction' (Sir. 51:23–27 NRSV)."[2] And in Hosea 11:4 we read, "I led them with cords of human kindness, with ties of love; I lifted the yoke from their neck and bent down to feed them."

Zugos also refers to bond service to masters in 1 Timothy 6:1 and to a pair of scales in Revelation 6:5. Second Corinthians 6:14 warns Christians not to marry unbelievers, saying, "Do not be yoked together with unbelievers." The word translated "yoked together" in this verse appears only here in Scripture. It is *heterozugeo*, a compound word from *heteros*, meaning another (who is different), and *zugos*.

We see the word *zugos* in Acts 15:10 and Galatians 5:1 to refer to the yoke of slavery of the Jewish law, particularly the requirement of circumcision, which the Judaizers wanted to enforce on Gentile converts. As Peter says in Acts 15: "Now therefore why are you putting God to the test by placing on the neck of the disciples a yoke that neither our ancestors nor we have been able to bear? On the contrary, we believe that we will be saved through the grace of the Lord Jesus, just as they will" (vv. 10–11 NRSV). Galatians 5:1 speaks against the same problem, again using the term "a yoke of slavery."

These stand in sharp contrast to the yoke of Christ, which is shared by him, which makes it easy. When asked what his yoke was ("Which is the most important law?"), Jesus replied, "Love God and love others." (See Matt. 22:36–40.) Which is indeed a light burden, when we shoulder it with his help.

APPENDIX OF HELPFUL WEB SITES

When studying the Scriptures, it can be helpful to use search engines like Google, but remember that almost anyone can put up a Web site, and they have the freedom to write whatever they want on that site, whether or not it is true. So some sites will have more credibility than others. This may seem obvious, but don't automatically trust Wikipedia or other sites that have no process for verification of the facts. Not everything you read on the Internet is true, so check it against other sources.

I did most of the research for this book in the reference section of the Wheaton College library, where I found hundreds of academic books published by credible publishers. A local Christian college or seminary is a great place to do serious research. Also, a copy of *Strong's Exhaustive Concordance* (which is available for all the major translations of the Bible) is an invaluable tool. You can get a print version or find an online one. *Strong's* lists every instance that each word in the Bible is used. So for example, if you look up "love" in *Strong's*, you'll find the 310 verses that contain the word *love* in the Bible. Each, with a short phrase of context, is listed, along with a number. The numbers correspond to the Hebrew or Greek word that is used in that particular verse. In verses that translate the word *agape* as "love," you'll see the number 25. You then go to the Greek dictionary section to see the definition and usage of *agape*.

The most important tool when trying to understand the Scriptures is prayer. As you study, ask that the Holy Spirit would speak to you, that he would reveal truth and renew your mind. Here are a few helpful and accurate online tools that I used while writing this book.

www.blueletterbible.org is a great site for studying without having to look up each individual word in a concordance. You can search by reference or by word. The KJV is the default version, and with that, if you look up a verse, you can see the *Strong's Concordance* number after each word. Click on the number, and it takes you to a Greek or Hebrew dictionary with the word, its meaning, and all other verses the word is used in. Click on the icons to the left of each verse and you can see that verse in several other versions, read commentary, and more.

www.biblegateway.com has the Bible online in over twenty English translations and many other languages. You can compare the same verse or verses in different versions, do a keyword search (including searching for verses that contain two words that are the same), or look up a verse by typing in the reference (e.g., John 3:16 or Psalm 23). This is one of several online Bible sites. It's great for doing word study. It also provides access to several commentaries.

www.eliyah.com/lexicon.html has *Strong's Concordance* online, along with a Hebrew and Greek lexicon. On this site, you can search by word, reference, or *Strong's* number. You can also search a thesaurus, encyclopedia, and other reference books.

www.biblestudytools.com is a very helpful site with dictionaries, encyclopedias, Bible translations, commentaries, and more, along with daily devotionals. Like *biblegateway.com*, it has over twenty English translations available to search, but more extensive commentaries and dictionaries.

www.netbible.org contains commentaries, *Strong's Concordance*, maps, sermon illustrations, and a lot of other resources, as well as the text of the Bible in various versions.

GREEK INDEX

NOTES

Afraid

1. C. S. Lewis, "The Christian Hope—Its Meaning for Today," *Religion for Life*, Winter 1952. Republished as "The World's Last Night" in *The World's Last Night and Other Essays* (New York: Harcourt, 2002), 109.

Anoint

1. W. E. Vine, *Vine's Concise Dictionary of the Bible* (Nashville: Thomas Nelson, 2005), 13.

Apostle

1. Rena Pederson, *The Lost Apostle: Searching for the Truth About Junia* (San Francisco: Jossey-Bass, 2006).

Believe

1. D. Guthrie and J. A. Motyer, eds., *The New Bible Commentary* (Grand Rapids, MI: Eerdmans, 1991, [originally Leicester, England: InterVarsity Press, 1970]), 927.

Blind

1. Keri Wyatt Kent, *Simple Compassion* (Grand Rapids, MI: Zondervan, 2009), 73.

Body

1. Craig A. Evans and Stanley Porter, eds., *Dictionary of New Testament Background* (Downers Grove, IL: InterVarsity, 2000), 415.
2. Dallas Willard, *The Spirit of the Disciplines* (New York: Harper and Row, 1988) 77, 92.

Break/Broken

1. Vine, 40.
2. David Bivin (publisher of *Jerusalem Perspective* and member of the Jerusalem

School of Synoptic Research), "'Binding' and 'Loosing,'" *www.jerusalemperspective.com/Default.aspx?tabid=27&ArticleID=1561.*

3. Rob Bell, *Velvet Elvis: Repainting the Christian Faith* (Grand Rapids: Zondervan, 2005), 49–50.

Burden

1. See Vine p. 43, which notes the one exception in Acts 27:10, where *phortion* refers to the cargo of a ship.
2. Willard, 9.

Call/Called/Calling

1. Vine, 46.

Care

1. William Barclay, *New Testament Words* (Louisville, KY: Westminster, 1964), 199.
2. Ibid., 201.

Chosen

1. From BibleGateway.com, *www.biblegateway.com/passage/?search=eph%201:4-6&version=TNIV.*

Church

1. Barclay, 70.

Clean/Cleanse

1. C. S. Lewis, *The Voyage of the Dawn Treader*, rev. ed. (New York: Macmillan, 1988), 90.

Compassion

1. Ceslas Spicq, *A Theological Lexicon of the New Testament*, Vol. 3 (Peabody, MA: Hendrickson, 1994), 320.
2. Barclay, 278.
3. Ibid., 279.
4. Ibid., 280.

Content/Contentment

1. Adele Calhoun, *Spiritual Disciplines Handbook* (Downers Grove, IL: InterVarsity, 2005), 96.
2. Lisa Graham McMinn, *The Contented Soul* (Downers Grove, IL: InterVarsity, 2006), 68.

Covenant

1. Spiros Zodhiates, gen. ed., *The Complete Word Study Dictionary, New Testament* (Chattanooga, TN: AMG, 1992), 424–425.
2. Ray C. Stedman, *Hebrews (IVP New Testament Commentary Series)*, Grant R. Osborne, ed., (Downers Grove, IL: InterVarsity, 1992), 89.

Cross

1. Judith Couchman, *The Mystery of the Cross* (Downers Grove, IL: InterVarsity, 2009), 35.
2. Stuart K. Weber, *New Testament Commentary, Matthew*, Max Anders, gen. ed. (Nashville: Holman Reference), 210.
3. James Strong, *Strong's Exhaustive Concordance of the Bible*, rev. ed. (New York: Abington Press, 1951), 122.
4. *The Complete Word Study Dictionary, New Testament*, 1309.
5. Weber, 256.

Deacon

1. "Appointment of the Seven," *Acts 6—IVP New Testament Commentaries, www.biblegateway.com/resources/commentaries/IVP-NT/Acts/Appointment-Seven*.
2. See for example the commentary on this passage by Pastor Buddy Martin, Founder and Senior Pastor of Christian Challenge International, at *www.christianchallenge.org/hebraic-foundations/Acts/Acts15.html*.

Disciple

1. Vine, 96.
2. Ray VanderLaan, "Rabbi and Talmidim," FollowTheRabbi.com, *www.followtherabbi.com/Brix?pageID=2753*.
3. Ann Spangler and Lois Tverberg, *Sitting at the Feet of Rabbi Jesus: How the Jewishness of Jesus Can Transform Your Faith* (Grand Rapids, MI: Zondervan, 2009), 33.

Doubt

1. John Ortberg, *Faith & Doubt* (Grand Rapids, MI: Zondervan, 2008), 23.
2. Ibid., 79.

Eye/Eyes

1. Richard Foster, *Freedom of Simplicity* (New York: Harper, 1981), 45.
2. Spicq, 472.

Faith/Faithful

1. Spicq, 110–111.
2. The entire chapter of Matthew 8 contains several stories of faith, or lack of faith. You may want to supplement your study of this word by spending some time meditating on and praying through this chapter.

Fellowship

1. Barclay, 173.

Fill/Fulfill/Fullness

1. Bell, 47–48.

Fire

1. Guthrie and Motyer, 871.

Forgive/Forgiven/Forgiveness

1. Kent, 177.
2. Lewis Smedes, "Five Things Everyone Should Know About Forgiving," October 5, 1997, *www.30goodminutes.org/csec/sermon/smedes_4101.htm*. I also recommend his book *Forgive and Forget*.
3. Frederick Buechner, *Wishful Thinking: A Seeker's ABC* (New York: HarperOne, 1973, 1993), 33.

Friend

1. Spangler and Tverberg, 66–67.
2. Spicq, 448.

Fruit

1. Vine, 149.

Gift/Gifts

1. A great resource for learning about and determining your spiritual gift or gifts is Network Ministries, founded by Bruce Bugbee, author of *What You Do Best in the Body of Christ*. Visit *www.networkministries.com*.

Good/Goodness

1. Spicq, 515–516.
2. C. S. Lewis, *Mere Christianity* (New York: MacMillan, 1952), 49.

Gospel

1. Barclay, 101.
2. Vine, 161.

Grace

1. *Strong's Exhaustive Concordance of the Bible*, 270.
2. Philip Yancey, *What's So Amazing About Grace?* (Grand Rapids, MI: Zondervan, 1997), 13.
3. Cathleen Falsani, *Sin Boldly: A Field Guide for Grace* (Grand Rapids, MI: Zondervan, 2008), 85.

Harvest

1. Stephen Renn, ed., *Expository Dictionary of Bible Words* (Peabody, MA: Hendrickson, 2005), 468.
2. Bible History Online, "Harvest," *www.Bible-history.com/isbe/H/HARVEST*.

Holy Spirit

1. Renn, 195–196.

Hope

1. I. Howard Marshall, A. K. Millard, J. I. Packer, and D. J. Wiseman, eds., *New Bible Dictionary* 3rd ed., (Downers Grove, IL: InterVarsity, 1996), 480.
2. Barclay, 76.

Humble

1. Bill Hybels with Rob Wilkins, *Descending into Greatness* (Grand Rapids, MI: Zondervan, 1993), 16–17.
2. Buechner, 48.

Hungry

1. Lynne M. Baab, *Fasting: Spiritual Freedom Beyond Our Appetites* (Downers Grove, IL: InterVarsity, 2006), 47.

Inheritance

1. Renn, 518.
2. Dietrich Bonhoeffer, *The Cost of Discipleship* (New York: Macmillan, 1963), 123.

Joy

1. C. S. Lewis, *Surprised by Joy: The Shape of My Early Life* (New York: Harcourt Brace Jovanovich, 1955), 17.
2. Renn, 541.

Justify/Justification

1. *New Bible Dictionary*, 637.
2. *Matthew Henry's Concise Commentary on the Bible* is available in the public domain. I've quoted from it as presented on *www.Biblegateway.com*.

Lamb

1. Dr. Richard J. Krejcir, "Understanding Apocalyptic Literature," *Into Thy Word*, 2007. *http://70030.netministry.com/articles_view.asp?articleid=31437&columnid=3801*.
2. Renn, 573.

Light

1. Vine, 219.
2. Spicq, 473.

Love

1. David Benner, *Surrender to Love* (Downers Grove, IL: InterVarsity, 2003), 44–45.

Mercy

1. Spicq, 478–479.
2. *Strong's Exhaustive Concordance of the Bible*, 84.

Messiah

1. Philip Yancey, *The Jesus I Never Knew* (Grand Rapids, MI: Zondervan, 1995), 52–53.
2. *New Bible Dictionary*, 760.

3. John Ortberg, *The Life You've Always Wanted* (Grand Rapids, MI: Zondervan, 1997), 117–118.

Miracle

1. C. S. Lewis, *Miracles* (New York: Macmillan, 1960), 134–135. As quoted in *The Quotable Lewis* by Wayne Martindale and Jerry Root, eds. (Wheaton: Tyndale, 1989).

New

1. Vine, 254.

One Another

1. The entire book of 1 John explores in great depth the connection between loving God and loving people.
2. Several church Web sites have information on this, including one from Trinity Baptist in Sikeston, MO, with a list of "one another" verses at *www.tbcsikeston.com/documents/One_Another_Commands.pdf*.

Parable

1. *New Bible Dictionary*, 868.

Patience/Patient

1. *Strong's Concordance*, 260.
2. Ortberg, 88–89.

Peace

1. Julian of Norwich, *Revelations of Divine Love*, translated by Elizabeth Spearing (London: Penguin, 1998), 22.
2. *Expository Dictionary of Bible Words*, 721.

Persecute/Persecution

1. Learn more about how to pray for the persecuted church at *www.opendoorsusa.org*.

Perseverance

1. Bill Hybels, *Who You Are When No One's Looking* (Downers Grove, IL: InterVarsity, 1987), 51.

Pharisee

1. Richard N. Ostling, "Religion: What Sort of Jew Was Jesus?" *Time*, April 12, 2005, *www.time.com/time/magazine/article/0,9171,1048374,00.html*.
2. Spangler and Tverberg, 168.

Pray

1. Walter Wangerin Jr., *Whole Prayer* (Grand Rapids, MI: Zondervan, 1998), 29.
2. Ibid., 35.
3. Marjorie Thompson, *Soul Feast* (Louisville, KY: Westminster, 1995), 31.

4. Philip Yancey, *Prayer: Does It Make Any Difference?* (Grand Rapids, MI: Zondervan, 2006), 30. I highly recommend this book.
5. Ibid., 128.
6. Richard Foster, *Prayer: Finding the Heart's True Home* (New York: HarperOne, 1992), 3.

Promise

1. Barclay, 87.

Proud/Pride

1. Jeff Cook, *Seven: The Deadly Sins and the Beatitudes* (Grand Rapids, MI: Zondervan, 2008), 33–34.
2. Barclay, 134.

Rest

1. Mark Buchanan, *The Rest of God* (Nashville, TN: W Publishing Group, 2006), 93. I highly recommend this book.

Resurrection

1. "Proving the Resurrection," *Matthew 22—IVP New Testament Commentaries, www.biblegateway.com/resources/commentaries/IVP-NT/Matt/Proving-Resurrection.*

Righteousness

1. Mae Elise Cannon, *Social Justice Handbook: Small Steps for a Better World* (Downers Grove, IL: InterVarsity, 2009), 35.

Rock

1. Guthrie and Motyer, 837.
2. Ibid.

Sabbath

1. Mark Buchanan, 127–128.
2. Ibid., 219.

Sacrifice

1. Willard, 75.
2. The whole book of Hebrews is a great place to do more in-depth study of this word, especially chapters 9 through 11.

Salt

1. Vine, 324.
2. *Strong's Concordance*, 169.
3. Craig Keener, *IVP Bible Background Commentary, New Testament* (Downers Grove, IL: InterVarsity, 1993), 57.

Salvation

1. Spicq, 345–346.

2. Ibid., 350.

Self-Control

1. Keathley's excellent article on this topic can be found at *http://Bible.org/seriespage/mark-10-self-control*. It is one in a series of articles entitled "Marks of Maturity: Biblical Characteristics of a Christian Leader."
2. Spicq, 60.
3. Keathley.

Sin

1. Barclay, 118–119.

Son of Man

1. Rodney Whitacre, *John* (*The IVP New Testament Commentary Series*), Grant R. Osborne, series ed., (Downers Grove, IL: InterVarsity, 1999), 90.
2. *New Bible Dictionary*, 760.
3. Merrill F. Unger, *The New Unger's Bible Dictionary*, R. K. Harrison, ed., rev. ed., (Chicago: Moody, 1988), 1211.
4. Spangler and Tverberg, 47–48.

Soul

1. *The Complete Word Study Dictionary*, 1494.
2. R. T. France, *The Gospel of Matthew* (Grand Rapids, MI: Eerdmans, 2007), 638.
3. Ibid., 639.
4. *The Complete Word Study Dictionary*, 1495.

Strength

1. The word is a compound of *oikos*, "a house," and *domeo*, "to build," but means to build anything. *Strong's Concordance*, 176.

Temptation

1. Unger, 1265.

Thirst/Thirsty

1. Spangler and Tverberg, 122–123.

Truth

1. Spicq, 72–73, 75.

Vine/Vineyard

1. *Strong's Concordance*, 8.
2. Ibid., 139.

Water

1. *Matthew Henry's Concise Commentary on the Bible*, public domain, as quoted on *www.Biblegateway.com*.
2. From an article at *http://Bible.org/seriespage/exegetical-commentary-john-4*

by W. Hall Harris III. Harris is Professor of New Testament Studies, Dallas Theological Seminary, and Project Director and General Editor for the NET Bible (New English Translation).

Wise/Wisdom

1. Leland Ryken, James C. Wilhoit, and Tremper Longman III, eds., *Dictionary of Biblical Imagery* (Downers Grove, IL: InterVarsity, 1998), 956.
2. Ibid., 957.

Witness

1. *Strong's Concordance*, 156.
2. Joel B. Green, Scot McKnight, and I. Howard Marshall, eds., *Dictionary of Jesus and the Gospels* (Downers Grove, IL: InterVarsity, 1992), 878.

Wonder/Wonders

1. Vine, 418.

Word

1. I'm not from a charismatic background, but I do believe that God can speak directly to the human heart. However, I think leadings from God should be tested against Scripture (and common sense) and that God will not contradict himself. While I don't give more weight to a *rhema* than to the *logos*, and we may not ever know the exact meaning of these two words, I think it's silly to pretend there is no difference in meaning between the two.
2. For more examples and rebuttal to the charismatic position, see *www.biblestudying.net/charismatic37.html*.
3. From *www.allaboutphilosophy.org/greek-philosopher-plato.htm*.
4. The quote and other information in this paragraph is from Antonia Tripolitis, *Religions of the Hellenistic-Roman Age* (Grand Rapids, MI: Eerdmans, 2002), 37–38.

Work/Works

1. Renn, 1063.

Yoke

1. Bell, 47.
2. *Dictionary of Biblical Imagery*, 956.

ACKNOWLEDGMENTS

I want to thank several people without whom this book would never have happened:

Thanks to my husband, Scot, and our amazing kids, Melanie and Aaron. You support this crazy calling of mine to write, and I couldn't do it without your help. You may not think doing your own laundry or making your own lunches helps me write, but it does! I love you.

Thanks to my editor, Andy McGuire, for having the vision for this project and for your encouragement during the writing process. And to my line editor, Ellen Chalifoux, for graciously listening to my defense of a certain Bible translation, and for your excellent attention to detail.

My agent, Chip MacGregor, convinced me I could write this book even when I thought I was sorely underqualified. Thanks for believing in me. It's an honor to be working with you.

Dr. Scot McKnight challenged me to make this book academically accurate and recommended resources to help me do that. Thanks for raising the bar, and of course for the endorsement (which I asked for during your busiest teaching season).

Thanks also to my girls: Jodi Walle, Pam Orr, Wendy Rosman,

and Bissy Elliott. Breakfasts at Panera, teaching together, vacations, praying together—I love doing life with you all.

This book required more research than any book I've written previously. I spent hours in the stacks at the Wheaton College Buswell Memorial Library, pouring through commentaries, Bible dictionaries, and encyclopedias. Thank you to all the staff who answered questions, showed me (several times) how to use the scanner to send copies to my email, and looked up a page number for my bibliography when I called ten minutes before the manuscript had to be sent in. I'm grateful to have a treasure like this library (and its staff) so close to home.

KERI WYATT KENT is the author of seven previous books and is a regular contributor to *Kyria.com* (formerly *Today's Christian Woman*), *Outreach* magazine, and *MomSense* magazine. Keri speaks at churches and retreats around the country and is a frequent guest on several shows on the Moody Broadcasting Network, including *Midday Connection*. Keri lives with her husband and two children in suburban Chicago.

This page is a continuation of the copyright page.

More from

Keri Wyatt Kent

WHY ARE WE IN SUCH A HURRY?

While juggling kids, errands, jobs, relationships, and church activities, many moms don't realize that their value is found not in what they do but *in who they are.* If this is you, and your energy runs out long before your day comes to an end, then maybe it's time to take a break and breathe.

MOPS author Keri Wyatt Kent wants to show you what Jesus meant when he said, "Come to me, all you who are weary and burdened, and I will give you rest." Filled with true accounts of moms making the journey away from "living on the edge," *Breathe* will help you slow down, grow spiritually, and make more room for God. Practical examples, "breathing exercises," and resources for further study will help you break free from the hectic pace of life and ultimately find rest through your relationship with Christ.

"In this thoughtful book, Keri Wyatt Kent leads us to a place where we can catch our breath—and keep it!" —Elisa Morgan, president and CEO, MOPS International

"Slow down. Find a comfortable chair. Fix a (decaffeinated) beverage and learn how to live one moment at a time." —John Ortberg, pastor and best-selling author, *God Is Closer Than You Think*

"Reading *Breathe* was like receiving a formal affirmation from God of my decisions to create more open spaces for pondering and prayer for the people I love, and for the pursuit of my true calling." —Lynne Hybels, Willow Creek Community Church